D0845854

The Leaning Ivory Tower

SUNY Series in Hispanic Studies
Gary Keller, editor

The
Leaning Ivory Tower

Latino Professors in American Universities

edited by
Raymond V. Padilla and
Rudolfo Chávez Chávez

STATE UNIVERSITY OF
NEW YORK PRESS

"The brain of a Cal State San Marcos multiculturalist" cartoon
© 1993 by the Oceanside *Blade-Citizen* and Mark Thornhill.
Published with permission.

"Senator Bill Craven is enlightened by the prod of political
correctness, wielded by an officer from the San Marcos politically
correct police" cartoon © 1993 by the Escondido *Times Advocate*
and Logan Jenkins. Published with permission.

Published by
State University of New York Press, Albany

© 1995 State University of New York

Production by Bernadine Dawes
Marketing by Nancy Farrell

Library of Congress Cataloging-in-Publication Data

The leaning ivory tower : Latino professors in American universities /
    edited by Raymond V. Padilla and Rudolfo Chávez Chávez.
        p.   cm. — (SUNY series in Hispanic studies)
    Includes index.
    ISBN 0-7914-2427-8 (alk. paper). — ISBN 0-7914-2428-6 (pbk. :
alk. paper)
    1. Hispanic American college teachers. 2. Hispanic Americans—
Education (Higher) I. Padilla, Raymond V. II. Chávez, Rudolfo
Chávez, 1951–   . III. Series.
LB2331.72.L43   1995
378.1'2'08968—dc20   94-28756
                                                           CIP

1 2 3 4 5 6 7 8 9 10

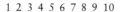

To my family.
To la lucha.
To our dreams.

—*Rudolfo Chávez Chávez*

॰ॐ॰

Para los profesores de la primera
ola que se sacrificaron para que otros
pudieran tener éxito.

—*Raymond V. Padilla*

Contents

Acknowledgments

Thanks to all of the authors who responded to our call for papers for this volume. We appreciate their willingness to share their personal experiences in American universities. Gary Keller's support and encouragement of this work is much appreciated. The SUNY Press staff was efficient and helpful. Thanks especially to Christine E. Worden, Lois Patton, Rosalie M. Robertson, Bernadine Dawes, and Nancy Farrell.

The anonymous reviewers provided valuable suggestions and support, as did members of the SUNY Press Editorial Board. Their suggestions helped us to improve the book. Thanks also to Terry Trimble and Donna Larson who were always cheerful and efficient in attending to numerous support activities. Thanks to our families for the gift of time.

Introduction

RUDOLFO CHÁVEZ CHÁVEZ AND RAYMOND V. PADILLA

The 1980s were a time of economic growth but also of greed; a time when concrete, ideological walls crumbled as conceptual (and equally ideological) walls were erected; a time when the language of diversity and pluralism was reintroduced to the banquet table of democracy but when intolerance and xenophobia also took their place at that same table. These were but a few of the contradictory trends during the past several decades that serve as a backdrop for this book.

The demographic facts of the nineties provide a reality check on the status of our diverse population. For example, one out of every four persons living today in the United States is of color, but one out of three will be a person of color in the year 2000. Demographic facts of this kind are having an inevitable impact on our educational institutions, from kindergarten to graduate school. They also place in a new context the racial and ethnic insensitivity, discrimination, outright racism, and other institutional and personal acts of inequality that have been considered "normal" in our society, including academia.

Although our American political system has made a consistent and noble attempt at freedom and democracy for all people, these efforts have been greatly undermined by acts of figurative or actual exclusion perpetrated by institutions and individuals who consciously or unconsciously fear the loss of white privilege. McIntosh (1989) contends that "white privilege is like an invisible weightless knapsack of special provisions, maps, passports, code books, visas, clothes, tools and blank checks" (p. 10). Thus, white privilege is an ontological knapsack where social reality is constructed to perpetuate the hegemonic structures that are deemed "normal."

Apple (1985) is well aware of the serious danger in overusing the concept of hegemony to explain the dominant cultural and economic reproduction observed by McIntosh (1989) as "white privilege" and

1

expressed metaphorically as an "invisible knapsack." But as evidenced by the personal narratives contained in this book, the concept of hegemony can provide an organizing framework for understanding some of the experiences of Latina and Latino professors in American universities. Clearly, hegemony is not "free-floating." It is bound to the social reality of the state. As Apple (1985) indicates, hegemony is not an accomplished social fact but "a process in which dominant groups and classes manage to win the active consensus over whom [sic] they rule" (p. 29). The state itself (which includes the institutions within the state) can be, and many times is, a site of racial group, gender, and class conflicts where "it must either force everyone to think alike or generate consent among a large portion of these contending groups. Thus, to maintain its own legitimacy the state needs [to] gradually but continuously . . . integrate many of the interests of allied and even opposing groups under its banner" (Apple 1985, 29–30). The whole process involves conflict, compromise, and active struggle to maintain hegemony.

The authors in this volume, through the power of narrative action, challenge the hegemony that is fostered and maintained by the colleges and universities in which these Latina and Latino academics function on a daily basis. Each of the writers presents the reality of the everyday; their stories and their experiences define the temporal structure that provides historicity and determines for these writers their situation in the world of "everyday life" (Berger & Luckmann 1967). This everyday life extends beyond the campus as the mass media provide a pathway to the "everyday world" that forms the context for the everyday life of individuals. The Latinos and Latinas in this volume were born in a certain era (post World War II), entered school in another era, and started working as professionals sometime during the seventies. "These dates, however, are all 'located' within a much more comprehensive history, and this 'location' decisively shapes [the writers'] situation" (Berger & Luckmann 1967, 28). Thus, the authors in this volume all experienced and were shaped to a greater or lesser degree by a specific historical context: The civil rights struggles of the fifties and sixties, Sputnik, the new math, the countercultural movement, the Cuban missile crisis, the assassinations of the Kennedys, Martin Luther King, and Malcolm X, Vietnam, moon landings, affirmative action, the grape boycott, Watergate, Bangladesh, ethnic studies, the Carter years, the Reagan years, arms for hostages, James Baldwin, César Chávez, Dolores Huerta, El Teatro Campesino, La Raza Unida Party, Rudolfo Anaya, Rodolfo Acuña, Sandra Cisneros, Edward James Olmos, Gabriel García Márquez,

Marti's poetry and vision, Nuyorican salsa, *pan dulce, arroz con pollo*, graduate school, sending out résumés and job applications, attending professional meetings, teaching, ethnic cleansing, the savings and loan debacle, apartheid, Mandela and de Klerk, the ever-growing national debt, AIDS, the Tomahawk chop, Zapotec guerrillas, NAFTA, Bill Clinton, dropouts, drive-by shootings, Rush Limbaugh, multicultural education, TV newsmagazines, political correctness, the changing demographics, and more.

The temporal structure of everyday life in the everyday world imposes predefined social structures on the "agendas" of any single day in the lives of the authors of this volume, as well as on their writings as a whole. "Within the co-ordinates set by this temporal structure [we] apprehend both daily 'agenda' and overall biography" (Berger & Luckmann 1967, 28). Indeed, the clock and the calendar compel our Latina and Latino authors to be women and men of their time. For it is within a temporal structure that everyday life retains its accent of reality.

Even though Latino and Latina academics may have been disoriented by covert and overt prejudices, marginalized, and made to question their own humanity in the everyday experience of academic life, these individuals have instinctively reoriented themselves. They have reasserted and reclaimed their authenticity through words and actions, through reading of the world, and through narratives such as those voiced in this volume. They have thus tried to reconfigure the reality of everyday life through pensive catharsis and contemplative historicity.

Each chapter in this book is an allegorical montage. Each reflects the context and complexity of the writer whose voice transcends the sense of individuality and isolation to unite with an ethnic community in order to access truth that is wrought not from physical or domineering power but from deep commitment to fairness, respect, and understanding of human strengths and shortcomings. Collectively, the narratives are connected by three overlapping themes. The first theme encompasses the writers' personal struggles, in varying degrees and in various forms, with covert and overt forms of racism. The second theme, marginality, is rooted in the questioning of prevailing and respected paradigms in established disciplines that despite universalistic claims display a provincialism that in the long run is neither reflective of nor responsive to the experiences of Latinas and Latinos. The third theme, valuing the self, focuses on personal identity and provides insightful discussions on how one might reconcile self-identity as a Latino or Latina with the behavioral expectations of academia.

Racism

Weinberg (1977) defines racism as a system of privilege and penalty based on one's race. It consists of two facets: (1) a belief in the inherent superiority of some people and the inherent inferiority of others, and (2) the acceptance of the way that goods and services are distributed in accordance with these judgments. Jones (1981) places racism into three categories: individual, institutional, and cultural. Individual racism is closest to racial prejudice and suggests a belief in the superiority of one's own race over another, while behaviorally it enacts an invidious distinction between races. Institutional racism is an extension of individual racism but also includes the manipulation of institutions so that one group benefits and maintains an advantage over others; institutional racism supports practices that operate to restrict on a racial basis the choices, rights, mobility, and access of groups or individuals. Although not necessarily sanctioned by law, these practices are nevertheless real. Cultural racism includes the individual and institutional expression of the superiority of one race's cultural heritage over that of another race.

The writers in this volume have in varying degrees encountered or witnessed all three categories of racism. Institutional racism was experienced by Richard R. Verdugo as ideological and institutional pressures that reinforce and maintain social order so that they can restrict entry into academia. In spite of possessing a doctoral degree, he was consistently denied opportunities in higher education. His publications were evaluated by a sociology professor even though they appeared mostly in economics journals. Verdugo's scholarly presentations were not sufficiently taken into account, nor was the fact that he was working outside of academia and thus did his research before and after working hours. His is by no means simply a victim's story. The loss to academia that this story represents can be made to bear fruit only if it stimulates those involved in hiring decisions to rethink job announcements, the interview process, and the invisible double standard that too often is invoked in the name of quality.

Covert institutional practices of racism are well illustrated by Raymond V. Padilla's "narrative memos," where he critiques the processes that he encountered in his applications for promotion to full professor. In one case, Padilla informs his department chair of the inadequacy of the review process. Two associate professors were judging his work. One of the associates had only one year in rank, the other lacked experience with doctoral students, and the full professor on the committee was not familiar with Chicano education, Padilla's area of expertise. Moreover, favorable judgments by knowledgeable full professors outside his department were accorded secondary importance. Reading between the lines, one can detect the department chair's protection and perpetuation of the status quo in the face of a review process that was clearly flawed.

Within the various networks in which most of us are engaged, we have heard many stories of the undeniable bigotry and intolerance that is experienced by Latinas and Latinos and about the privilege and power that is usually concentrated in the European American old guard (and increasingly the nouveau guard of special interest groups). We foresee that the narrative by Tatcho Mindiola, Jr., will surely become a classic description of how racist hegemony unfolds and how individual, institutional, and cultural racism are threaded into everyday life. Mindiola's department chair told him that tenure and promotion standards had changed during his employment, and that he now needed more publications. This revelation was made in the context of Mindiola's having knowledge that the wife of one of the tenured professors in the department also was "going up" for tenure in the same department and that the tenured professor and his nontenured wife were part of the "influential political group in the department." The department chair, under the guise of being a supporter, provided advice to Mindiola and after the third meeting told Mindiola that he would probably be denied tenure.

Mindiola's tenure and promotion story is filled with intrigue and implicit malice and contempt for his person as evidenced by the arbitrary changing of rules that eventually led to a discrimination lawsuit filed against the university. After retaliatory behavior against Mindiola by his chair, the lawsuit was amended to include an "allegation of retaliation." It would be simplistic to think that the denouement of the complex social drama narrated by Mindiola rested entirely on one incident. Nonetheless, the public act in which the university president called him "Taco," instead of Tatcho, illustrates the banal and sometimes cavalier way in which institutional racism manifests itself. A university president presumably serves as the moral, ethical, and academic helmsperson of a public institution. Strangely, Mindiola believes that the opposition to his bid for tenure was motivated not so much by prejudice but more by a department's need to tenure "one of its own." Yet university documents revealed that other non-Chicano faculty with equal or lower accomplishments had been promoted and tenured. Thus, Mindiola's narrative reveals the fine texture of institutional patterns that conceal the practice of discrimination and resist its elimination.

Hermán S. García's narrative describes what he experienced as institutional discrimination. His academic work questioned, he responded by decentering faculty from the dominant culture and challenging students' positivistic notions of culture, knowledge, and truth. He demanded that they frame their critique of his work from a less domineering and ethnocentric point of view that does not totalize "truth." He uses a critical theory lens to perceive his Otherness as a Chicano, as an academic, and as a person who simply wants to teach and learn within the academic culture. This is juxtaposed against an institution's "unearned entitlement" (McIntosh 1989) to cultural capital and how it uses that gratuitous entitlement to undermine García's humaneness. This narrative reads like a rear-view mirror with the inscription "Objects in mirror are not what they appear to be."

Dulce M. Cruz challenges the subtle and not so subtle manifestations of institutional racism. She was assigned to teach composition to "foreign" students. She learned that the assignment was based on her own foreignness, although she was raised and socialized in the United States. People were "stunned" when Cruz revealed her research interest in nineteenth-century British literature; they would ask why she wasn't interested in the literature of "her people." Later, when her own intellectual preoccupations led her to focus on ethnic literature, she found herself facing the "brown-on-brown" research taboo (Reyes & Halcón 1988). Reflecting on a conversation she had, Cruz writes:

> When I explained that I had done research on highly literate Dominican Americans . . . [the] immediate response was "Oh, so you must be a Dominican American yourself." "Yes I am," I answered, and by the end of the conversation I was angry. It is a no-win situation. Had I done research on a typical mainstream subject, my right and ability would have been questioned. I do research on my own community and I am suspect, considered narrow, ethnocentric, and incapable of being objective.

Racial incidents in higher education, similar to the ones described by our narrators, were not well documented by the popular media until the late sixties and early seventies when civil rights legislation compelled most universities to employ members from ethnically distinct groups. Once employed, such individuals and groups became a source of challenge to prevailing personnel practices in higher education, particularly with respect to employee retention, tenure, and promotion. When individuals reported discrimination, bias, or underrepresentation of ethnically distinct groups, too often the university authorities considered them as "isolated incidents" even though they resulted in stereotyping, condescension transmitted as compliment, and the second-guessing and undermining of the academic work of Latino and Latina professors, not to mention of their talents and humanity. Such incidents are invisibly normal and endemic to the academic landscape (Aronowitz 1981). To characterize them as "isolated" only serves to perpetuate the status quo and stifles the dialogue that is needed to overcome them. In this context, the present volume is not about "isolated incidents," just as it is not an attempt to chastise anyone by personalizing injustices that the authors have seen and experienced. It is, rather, a cogent and disturbing portrait of academic life in American universities as experienced by Latina and Latino academics.

Marginality

Practicing democracy is very much a subjective act—an act based on personal agency and a conviction for action, dialogue, and interaction with other selves in everyday activities. One also must continuously recreate the cultural terrain that enhances and sustains democratic practice. If not practiced as a subjective act, democracy remains, for all practical purposes, an abstract ideal better left to rhetorical debate. As a subjective practice, democracy creates a lifestyle that is ruled by committed personal action and an implicit commitment to historicity.

The academic cultural terrain, as lived by the contributors to this volume, suggests a constricted democratic practice where the very act of living can reside on the margins. So these narrators have created epistemological constructs that will promote a more democratic practice. To do so it has been necessary for them to step out from the margins onto the unknown and face the complexity of their humanity as well as the covert and overt racist acts carried out by entrenched forces in academia. As Rosaldo (1989) insightfully reminds us, "we often improvise, learn by doing, and make up things as we go along" (p. 92). Life, as it is lived, continuously forces us to live with ambiguity, uncertainty, and even a simple lack of knowledge. Then the day arrives when life's experiences clarify matters.

Even though marginality has many aspects that are difficult to pin down, it is a central theme for many of the writers in this volume. The narrators are marginalized but somehow integrated into their respective institutions. Although not necessarily marginalized in an economic or political sense, they are exploited in various ways, and many times their creativity is repressed. While not necessarily marginalized socially and culturally, they are nonetheless stigmatized and excluded from many of the social networks in academia (see Perlman 1975). In introducing her edited volume of short stories and poetry, Anzaldúa describes marginality within the context of "womaness" and "of color," but her observations are relevant to the present discussion:

> The world knows us by our faces, the most naked, most vulnerable, exposed and significant topography of the body. When our *caras* do not live up to the "image" that the family or community wants us to wear and when we rebel against the engraving of our bodies, we experience ostracism, alienation, isolation and shame. Since white AngloAmericans' racist ideology cannot take in our faces, it, too, covers them up, "blanks" them out of its reality." ... Some of us are forced to acquire the ability, like a chameleon, to change color when the dangers are many and the options few. Some of us who already "wear many changes/inside of our skin" have been forced to adopt a face that would pass. (Anzaldúa 1990, xv)

Marginality becomes a constant "balancing act" that undermines the humanity and ethnic integrity of many of the writers. Dulce Cruz, for example, wrestles with an oppressive hegemony and conquers it by accepting her cultural complexity—a complexity that is created by crossing cultural borders. She actively rejects stereotyping and racial myths that abound in our race-conscious American culture. Cruz tells how she was "designated as the spokesperson for all Hispanics and Blacks." She remembers the condescension of a faculty member who thanked her for "giving voice to the oppressed" when in actuality the faculty member was "congratulating herself for being liberal enough to 'empower' [Cruz] as if power can or should be given!" Cruz painfully speaks of her marginalization. "No matter what we do (get a Ph.D., become wealthy, move out of the neighborhood), we are still separated and boxed into categories like 'ethnic' and 'minority.' "

The account by Adalberto Aguirre, Jr., is only incidentally about a poor farmworker who excels in academia. The marginality Aguirre experiences comes as institutional hypocrisy and the feigned efforts to fulfill the mission of diversity in a multicultural world. He challenges pseudomulticultural academic values by "speaking the unpleasant" and thus gives us insight into what it is like to live as a "stranger in academic paradise." To his students and to his academic colleagues, Aguirre is a "stranger" who by his strangeness is kept at the margins. He argues that minority faculty are placed in an "organizational niche from which [minorities] emerge only when academe needs them to legitimate its own response." Aguirre, along with many of the other writers in this volume, believed in the myth that publishing was the brass ring to tenure, promotion, and academic success. Yet maintaining an "academic presence" within those networks that would indeed assist in one's academic career has been tenuous. Aguirre threads several examples that poignantly illustrate the hegemonic qualities of reciprocal exclusivity (Fannon 1963) expected by those in power. That is, ethnically distinct men and women, and to a lesser degree European American women, are compartmentalized into a climate that fosters academic apartheid by keeping such groups on the margins.

The marginalizing of a group can be very useful for those in power. The case study by Gerardo M. González, Francisco A. Ríos, Lionel A. Maldonado, and Stella T. Clark reveals what can happen when ideological crossfire is used to undermine and eventually divide the forces working for a more democratic nation. Besides being a story of the insidiousness of racism in everyday life and the calculated heavy-handed use of power and privilege, the authors' account illustrates the "unearned advantage" (McIntosh 1989) that can be used by a community inside as well as outside the university as a bully stick to forge its hegemonic superiority and shape the hypocritical ideology of a university campus. The case study revolves around an incident where a state senator made a statement about migrant workers that was widely interpreted as racist. Adding to the controversy, the new administration building at the authors' university campus was to bear that senator's name. The case study methodically illustrates how members of the Latino association on campus were alienated and compartmentalized (i.e., marginalized). Their marginalization gave the majority community the ability to bestow the senator's name on the new building. Yet critical lessons were learned about the significance of bringing those who are marginalized into the mainstream via the practice of coalition politics. So the "margins" can become frontiers—cultural borders of the academic terrain where the Other takes a central role in configuring a counterhegemonic epistemology and pedagogy. As Giroux (1992) reminds us:

> Indeed, such a task demands a rewriting of the meaning of pedagogy itself. It means comprehending pedagogy as a configuration of textual, verbal, and visual practices that need to engage the processes through which people understand themselves and the ways in which they engage others and their environment. It recognizes that the symbolic presentations that take place in various spheres of cultural production in society manifest contest and unequal power relations. As a form of cultural production, pedagogy is implicated in the construction and

organization of knowledge, desires, values, and social practices. At stake here is developing a notion of pedagogy capable of contesting dominant forms of symbolic production. (p. 3)

María Cristina González's personal narrative contests dominant forms of symbolic production by dragging from the academic margins to her ontological heart the value of personal and familial story, as language linkages not only to her rich past but to a deeper understanding of the dominant society that marginalized her in the first place. She recontextualized her cultural past, her traditional indigenous self, and the learning of "principles implicitly, etching them indelibly into [her] character." González challenges the positivist reader by illustrating that intellectual pursuits are more than one-dimensional jaunts into a mythic monocultural world that truly does not exist today (if it ever did). She writes honestly about her graduate school socialization and the entrenched positivism that would drive a wedge between her Chicana and her academic voices. The irony of her self-imposed exile from the margins into the perceived academic mainstream was a loss of her "creative" voice in an aseptic terrain that rewarded memorization and rebuffed originality and deep-felt insights. Throughout her narrative she weaves the remembrances of Papa M.R.'s traditional wisdom and shares with the reader her anguish and surprise as she finally realizes that the margins she roams are the terrain where we can "construct our own rhetorics of strength and dignity." She encircles and re-authenticates her ethnic, linguistic, and cultural richness, and thus turns the marginal into the essential. González redraws and expands the boundaries of the ideological turf that prescribes how an academic can think, act, and practice her calling.

Valuing the Self

After reading each of the narratives in this volume, one is left with a sense of overwhelming unease. The reader will encounter covert and overt anti-Latino prejudice in each of the stories. One quickly realizes how racism is an ideological poison that is historically and socially created and that is introjected into "social practices, needs, the unconscious, and rationality itself" (Giroux 1992, 113). At the same time, each narrative communicates some form of marginality. In this context, valuing the self becomes vital to personal and academic survival. In order to face the adversity of everyday life in academia, valuing the self becomes a necessity. Indeed, valuing the self becomes the metaphorical glue that all of the authors adhere to in order to protect authenticity and preserve their integrity. Yet valuing of self is an ontological struggle, a negotiation between two distinct typificatory schemes (Berger & Luckmann 1967) of the Latina or Latino academic's everyday life: that of ethnic identification as opposed to academic socialization as a scholar. While the narrators do genuinely value their persons, some of them display a glimpse of guilt as they find success in academia. Others, in their efforts to be forthright but not resentful, seem conspicuously ambiguous about their success.

María E. Torres-Guzmán frankly describes her journey through academia and the choices that any professor going through the tenure process must confront. Yet, as she is a person of color and a single mother, her choices reveal a portrait of the Other that attests to the rethinking of academic social systems and what undergirds their existence. Accepting a social system at the workplace is one thing, accepting its cultural sterility and its intolerance for diversity is another. By valuing her person, Torres-Guzmán challenges the paradigm of institutional intolerance and ignorance. She assists the reader to reconfigure the multiple and diverse conceptions that undergird an academic social system. Torres-Guzmán covers several topics circumstantial to her face-to-face encounters with the Other. The Other are students, departmental colleagues, the institution itself that implicitly devalued and set limits on her naturalistic knowledge base, her ethnicity, and her bilingual/multicultural capacities. She learned to "value the self" by setting limits not on herself but on those around her who devalued her every move, her expertise, her essence as a human being, and her time.

A. Reynaldo Contreras's story hides more then it tells. His valuing of self is expressed not so much as a declaration of autonomy by an academic, but more as a negotiation to nurture his deep-felt sense of connectedness to his family and to his community. Valuing the self, as Contreras teaches us, can become one's commitment to helping others and seeing them through the rough spots. In Contreras's story, however, there is an underlying demureness that hides the destructiveness of accepting the status quo. His story poignantly illustrates how the myth of meritocracy within academia is used as a backdrop to undermine needed reforms of the hiring, tenure, and promotion process. His "playing by the rules" only served to ghettoize his position by perpetuating the one-slot-for-minorities hiring rule. There is also a contradiction to his story that needs resolution: He naively accepted the meritocratic ideology of the institution—an institution with no conscience and no loyalty that continued the pervasive cycle of racial prejudice under the guise of "academic standards."

Ana M. Martínez Alemán illustrates the energy and commitment that it takes to value the self when one's cultural sphere becomes a tiny island in the sea of the Other. Not valuing one's cultural complexity may lead to complicity in one's oppression, as Ana M. Martínez Alemán suggests: "To be a professor is to be an Anglo; to be a Latina is not to be an Anglo. So how can I be both a Latina and a professor?" She concludes: "To be a Latina professor means to be unlike and like me. *¡Qué locura!* What madness!" Her fear of losing her cultural roots (and her resolve not to) leads her on a journey of self-doubt and reaffirmation that gives her narrative a poetic quality. Her narrative serves as a testimony to the importance of diversity and the courage that it takes to share that diversity with the Other within an interactive climate of difference.

The epilogue of this volume, by Roberto Haro, clearly portrays the social forces and hiring practices that Latinas and Latinos face in higher education administration. This chapter captures the theme of valuing the self in its "opposite." That is, this chapter exemplifies how higher education as an institution spreads its racist poison by subtly devaluing, undermining, and creating double standards for Latinas and Latinos who aspire to higher academic administration. It seems almost incomprehensible to what extent the devaluing process is practiced and accepted in order for an institution to hire its own. Yet Haro patiently and thoroughly takes the reader through his data-gathering techniques, research methods, and, finally, several most interesting subheadings, including academic preparation, experiential background, and scholarly/teaching accomplishments. Each of the subheadings adds to the entire puzzle, which finally reveals a disturbing portrait of the hiring process of academic administrators in higher education. To admit that such double standards exist today in the selection of vice presidents and presidents in higher education is to admit to one's complacency. Yet collectively we let such practices continue.

Ontological Holograms

The various chapters in this volume are ontological holograms of Latina and Latino survival and success in academia. They also envision the reconstruction of academia so that, among other things, it will have a more diverse professoriate. The stories, the portraits, the holograms (depending on the perspective that the reader wishes to take), provide insights into American academic life at the end of the twentieth century. These narratives express a "language of hope and possibility" (Giroux 1988) that reaches into the reader's ontological innerworkings and demands both a reflective evaluation of authentic human interactions and a rejection of anesthetized thoughts and feelings in the face of inequality and exclusion.

We hope that this book will stimulate academia to rethink how it produces, reproduces, and re-presents the meaning and practice of democracy (Giroux 1992) in the hiring, retention, tenure, and promotion of Latinas and Latinos in academia. This book suggests to presidents, vice presidents, deans, department chairs, search committees, and faculty that the concept of democracy must be reconstructed to include the voices of the Other. The authors included in this volume directly and indirectly declare that they too are part of our living democracy—sometimes meekly asking, at other times consciously challenging, and at still other times saying: "We are here. We will not go away. We will not change to meet your notions of what an academic should be or how an academic should look or act." This stand in support of fundamental democracy is in sharp contrast to recent examples of so-called educational reformists who have wanted to suppress democratic expression by eliminating opposition and difference (Bloom 1987; DíSouza 1991; Hirch 1987; Ravitch 1990; Ravitch & Finn 1987).

Within our popular culture there are innumerable images of a not-too-distant past that portray acts of undeniable violence, such as hate crimes. San Juan (1992) points out the still-prevalent manifestations of racism that continue to be as violent as in the near and distant past. During the past decade, examples of such hate crimes have ranged from the killing of African Americans in the Howard Beach and Bensonhurst incidents, to urban rebellions in the early and late eighties in Miami, Florida, antibusing attacks, the 1982 killing of Albert Chin (a Chinese American mistaken for a Japanese) by unemployed auto workers, the harassment of students of color at several campuses throughout the country, the slaying of a man of Ethiopian descent by neo-Nazi skinheads in Portland, Oregon, and the willful murder of five Asian children and the wounding of thirty others by a white gunman with a hate psychosis. These are only a few of the many examples of the racial violence that has been endured by people of color—the Other. San Juan reports that, in the eighties, "racial attacks increased from 99 in 1982 to 276 in 1986" (1992, 1). As San Juan argues, by no means can these be construed as "isolated incidents."

It is characteristic of the human condition to emphasize our successes and strengths and to deemphasize our failures and weaknesses. We do not want to think about or feel the uncomfortable. Institutions and the people that make those institutions are not any different. However, we can let discomfort become a path to reflection and democratic action in our practice. The stories contained in this book, although sometimes uncomfortable and by no means "isolated incidents," genuinely share with the reader experiences that will further the dialogue and that may enhance the recruitment, retention, tenure, and promotion of Latinas and Latinos. The authors do not write from the standpoint of "victims." Rather, they write as authorities who "speak the unpleasant," as Aguirre suggests in this volume. Each author places before the reader a story rich in introspection, and sometimes self-doubt, but almost always with the rediscovery of courage within.

Each story is a perspective, a slice of academic life. Collectively, the multiple perspectives in this volume provide a totality that is penetrating and disturbing but essential if we are genuinely to diversify our present and future professoriate. Equally important, the accounts capture and challenge the topography of the academic cultural terrain as it is constructed and perceived by the writers: a cultural terrain that has been created to limit and exclude, based on and bound to cultural, racial, gender, religious, and class manifestations and oppressive hegemonic traditions. The power of the narratives is that they constitute a counterhegemonic force, a force that if actively engaged will enhance the practice of democracy for all.

The Leaning Ivory Tower, then, is a critical collection of multiple constructed realities that can be understood best if placed in a holistic framework (Lincoln & Guba 1985). Each author, struggling with her or his own reality, is a study in authenticity and the engagement of liberation through self-critique. Through struggle with an oppressive academic world, the authors not only pursue their own liberation but simultaneously serve as liberating sponsors by restoring humanity back to those who oppress them. As Freire (1972) noted a generation ago:

> It is only the oppressed who, by freeing themselves, can free their oppressor. The latter, as an oppressive class, can free neither others nor themselves. It is therefore essential that the oppressed wage the struggle to resolve the contradiction in which they are caught; and the contradiction will be resolved by the appearance of a new man: neither oppressor nor oppressed, but man in the process of liberation. If the goal of the oppressed is to become fully human, they will not achieve their goal by merely reversing the terms of the contradiction, by simply changing poles. (p. 42)

Thus *The Leaning Ivory Tower* is not just a metaphor for what is. It also confronts, reconfigures, and challenges us to redraw our paradigmatic and conceptual borders so that the democratic process will be a liberating practice evidenced throughout academia.

Finally, we want to alert the reader to the need to continue to make public the lived experiences of Latina and Latino professors in American universities. This book breaks new ground in that the private stories of Latino and Latina professors are finally brought out into the public discourse. Many more such stories need to be told. After such narrative materials become abundant, there needs to be a collective effort to engage in analysis and critique of these experiences. Only such critical study will permit us to reap the positive results of having made our abode in a leaning ivory tower.

References

Apple, M. W. (1985). *Education and power*. Boston: Ark Paperbacks.

Anzaldúa, G. (1990). Haciendo caras: una entrada. In G. Anzaldúa (Ed.), *Making face, making soul, haciendo caras: Creative and critical perspectives by women of color* (pp. xv–xxviii). San Francisco: Aunt Lute Foundation.

Aronowitz, S. (1981). *The crisis in historical materialism*. New York: Praeger.

Berger, P. L., & Luckmann, T. (1967). *The social construction of reality: A treatise in the sociology of knowledge*. Garden City, NY: Anchor Books.

Bloom, A. (1987). *The closing of the American mind*. New York: Simon & Schuster.

DíSouza, D. (1991). *Illiberal education: The politics of race and sex on campus*. New York: Free Press.

Fannon, F. (1963). *The wretched of the earth*. New York: Grove Press.

Freire, P. (1972). *Pedagogy of the oppressed*. New York: Seabury Press.

Giroux, H. (1988). *Teachers as intellectuals: Toward a critical pedagogy of learning*. Westport, CT: Bergin & Garvey.

Giroux, H. (1992). *Border crossings: Cultural workers and the politics of education*. New York: Routledge.

Hirch, E. D., Jr. (1987). *Cultural literacy: What every American needs to know*. Boston: Houghton Mifflin.

Jones, J. M. (1981). The concept of racism and its changing reality. In B. P. Bowser & R. G. Hunt (Eds.), *Impacts of racism on white Americans*. Beverly Hills, CA: Sage.

Lincoln, Y., & Guba, E. (1985). *Naturalistic inquiry*. Beverly Hills: Sage.

McIntosh, P. (1989). White privilege: Unpacking the invisible knapsack. *Peace and Freedom*, July/August, pp. 10–12.

Perlman, J. (1975). Rio's favelas and the myth of marginality. *Politics and Society*, 5, 121–60.

Ravitch, D. (1990). Diversity and democracy: Multicultural education in America. *American Educator*, Spring, pp. 16–20, 46–48.

Ravitch, D., & Finn, C. E. (1987). *What do our 17-year-olds know? A report on the first national assessment of history and literature.* New York: Harper & Row.

Reyes, M. L., & Halcón, J. (1988). Racism in academia: The old wolf revisited. *Harvard Educational Review, 58 (3)*, 299–314

Rosaldo, R. (1989). *Culture and truth: The remaking of social analysis.* Boston: Beacon Press.

San Juan, E., Jr. (1992). *Articulations of power in ethnic and racial studies in the United States.* Atlantic Highlands, New Jersey: Humanities Press.

Weinberg, M. (1977). *A chance to learn: A history of race and education in the U.S.* Cambridge: Cambridge University Press.

CHAPTER 1

A *Chicano Farmworker in Academe*

ADALBERTO AGUIRRE, JR.

It is predictable by now. As I lecture on the relationship between minority status and educational attainment, a student will ask: "What made you pursue an education?" Is the student curious, or am I the curiosity? Over the years, I have framed the following response to the question.

> My family was part of the Chicano migrant worker stream in Texas. When I was fourteen years old, my father had contracted (the family) with a rancher in Plainview, Texas, to weed his cotton fields. The pay was attractive—thirty cents an hour per worker! Since there were six workers in the family, this translated into major economic gains.
>
> On one particular day, the temperature was around 110 degrees, the flies were buzzing louder than ever, and the ground was harder than usual. I stopped working. I watched the cars traveling on the highway that ran alongside the cotton field. I saw families traveling in air-conditioned cars. Mom, dad, and the kids looked happy. It just didn't seem fair. I decided then that that summer would be my last as a migrant farmworker.

Most students like my response to the question. I believe that students like my response because it reinforces their belief that minority faculty succeed out of a desire to escape victimization and misery in society. I also believe that students like my response because it offers hope to working-class and minority persons. Thus, for some students I become a symbol of unbridled hope. Regardless of why students like my response, the question reflects a general perception students have of me: that I am a minority person first, and a professor second. To them I symbolize a stranger in academe, and my *strangeness* resides in being

The ideas discussed in this essay have evolved from conversations with numerous persons—in particular, the late Tomás Rivera, Richard Verdugo, Hisauro Garza, Ruben Martínez, Raymond V. Padilla, Tony Hernández, and Gloria Cuadraz.

17

someplace where I'm not supposed to be. I then wonder, Is what I see in the eyes of my students the same things I see in the eyes of the faculty around me? Am I also a stranger to them?

Strangers in Academe

The research literature notes that working-class background (Ryan & Sackrey 1984, Hochschild 1988), ethnicity (Aguirre 1987, Garza 1988), race (Bell 1986, Smith & Witt 1990), and gender (Sandler & Hall 1986, Johnsrud & Wunsch, 1991) are instrumental in shaping a person's presence in academe. These status characteristics transform persons into strangers in academe—the working class, women, and minorities. The social expectations, for example, that structure the ordering and sorting of these status characteristics in everyday life constrain individuals who possess them from participating in some sectors in academe (Aguirre, Martínez, & Hernández, 1993). Consequently, when individuals possessing one or more of these status characteristics enter academe, they become strangers in context because they are not expected to be there. In this sense, participation in academe is not part of the life experience of individuals possessing those status characteristics. In his study of minority law professors' lives, Delgado (1988, 12) notes how difficult it is for minority persons to negotiate their presence in academe: "A young Hispanic professor teaching at a major school approached a senior white male colleague. . . . The professor appeared not to recognize her and asked her to please see his secretary for an appointment—the treatment he routinely applies to students."

When, then, do minority faculty have a meaningful presence in academe? When are they not treated as strangers in academe? From my discussions with minority faculty I have made the observation that a meaningful context is created in academe for minority faculty only when academe is faced with an issue or decision involving a minority person. It thus appears that minority faculty are placed in an organizational niche from which they emerge only when academe needs them to legitimize its own response to an issue or decision involving a minority person. As a result, minority faculty are institutionalized as *"shape changers"* in academe—their image is altered to mirror the type of response academe expects from them. This is not to imply that minority faculty are the only *"shape changers"* in academe. White faculty are capable of being *"shape changers"* too. However, white faculty only undergo the shape-changing process when they have something to gain. In contrast, minority faculty are so constrained in their organizational niche within academe that *"shape changing"* is perceived by them as meaningful institutional participation, even though they usually have nothing to gain.

In addition, input from minority faculty is actively solicited when either the campus or the department screens a minority applicant for a faculty position. However, minority faculty are rarely asked to play a similar role in screening nonminority candidates. Their participation in only certain types of activities places minority faculty in a segregated context in academe. The minority faculty person is now even more a stranger in academe—her or his presence is now peripheral and segregated in academe. I then wonder, Do nonminority faculty know that their behavior toward and expectations for minority faculty reinforces the peripheral and segregated presence of minority faculty in academe?

The Utility of Minority Faculty

Sometimes academe creates a decision-making context for minority faculty that enhances the legitimization of organizational decisions that could be perceived as *"suspect"* if minority faculty are excluded from the decision-making activity. For example, several years ago the College of Humanities and Social Sciences at my campus, the University of California at Riverside, recommended disestablishing the Chicano Studies Program. At the time, the Chicano Studies Program had five tenured faculty with joint appointments, a faculty-student ratio that was in the top five on the campus, and a high profile among other Chicano Studies Programs across the country. To the casual observer the Chicano Studies Program looked strong and healthy. The decision to disestablish the program thus came as a surprise to the Chicano faculty, staff, and students.

In an attempt to placate the Chicano community, the dean of the college asked the Chicano Studies faculty to prepare a programmatic review. The programmatic review was presented as the best argument against the disestablishment of the Chicano Studies Program. The Chicano faculty, staff, and students spent countless hours documenting course enrollments, extramural support, research productivity, teaching evaluations, and so on. In the end, a twenty-five-pound document was produced that contained a major finding of interest to all: The extramural review team composed of faculty from the other UC campuses ranked the Chicano Studies Program, based on its program size and campus size, among the top five academic units in the UC system. The Chicano campus community breathed a sigh of relief because it believed that the document insured the continuation of the Chicano Studies Program.

The academic senate on campus did not think so. While the senate agreed that the document identified Chicano Studies as a strength of the campus, the senate felt that Chicano Studies was too narrow to fit within a curriculum focused on comparative academic study. Chicano Studies was portrayed by the senate as a *"narrow"* discipline. As a result, the senate voted to disestablish the Chicano Studies Program, but passed legislation that established an Ethnic Studies Program that would be comparative in its course offerings. The immediate question for the Chicano Studies faculty became: Do we fit within an Ethnic Studies framework? An answer can be found in the fact that only one of the Chicano Studies Program faculty became a member of the Ethnic Studies Program.

I offer the preceding example as an illustration of what happens when minority faculty are involved in decision-making activity that is utilized by academe to remove the *"suspect"* quality of its decisions. The efforts of the Chicano faculty, staff, and students were not completely in vain—they did get the university to acknowledge the presence of Chicano Studies on campus. However, the academic senate utilized the academic viability of Chicano Studies to remove its presence from the campus. Several months after the academic senate reached its decision, I had the opportunity to talk with one of the key senate members involved in the decision. As I recall, he said to me: "What is the Chicano community complaining about? We disestablished Chicano Studies, but gave them Ethnic Studies? What's the difference?" It was precisely at that point that I saw in his eyes what I see in my students' eyes—I am a stranger in academe.

Academic Networks

I remember my advisor saying to me several times as I was completing my Ph.D. dissertation: "Never stop publishing." The act of publishing took on symbolic meaning and demanded twenty-four-hour attention. It became my newborn baby. I had to nurture it much as I would a newborn baby. Parents tend to bestow a lot of attention on their children with the hope that their children will grow up to show society that they had responsible parents. In this sense, I paid attention to my research and publishing activities so they would show that I was a responsible scholar. I believed that hard work and commitment would bring their rewards. But things are not always what they seem nor what we want them to be.

Strangers in academe must bear the cost of attempting to maintain presence. They are constrained from entering those networks, or collegial relations, necessary to establish presence in one's academic career. For example, according to Levin (1987), law professor Rebecca Shepard finds that a woman lawyer on a law school faculty is still subject to male bias: "If she came upon a knot of McKinley professors standing around the doorway of one of their offices, she would find herself ignored, and if she attempted to join the conversation, the men would look at their watches, mumble something about how late it was, and wander off" (p. 26).

The exclusion of faculty persons by other faculty as a result of their status characteristics limits their ability to negotiate their contextual presence in academe. It is not unexpected to find in academe, for example, women and minority faculty interacting more often with each other than with white male faculty. Consequently, white male faculty often refer to women and minority faculty as "*clannish.*" In a sense, women and minority faculty are blamed for being themselves in order to avoid drawing attention to the structural constraints on their presence in academe. For racial and ethnic minority faculty, their exclusion from networks controlled by white male faculty is simply an extension of their subordinate position in society. According to Reyes and Halcón (1991), the racism experienced by minority faculty can be observed in minority-majority faculty relations, especially in the manner in which minority scholars and their research are evaluated by majority faculty: "The practice of hiring underrepresented minorities only for certain specialized ethnic departments, of limiting their numbers in mainstream departments, of fueling and perpetuating the myth that they are not fully qualified for academic positions, the continual devaluing of minority research . . . are all manifestations of covert racism" (p. 181). Similarly, Lafontaine and McKenzie (1985) note that the sexism, or sexual bias, experienced by women in academe can be observed in male-female faculty relations: "because social norms designate administrative positions in higher education as male, women occupants are always seen as women occupants . . . women invariably are viewed, and exist, as 'outsiders' " (p. 20).

Secondly, women and minority faculty are often excluded from those networks instrumental in determining continuity in one's presence in academe. Could it be that publishing and research are not the primary vehicles for establishing continuity in one's presence in academe? Do networks play a more important role? Was there something I neglected doing for my newborn baby? While a data set does not exist from which one could "crunch numbers" to show that network activities sometimes play a more important role than publishing and research do in determining continuity in a person's academic progress, one does hear through the academic grapevine (for minority faculty) about cases in which things were not as they should have been. For example, one hears about the Chicano sociologist who was denied tenure because his publications were in Chicano journals; the Asian American historian who was not recommended for promotion because her research was considered to be too "journalistic" in quality; the Black legal scholar who was not promoted to full professor because his writings were too critical of the legal system. The grapevine is full of stories—in most instances, the stories illustrate the powerless position of minority faculty in academe—a position of powerlessness that is fueled by the exclusion of minority faculty from networking activities in academe.

There are exceptions, but they hardly ever involve women and minority faculty; they are usually white male faculty who do not worry about publishing because their networks will review their work as being central and groundbreaking in the discipline. Some participants in academe have continuity in their presence because their work (research and publications) has future promise—it just needs time to mature. Strangers in academe, however, do not enjoy this luxury, because their work is evaluated not for promise, but for production; it has had enough time to mature.

A Recollection

A while back I submitted the first paper I ever wrote on Chicano faculty to one of the mainstream journals in my discipline. Before submitting the paper, I sent it out for comments and suggestions to persons in the field who had a high probability of serving as outside readers for the journal. (It has always been of interest to me that when senior white faculty submit papers for journal review, they often include a list of "suggested" reviewers for the paper.) I had a good feeling about the paper when I submitted it to the journal. Its publication in the journal would certainly promote the perception that Chicanos were capable of producing articles worthy of publication in the mainstream sociological journals.

Within a week, a letter arrived bearing the journal's address. My first feeling was that the article was "so good" that it had been accepted for publication without external review—I had heard that that happens sometimes. However, it did not happen to me. In three sentences the journal's editor said that he was using his authority as editor not to send out the paper for external review. According to the editor, the paper was of limited interest to the members of the American Sociological Association and the topic itself was not promising enough. Interestingly, an article dealing with Chicanos was published in the next quarterly issue of the journal. The journal's authors were white academics.

A Reflection

Finally, after listening to countless stories from colleagues about who survived or did not survive an academic review, I have reached two conclusions about academe: (1) Strangers in academe must work harder in order to maintain continuity in their academic presence; (2) some faculty in academe do not work as hard as others because they are shielded by their membership in certain academic networks. I now realize that faculty do not all subscribe to the same work ethic.

Simple hard work is not sufficient to maintain one's presence in academe. Most working-class, women, and minority academics I have met generally feel that no matter how hard they work, they will still not have access to networks that play a crucial role in sponsoring presence in academe, especially those networks that serve as the gatekeepers for strangers in academe. According to Moore (1988), these networks determine academic presence, because participation within them identifies one as a legitimate keeper of the guard: "The gatekeepers determine who is qualified and who is not; what rules to apply, break, or modify as it suits their objects" (p. 118). Perhaps my adviser should have told me, "Never stop publishing if you are not part of a network."

Role Models

During the 1960s, the postsecondary education institution was accused of "window-dressing" its minority faculty. The postsecondary education institution was attacked for its recruitment of minority faculty in order to showcase the institution's open environment. The affirmative action debates that criticized the window-dressing activities of the postsecondary education institution promoted the concept of "role model" as a new recruiting strategy. As a result, the postsecondary education institution embraced the role model concept in its acceptance of affirmative action guidelines. The questions surrounding the application of the role model, however, are far from simple: Role models for whom? Are role models symbols of increased access? Are role models vehicles for opening doors in academe? What is expected of role models in academe?

Delgado (1991) identifies one conceptual problem with being a role model for minority faculty: "To be a good role model, you must be an assimilationist, never a cultural or economic nationalist, separatist, radical reformer, or anything resembling any of these" (p. 1227). In its application, the role model concept requires at least two things. First, the persons selected to serve as role models must be static participants in academe. Role models have meaningful presence in academe only as long as they neither initiate nor participate in initiatives designed to open the doors of academe for others. Second, the persons selected to serve as role models must in their behavior reflect what is possible, but not what is probable. The role models become the postsecondary education institution's "carrot" to others on the outside—"we have one of the very few." As such, role models reinforce the concept of "very few" rather than "why not more." As a result, role models are simply window dressing for the postsecondary education institution (Aguirre & Martínez 1993).

The role model concept has hidden costs for strangers in academe. Minority faculty, for example, are expected to develop minority courses, advise minority students, and perform numerous committee assignments focused on minority affairs. This is a given for minority faculty because it legitimizes the postsecondary education institution's decision to open its doors to a stranger. In a sense, the stranger is constrained to those institutional contexts and activities that reflect his or her status characteristics in order to show other institutional members that he or she is not a "lost stranger" in academe. Vivian Twostar, the Native American anthropologist portrayed in *The Crown of Columbus*, reflects on the cost of being a role model: "Mine was not an orthodox promotion case . . . there was the matter of special counseling roles I had to fulfill for the Native American students. . . . The 'community service' portion of my resume bulged at the seams—I was a natural double bull's-eye for every college committee that lacked either a woman or minority" (Erdrich & Dorris 1991, 17).

The price of serving as a role model in academe might be too high for a woman and/or minority person to pay. Role models are expected to work not only harder, and with a larger constituency, but in context and activities that might not serve a useful purpose in promoting their presence in academe. Why then is it that women and minority faculty in academe are most often found in the junior ranks and in the lower levels of the senior ranks? I have come to believe that women and minority faculty are given an extended presence in academe only when there is no one left—especially when no white male faculty are left for promotion or advancement opportunities. Thus, the role model concept is instrumental in keeping women and minority faculty powerless in academe because academe fabricates their presence.

Finally, I tell my students, especially my Chicano students, to consider the "absurd" quality of being a role model. I tell them that if they accept the role model concept, they remove themselves from the general Chicano experience. Belief in oneself as a role model requires alienation—"I am so different, that's why I am here." Consequently, they are removed from the Chicano experience because they now seek answers to the questions: Different from whom? Similar to whom? If you can be a role model only by reflecting a competing Chicano experience, yet this competing Chicano experience does not move you closer to the white experience—after all, the phenomenological basis for role models is that they mirror aspects of the white experience—then for whom are you a role model? You might become a non-Chicano in the Chicano experience, but you always will be a Chicano in the white experience. The reality of losing one's identity as a Chicano results in a personal loss of self and belonging (see, for example, Navarrette, 1993).

Speaking the Unpleasant

Sometimes things need to be said that are not very pleasant, especially when we focus on an institution viewed by many as "paradise." The purposeful exclusion, however, of some persons from full participation in academe is not a pleasant thought. Those of us in academe are directly and indirectly involved in gatekeeping activities that exclude some persons from full participation. Some persons are just not welcome in academe no matter how hard they try.

What I hope to have made clear in this essay is the operation in academe of competing work ethics in which some work harder than others. Secondly, the exclusion of strangers (women and minority faculty) in academe from networks controlled by white male faculty limits the progress and continuity of strangers in academe. Thirdly, the role model concept is instrumental in maintaining strangers in academe as peripheral and segregated participants. To illustrate the preceding three observations I have provided a variety of examples. Just about every faculty person in academe has at some point in their academic career come into contact with one of the preceding three observations, if not all three.

Someone will ask: "Where is your data?" My only response is that some aspects of the life experience are not subject to empirical verification. Some things in life just are. As such, the observations I have offered in this essay are data of sorts in that they define real intersections in the life experience of strangers in academe. Thus, these observations are not subject to the scope conditions of empirical reality because they represent contextual reality—it is an open window with which to see how things really are.

For the curious, yes, I have traveled a long way from the cotton fields and my origins as a Chicano migrant farmworker. The journey so far has been an exceptional one. Not because I have traveled it, but because I am still surviving. The costs of the journey have been immense. I have lost some of my self in the journey. The journey has transformed me into a curiosity for my students and colleagues—"He has a Stanford Ph.D." However, not even Stanford, with its academic splendor, was enough to transform me in the eyes of students and colleagues. To them I am a stranger. I am a Chicano farmworker in academe. The field is still a field.

Finally, I remember that several years after the completion of my Ph.D. I found myself asked by my father and his friends to explain how academe works. At the time, my father and his friends were on strike at a steel-welding plant in south Texas. Faithful to my discipline, I gave them a discourse on the sociological nature of the academic profession. Would they understand how complicated academe was in its operation? After all, these persons did not possess Ph.D.'s. I talked, and they listened politely, sometimes asking a brief question. After I finished, my father looked at his friends, they looked at me and smiled, and my father said: "It's just work. I thought there was something special about it. But it sounds like you have to know more than what you understand in order to survive." Since then I have often wondered about my father's response. Could it be that academe is a paradise because we pretend not to be what we accuse the real world of being—simple?

References

Aguirre, A., Jr. (1987). An interpretative analysis of Chicano faculty in academe. *Social Science Journal, 24*, 71–81.

Aguirre, A., Jr. & Martínez, R. (1993). *Chicanos in higher education: Issues and dilemmas for the 21st century*. ASHE-ERIC Higher Education Report No. 3. Washington, DC: George Washington University School of Education and Human Development.

Aguirre, A., Jr., Martínez, R., & Hernández, A. (1993). Majority and minority faculty perceptions in academe. *Research in Higher Education, 34*, 371–85.

Bell, D. (1986). Strangers in academic paradise: Law teachers of color in still white schools. *University of San Francisco Law Review, 20*, 385–95.

Delgado, R. (1988). *Minority law professors' lives: The Bell-Delgado survey.* University of Wisconsin–Madison Law School Institute for Legal Studies Working Paper Series 3. Madison: University of Wisconsin.

——— (1991). Affirmative action as a majoritarian device: Or, do you really want to be a role model? *Michigan Law Review, 89*, 1222–31.

Erdrich, L., & Dorris, M. (1991). *The crown of Columbus.* New York: Harper.

Garza, H. (1988). The "barrioization" of Hispanic faculty. *Educational Record, 68*(4)/69(1), 122–24.

Hochschild, J. (1988). Race, class, power, and equal opportunity. In N. Bowie (Ed.), *Equal opportunity* (pp. 75–111). Boulder, CO: Westview Press.

Johnsrud, L., & Wunsch, M. (1991). Junior and senior faculty women: Commonalities and differences in perceptions of academic life. *Psychological Reports, 69*, 879–86.

Lafontaine, E., & Mckenzie, B. (1985). Being out on the inside in higher education administration: Women's responses to role and status incongruity. *National Association for Women Deans, Administrators, and Counselors Journal, 48*, 19–25.

Levin, M. (1987). *The socratic method.* New York: Ivy Books.

Moore, W. (1988). Black faculty in white colleges: A dream deferred. *Educational Record, 68*(4)/69(1), 117–21.

Navarrette, R., Jr. (1993). *A darker shade of crimson: Odyssey of a Harvard Chicano.* New York: Bantam Books.

Reyes, M. de la Luz, & Halcón, J. (1991). Practices of the academy: Barriers to access for Chicano academics. In P. Altbach & K. Lomotey (Eds.), *The racial crisis in American higher education* (pp. 167–86). Albany: State University of New York Press.

Ryan, J., & Sackrey, C. (1984). *Strangers in paradise: Academics from the working class.* Boston: South End Press.

Sandler, B., & Hall, R. 1986. *The campus climate revisited: Chilly for women faculty, administrators, and graduate students.* Washington, DC: Association of American Colleges, Project on the Status and Education of Women.

Smith, E., & Witt, S. (1990). Black faculty and affirmative action at predominantly white institutions. *Western Journal of Black Studies, 14*, 9–16.

CHAPTER 2

"Getting Tenure at the U"

TATCHO MINDIOLA, JR.

This essay discusses a Chicano professor's experiences in a tenure dispute that occurred at a major university in one of the country's largest and most populous states. The dispute brought to the fore several issues pertinent to minority professors in the universities. Although the primary face of the issue was the manner in which tenure is granted, relevant issues, such as departmental politics and discrimination, surfaced along the way to complicate matters and to make protracted what ought to have been a relatively simple, clear-cut solution.

Before it was all over, certain of the participants within the university felt that it had become a matter of protecting institutional integrity, and elected officials became involved because they perceived the dispute to be a matter of institutional discrimination aided by the use of public funds. It is a story, then, of intellectual and personal integrity, social justice, luck, inadvertent blunders, and the exercise of political power.

Background

Tenure is the single most important accomplishment in the career of an academician. At the end of a probationary period, usually between three and six years, a university professor is given a rigorous review and evaluation in three distinct areas. In the first of these, research and publications, the review committee considers the tenure candidate's fitness as a scholar. Generally, publication presents concrete evidence of a professor's research and scholarly activities and thus it is normally given additional weight relative to the other areas. In the second area, service to the university, the candidate may offer membership in committees, participation with student groups, and community service that reflects positively upon the image of the university. The third and last area is teaching. Credit for teaching is either conceded outright or is given weight according to a number-based teaching evaluation prepared by students at the end of each class taught by the candidate.

Tenure is not just an important honor bestowed upon a professor. It is, in fact, the legitimization of a career. If a professor is denied tenure, a career in a chosen profession might be over. It is difficult and rare for a professor denied tenure at one institution to rebound and continue at another institution. A professor granted tenure, however, has lifetime employment at the university where it is granted. Furthermore, while tenure itself is not transferable, it is usually the sine qua non for a professor to move from one university to another. A tenured professor, for example, may be removed from a position only for malfeasance, violation of civil or criminal laws, or financial exigencies (Wessells 1980). Only federal judges and tenured professors enjoy this privilege.

The rationale for granting tenure to a professor is that it allows for the unhindered pursuit of truth. Tenured professors can pursue controversial intellectual activity without fear of political or economic reprisal (Metzger 1979). In recent times, though, tenure has protected professors less for unfettered intellectual pursuit than for political and social activities that might make university administrators uneasy. For most professors, it can be safely asserted that tenure serves as little more than job protection. This is not entirely true, however, in the case of Chicano and other minority professors who are more apt to engage in research and other activities that question and criticize the status quo.

The Antecedents

When the dispute arose over the granting of tenure to the professor in this case, at issue was the question of joint appointments between various specialized programs and traditional academic departments. As these programs came into existence, their academic course offerings cut across various traditional disciplines and thus no one department could have full administrative jurisdiction. A joint appointment, then, meant that a faculty member had dual responsibilities, divided half and half between the program and an academic department.

A director would administer the program in a manner similar to that of a department chairman in a regular discipline, with the exception that the program did not have the authority to grant tenure to its faculty. The programs themselves did not all have full academic standing in the sense that not all granted degrees. When students completed the program curriculum, they would be issued a certificate as an addendum to a degree in a major discipline. Virtually all program course offerings were cross-listed with an academic department, a department in which a particular faculty member held a joint appointment.

Considering the jealously guarded autonomy of academic departments, joint appointments were fraught with the potential for controversy and dispute. There was, for example, the question of hiring. A candidate suitable to a program might not be acceptable to a department, and vice versa. There were also questions of course offerings, salary increases, and other administrative details that were the joint responsibility of the program director and the department chair.

In actual practice, a review of correspondence between colleges and departments and programs at the university, in the period prior to the professor's dispute, reveals that joint appointments tended to work well and were characterized by a spirit of cooperation and collegiality. Only two programs were the source of controversy. These were the Chicano Studies Program and the Black Studies Program.

At the time of the professor's employment in a joint appointment, there were five such appointments available in Chicano Studies and five more in the Black Studies Program. The responsibilities attached to his appointment were stipulated in the professor's letter of appointment, which stated in general terms his obligations to the department and to Chicano Studies. The professor's dual responsibilities were further outlined in a policy statement issued by the chancellor of the university.

The duties of a faculty member in the ethnic studies programs, according to the policy statement, would be considered in the evaluation of professors holding joint appointments. Furthermore, the director of each ethnic studies program would be involved in the evaluation of associated faculty. This statement became necessary because of disagreements over the role to be played by program directors in the evaluation of faculty holding joint appointments.

At issue was the authority of the director over the program's portion, nominally 50 percent, of the joint appointment. The chancellor's policy statement was intended to clarify the issue of the distribution of authority. However, disagreements continued, particularly where hiring and salary increases were concerned.

The professor in question was the first to hold a joint appointment between the Chicano Studies Program and an academic department. Moreover, the professor was the first Chicano ever employed in the department. The joint appointment called for the professor to teach and conduct research relevant to his discipline. Additionally, he was to help develop the newly established Chicano Studies Program. The latter entailed curriculum development and recruitment and retention of faculty and students. Also, because the university wanted Chicano Studies to stand as a symbol of its commitment to the Chicano community, the professor was to act as a liaison between the university and a variety of organizations and individuals in the Chicano community.

It was implicit in the professor's joint appointment that consideration would be given to the above activities in the professor's tenure review, to come after the standard probationary period. The professor's tenure was the first in which a joint appointment between Chicano Studies and an academic department was involved. Thus, there was no previous experience from which to draw procedural guidelines.

Department Politics

During the summer preceding his tenure candidacy, the professor became aware of a rumor that certain members of the department favored the granting of tenure to a white female who was to be considered at the same time as the professor, and that a strategy for removing the professor from consideration was being devised. There is always pressure, whether real or imagined, to limit the number of tenure appointments in any department. The female professor was the wife of one of the tenured professors, and together they were part of the most influential political group in the department. The professor was alerted to the possibility of a negative decision because of the rumors and from the result of three meetings he held with the chair of the department.

The meetings with the chair gave substance to the rumors. In the first meeting, the chair expressed concern that the professor did not have enough publications to be awarded tenure. He stated that standards had changed during the professor's employment and that more publications were now required. He advised that a one-year delay before the professor offered himself for tenure would allow the professor more time to publish additional articles. The professor rejected the advice. During his probationary period, the professor had been granted a one-year extension in order to complete his dissertation. He did not think it prudent to seek a further delay. Besides, the professor felt that, according to the available criteria, he deserved tenure.

In the second meeting, the chair again expressed concern over the professor's chances of being tenured. His reading of the faculty in the department, who would conduct the review, did not indicate a favorable disposition. He stated that perhaps the professor should seek tenure in another area, and he mentioned two departments that he thought might be interested. He convinced the professor to at least pursue exploratory conversations in order to assess the possibilities. After doing so, the professor informed the chair he would not seek tenure in another department.

In view of how things were going even before tenure proceedings began, the professor employed the counsel of an attorney for the duration of the tenure process. The attorney's first advice to the professor was to keep a record of any and all conversations pertaining to his tenure case.

In the third meeting, the chair indicated that denial of tenure was now a virtual certainty. The chair had spoken, however, with university officials about the situation, and these officials were interested in retaining the professor's services as the director of the Chicano Studies Program in a nontenured administrative position. At the time, an interim director headed the program. An unsuccessful bid for tenure, the chair continued, would make it difficult for the university to employ the professor in an administrative position. It would be difficult for the university to retain someone in an administrative capacity who had been rejected for tenure by one of the departments.

The solution to the dilemma, as put forth by the chair, involved the professor's resignation prior to any tenure consideration. This would preclude the stigma that denial of tenure would bring and thus it would make it easier for the university to retain his services. This proposed solution was adamantly rejected by the professor and it prompted a heated exchange between the professor and the chair of the department.

The Tenure Decision

The department's deliberations over the professor's tenure were lengthy and characterized by strong opinions for and against granting him tenure. In the end, the department voted six to five not to grant tenure. The recommendation was based upon there being an insufficient number of published scholarly articles. Chicano Studies, in contrast, strongly recommended the granting of tenure on the basis of outstanding service to the program and a more than acceptable record of scholarly achievement and publications, especially in light of the professor's dual responsibilities.

The negative decision by the department sparked controversy not only on campus but in the Chicano community as well. Students from various Chicano organizations on campus wrote letters to the department and began meeting with departmental faculty and other university officials. They were joined by representatives from a number of Chicano community organizations and other prominent individuals.

The professor notified the department that he would appeal their decision as provided for in university rules and procedures. The basis of the appeal was to be the department's failure to consider the joint appointment and give proper weight to the professor's duties and obligations to Chicano Studies. It was clear from their written evaluations that the department did not consult with Chicano Studies and that little, if any, consideration had been given to the joint appointment and the assessments that were submitted by the Chicano Studies tenure committee. Prior to the appeal, the faculty in the department were lobbied by members of a coalition composed of students and representatives of the Chicano community. On the day of the appeal, a Friday, approximately seventy-five members of the coalition appeared before the faculty to read statements of support.

The appeal and the discussion that followed lasted for several hours. When a vote was finally taken, it was seven for tenure, three against tenure, and one abstention. The abstention came from a committee member who wanted more time to consider his vote and who stated that he would return on Monday with a decision.

On Monday, the committee member who had abstained changed his vote in favor of granting tenure. The amended vote was now eight for tenure and three against. Two other faculty members, however, who had initially voted to grant tenure during the appeal vote, changed their votes over the weekend. Thus, instead of an eight-to-three vote, the amended vote was six to five in favor.

The professor protested that, procedurally, votes could not be changed after the close of official deliberations. The professor's objections fell upon intransigent ears, and the six-to-five vote moved forward to the next week. It was accompanied by a letter in which the professor objected to unusual procedures that had taken place.

At the next level, the College of Social Sciences, the department's recommendation to grant tenure was rejected. The dean of the college recommended a denial of tenure. Once again, the joint appointment played no part in arriving at the recommendation. In view of the anticipated complexity of the negotiations to follow, the professor formally introduced his attorney into the process. This became necessary as the discussions moved forward to the provost and the chancellor of the university.

The argument in defense of the professor's tenure, as stated by the professor and his attorney, stressed the matter of the joint appointment and the attendant obligations to the Chicano Studies Program, neither of which had thus far been considered in the tenure review and subsequent decisions. These officials were not persuaded by the argument and steadfastly refused to sustain the department's decision to grant tenure. They countered by stating that they recognized the professor's worth to the university and therefore were willing to consider making him the permanent director of Chicano Studies in a purely administrative capacity.

The professor was very hesitant about accepting the offer. He felt that, all things considered, he had earned tenure. After lengthy negotiations, an agreement was reached that called for the professor's appointment as director of Chicano Studies. A provision was included by which the professor would be reviewed again for tenure every five years until it was granted to him.

It was a jewel of an agreement, but it was ultimately rejected by the president of the university system. In its stead, the professor was offered a standard three-year contract for employment in an administrative nontenured position. No provision for a future tenure review was included. It did, however, allow for continued teaching in his academic discipline within the department. It was the only kind of contract to which the president would agree.

After much consultation and thought, the professor reluctantly agreed to the offer. In his letter of acceptance, he made it clear that his acceptance did not imply that he was waiving his right to litigate the tenure issue in court. A year and half after accepting the contract and after clearing Equal Employment Opportunity Commission grievance procedures, and two days before the grace period to litigate was to expire, the professor filed a discrimination suit in federal court.

The Lawsuit

The lawsuit alleged discrimination based upon the nature of the joint appointment. The university could not place Chicanos in joint appointments between Chicano Studies and academic departments, expect fulfillment of a faculty member's obligations to both units, and then ignore the division of responsibility at the time of tenure decisions. This was discriminatory at the time of tenure decisions. This was discriminatory, the suit alleged, because other, non-Chicano professors were not required to accept joint appointments as a condition of their employment. Therefore, no other professors were obliged to serve two masters. In effect, the suit stated that the university could not have it both ways.

After the lawsuit was filed, the professor was notified by the chair of the department that he would not be allowed to teach courses in the department. The professor objected and reminded the chair that his contract stipulated a teaching opportunity. The chair refused to comply. The professor carried his objections to the provost but was told that it was strictly a matter between the department and the professor and that the department could, if it chose to, exercise its prerogative over who taught courses. The lawsuit was amended to include an allegation of retaliation.

The decision to file a lawsuit was not an easy one for the professor to make. For one thing, the lawsuit raised the possibility that the university would not reappoint him as director of the Chicano Studies Program at the end of the three-year contract. This would leave the professor without the economic resources needed to continue the litigation, and it had been for that very reason that he had accepted the contract in the first place.

Moreover, universities and other institutions have, over the years, chipped away at laws allowing for discrimination suits to be filed and have made proving discrimination extremely difficult. More importantly, the courts have a tradition of deferring to institutions of higher learning in purely academic matters. Their attitude has been that decisions concerning educational matters are best left to the educators. Thus, courts are very reluctant to question personnel decisions that are based upon educational grounds, such as the quality of research or competence in teaching (Gray 1985).

This reluctance on the part of the courts makes it even more difficult to prove discrimination, because discrimination often is hidden under the guise of an educational decision. Furthermore, research revealed that the university against which the professor filed suit had not lost a case in court on any matter during the thirteen years preceding the professor's lawsuit. All of this confirmed how difficult it is for an individual to prevail in a lawsuit against an institution of higher education.

The Luck of the Draw

A further reason for the professor's uneasiness concerned the conservative judicial temperament of the majority of the judges in the federal district in which the case was filed. They were not likely to rule in favor of the professor. Because of this, a jury trial was contemplated. Federal regulations require, however, that both parties to a suit agree to a jury trial. Whether the university would agree to a jury trial was problematic, at best. This was rendered moot when the judge was assigned. Judges in federal district courts are randomly assigned to hear lawsuits according to the kind and type of lawsuit filed. As it turned out, the only Mexican American judge in the district was assigned to hear the case. The "luck of the draw" could not have been more favorable to the professor.

The judge had a civil rights background and, in the informal characterization of attorneys, he had the reputation of being a plaintiff's judge. While in private practice he had been involved in filing lawsuits against school districts for discriminating against Chicanos. He was also a longtime member of a major civil rights organization in the Chicano community. This particular judge considerably enhanced the chances of the professor's case, but the significance of this was not readily grasped by attorneys for the university.

The Faux Pas

During the negotiations for renewal of his contract as director of Chicano Studies, the professor met with the president of the university system on three separate occasions in an effort to obtain a clause in the contract that would call for a tenure review. Each time the president refused. In fact, during the final meeting, the president expressed the sentiment that the professor would probably never receive tenure at the university.

In the course of the entire tenure dispute there were two other instances, in line with his duties as director of Chicano Studies, that required that the professor interact with the president of the university system. As a result of this interaction, the professor and the president became acquainted with one another beyond the cursory contact that otherwise would have been the case.

The first occasion was a summer scholarship program administered by the Chicano Studies Program. The scholarship program was funded by the government of Mexico and it provided for up to twenty-five Chicano students to study for six weeks at one of Mexico's most prestigious colleges. The intent of the program was to foster a better understanding of Mexico among Chicanos through the study of Mexico's history, economic and political system, and social problems.

Every year representatives from the university and the college met to sign an agreement that spelled out each institution's obligations. The host duties for the signing of the agreement alternated each year; one year representatives from the university went to Mexico, and the next year a delegation from Mexico visited the university campus. The professor was responsible for arranging the details of the scholarship program every year, and this necessitated interaction with the president on a regular basis.

One year, the president led the delegation to Mexico. On this particular trip, the agenda included not only the signing of the scholarship agreement but also the beginning of negotiations for joint conferences and research projects. The delegation included the professor, other Chicano faculty, and university officials. The itinerary called for the delegation to spend a total of three days in Mexico. Throughout the visit, the professor had continuous interaction with the president. All of this is important in order to understand the faux pas that will soon be described.

The second occasion was the professor's efforts to secure a line-item appropriation for Chicano Studies from the state legislature. A line-item appropriation is a mechanism by which special university projects may be funded directly by the legislature. The line item sought for Chicano Studies would establish a visiting scholar's program, expand its efforts to recruit students, and purchase equipment.

The request was initiated by the director of Chicano Studies, and it had to have approval from university officials before it could be forwarded to the legislature. It was in fact approved at the appropriate levels of authority within the university, and this included the president's office at the system level.

Assisting the professor were two local Chicano state representatives. One served on the appropriations committee that reviewed all budget requests from state agencies. The other representative was the newly elected chair of the Chicano Legislative Caucus, which consisted of twenty-two Chicano and nine Anglo legislators.

Given that a legislative request involves a certain amount of lobbying, the professor suggested that a meeting of the Chicano Legislative Caucus be convened on the university campus, with Chicanos Studies acting as host. The purpose of the on-site meeting was to showcase the program and its faculty; in short, to gain support for the line-item request.

The president hosted a lunch for the legislators. In the course of his introduction, preparatory to a short speech he was to deliver, the president committed a faux pas that was interpreted as a display of insensitivity and that would later have a significant effect upon the tenure issue.

The blunder involved the professor's first name, which is *Tatcho* (pronounced, *Ta-cho*). Admittedly *Tatcho* is an unusual name even among Chicanos. The mispronunciation of his first name, at least upon initially meeting someone, is something with which the professor has had to live all of his life. This is especially true when Anglos try to pronounce the name. It should also be stated, however, that people quickly learn how to say the name properly, once they are given the correct pronunciation.

The professor introduced the president to the legislators at the luncheon. The mood of the luncheon could be characterized by cordiality and good will. In his brief introductory remarks, the professor sought to put the president in the best possible light by stressing the president's support for Chicano Studies, as evidenced by his trip to Mexico.

After the president was introduced, he received a polite round of applause as he stepped forward. He strode to the podium in his usually confident manner, turned to face the audience, and in his southern drawl, he said, "Thank you, *Taco!*"

The president's mispronunciation of the professor's first name aroused a ripple of laughter among members of the caucus. The president then launched into his speech, in which he cited the university's strengths and accomplishments, and he made an appeal for more funds for research and faculty salaries. This portion of his speech lasted approximately twenty minutes.

He then proceeded to discuss the enrollment of Chicano students on the four campuses that make up the University system. He praised the system's open admissions campus for its Chicano students. He acknowledged that the main campus, where the legislators were present, did not have a similar record, but he quickly pledged his commitment to improve the situation. The president then looked over to where the professor was standing, gestured towards him with his hand, and the following ensued:

PRESIDENT: Now, I know that *Taco* is not going to let me leave this room without mentioning his line-item request. (*Muffled laughter from the audience*)

I've said this privately, and *Taco*, I'll now say publicly, that I support your line item request.... (*More muffled laughter, coupled with incredulous looks in the professor's direction.*)

Taco has been doing a fine job as director of Chicano Studies.... (*Still more muffled laughter, some unclear comments.*)

... *Taco*, you have my...

CHAIRMAN OF THE CAUCUS: *(Interrupting the president.)* It's Tatcho! not
                           Taco! *(Laughter, unclear comments.)*

PRESIDENT: Beg your pardon?

CHAIRMAN OF THE CAUCUS: It's Tatcho, Tatcho, not *Taco*, and the univer-
                           sity is not going to receive it's appropriations
                           next year until you learn to say it correctly.
                           *(An outburst of laughter, coupled with scat-
                           tered applause.)*

PRESIDENT: *(Turning red in the face and looking down at the podium.)*
              Oh, I beg your pardon.

The president quickly made a few more complimentary remarks
about Chicano Studies and ended his speech with a call for support
from the caucus. He received a polite round of applause that was mingled
with much comment. The president's blunder left him stigmatized and
discredited in the eyes of the caucus. This, however, did not surface or
have any consequences until several months later when the issue of the
professor's tenure came before the caucus.

The Importance of the Judge

The lawsuit against the university continued to unfold, and the judge's role
began to assume major significance. The professor's attorney filed a motion for discovery of evidence in which he asked that all records pertaining
to the university's tenure decisions from the time of the professor's employment to the present be made available. This covered a period of ten years.

The university in its countermotion objected on the grounds that
there should be a time restriction of only five years and that only those
records pertaining to tenure in the department should be made available. In the preceding five years, only two tenure decisions had been
made in the department. This would have made just those two files
available.

The judge ruled in the professor's favor. Given that confidentiality
of personnel decisions is part and parcel of the judicial deference traditionally accorded to higher education, the judge's ruling was a major
victory for the professor. More so as the evidence discovered in large
measure substantiated his case.

The university's tenure records revealed the following:

- Professors who did not hold joint appointments had been granted tenure with records of scholarly achievement equal to or less than that of the professor. One such individual had been granted tenure in the same year as the professor had been denied tenure.
- The joint appointments between the ethnic studies programs and departments were fraught with conflict, controversy, and disputes over hiring, salary, and jurisdiction. In comparison, joint appointments involving Anglo professors were characterized by cooperation, harmony, and a spirit of collegiality.
- Accomplishments other than scholarly publications were recognized in some instances as a contributing and significant factor in the awarding of tenure.

In the midst of these discoveries, the university made an announcement that helped to bolster the professor's case. The university eliminated ethnic joint appointments between the ethnic studies programs and departments. Henceforth, all Chicano and Black faculty would have regular appointments. In announcing their decision, the university acknowledged the controversy surrounding such joint appointments and was in fact admitting that they did not work. It is not apparent whether university officials were aware of the implication that this decision would have in the related and pending federal lawsuit.

Entrenchment and Victory

Federal lawsuits require that both parties jointly prepare and submit a document that spells out which facts in a case are in dispute and which are in agreement. At the end of this process, the attorney general's office, which is required to represent the university, conceded to the professor's attorney that the facts favored the professor and that the university in all probability would lose the lawsuit if it were allowed to go to trial. The assistant attorney general assigned to the case also stated that he would inform his superiors in Austin, as well as the university's attorney, of his opinion and he would recommend to the university that it seek an out-of-court settlement.

When informed of the recommendation, the president refused to accept the recommendation of a settlement and determined that the case would go to trial. His rationale was that the integrity of the tenure process had to be protected. A week before the trial was to begin, the professor's attorney was notified that the court date would have to be postponed because the preceding trial was taking more time than had been anticipated. It was at this point that the network of attorneys in the federal courts system contributed some assistance to the professor's case.

A former law associate of the professor's attorney served as a law clerk for one of the federal judges. This law clerk had become the friend of the law clerk of the judge who was slated to hear the professor's case. Through this informal network, the professor's attorney gained an impression of how the judge viewed the case. When informed of the postponement, the professor's attorney requested that both sides meet with the judge in his chambers in order to solicit his opinion. The university was unaware that the professor's attorney had arranged the meeting.

During the meeting, the judge apologized for the postponement and said he wanted to relay his thinking on the case, based upon the evidence submitted thus far. He stated that it appeared to him that the professor had a meritorious case and he urged an outside agreement. The judge acknowledged the possibility that the university might submit additional evidence that could change his opinion, but he said he doubted that this would occur since rules governing federal lawsuits require most, if not all, of the relevant evidence to be submitted prior to the beginning of a case. The judge closed the meeting by again recommending an out-of-court settlement and requesting that he be kept informed of the case's progress. When this information was relayed to the president, he again refused to consider a settlement.

Chicano Power

Shortly thereafter, the professor received an inquiry about the lawsuit from one of the local Chicano state representatives. The representative was apprised of the progress of the case. The state representative then contacted the attorney general's office and he confirmed that the assistant attorney general handling the case, and the judge who would preside over it, had recommended an out-of-court settlement.

The president's adamant refusal to follow his legal advice angered the Chicano state representative. He took the matter before the Chicano Legislative Caucus for their consideration. They readily agreed to become involved.

As stated above, the caucus members already had developed a negative perception of the president because of his faux pas involving the professor's first name. This perception was not ameliorated when they learned that the president steadfastly refused to settle the case even though the university had been advised to do so by its counsel and by the presiding judge.

The president was approached several times by caucus members, who encouraged him to settle the case. Each time he refused. The president's refusal was interpreted by the caucus as a blatant display of arrogance and entrenchment, and it was taken as a direct challenge.

There followed several heated exchanges between caucus members, and the president and other university officials. The president's continued refusal prompted the caucus to send him a strongly worded letter, which, in part, read as follows:

> Generally, Hispanics . . . have not quite penetrated our higher education system in any significant fashion, whether we speak about students or faculty. Part of this can be attributed to the fact that we have continued to fail to make a stronger effort in adequately recognizing the needs of this special population. This is ironic when you consider the fact that for the last two decades, the public outcry for more Hispanic representation in education has intensified. Furthermore, more and more state and federal legislation continues to address this issue. Yet, the problem does not seem to be disappearing. It is irresponsible actions and decisions like yours that create an obstacle to this.[1]

Word of the situation began to spread beyond the Chicano Legislative Caucus to other legislators. The university was creating for itself the image of a racist institution. Advised that his intransigence was threatening the university's reputation, not to mention its budget, the president began to soften his position and undertook a series of strategies designed to show good faith on the part of the university and to improve relations with the Chicano Legislative Caucus and other legislators.

He first announced that the professor would be allowed to undergo another complete tenure review in order to correct any mistakes that may have occurred in his initial review. The offer was refused on the grounds that a review had already been conducted. What mistakes might be discovered would not be corrected but covered up.

The president then announced that the professor would be reviewed for special tenure in the Chicano Studies Program. He ordered the formation of a committee to review the professor's credentials. This offer was also refused on the grounds that only departments have authority to grant tenure. The Chicano Studies Program lacked departmental status. Tenure in the program was tantamount to "second-class tenure" and would be viewed as such by the broader academic community on campus. The faculty committee appointed by the president also refused to review the case, citing similar grounds.

The president then informed the caucus that the professor would not accept his offer of tenure. The caucus, meanwhile, had been briefed as to the anomalous nature of tenure in the Chicano Studies Program—that it is, in fact, an offer of "second-class tenure." This latter point struck a responsive cord among members of the caucus and in the end it served only to reinforce their negative perception of the president.

Strongly worded messages continued to be sent to the president. Caucus members on the appropriations committee sent word that the university's budget would be held up in committee. Also, they were prepared to hold public discussions on the issue if an out-of-court settlement was not reached.

As it became evident that few options remained, the president at last relented. He agreed to tenure the professor in the department. He refused, however, to approve a promotion to associate professor. Except in rare circumstances, a promotion to associate professor normally accompanies the granting of the tenure. On this point the president was adamant.

The Judge and Resolution

After years of litigation and administrative and political maneuvering, countless hours in meetings and discussions, on the face of it the case appeared to be resolved as it had all along been anticipated it would be— that is, in the professor's favor. Pressure from his attorney, family, colleagues, and close friends began to mount on the professor. All agreed that he ought to accept the president's offer. His acceptance of it would bring the case to a close.

Despite the temptation to accept the offer, put the matter to rest once and for all, and continue with his career, the professor was nevertheless hesitant. His reluctance stemmed from the president's refusal to approve the promotion to associate professor. He feared he would be victim of a subtle form of reprisal that would have him remain an assistant professor for a very long time, quite likely for his entire career. Not only that, the professor felt that he deserved the promotion. The situation was a delicate one.

The professor consulted with representatives from the Chicano Legislative Caucus. A large contingent of legislators was going to be on campus as part of a public relations tour sponsored by the city. The caucus had scheduled a private meeting with the president during this visit for the purpose of discussing the issue of the professor's promotion.

At the meeting, strong opinions were expressed by members of the caucus and by the president. The president's position stipulated that it was time for the professor to compromise and accept the offer of tenure, even if it did not include promotion. The chair of the caucus agreed with him and this served to calcify the president's position even more as he refused to change his mind about promotion. Pressure, meanwhile, continued to mount on the professor to accept the offer.

A strategy was finally devised whereby the promotion issue would come before the judge, who had asked to be kept informed as to the progress of the case. The professor agreed to abide by the judge's opinion on the issue. If in the judge's opinion he ought to accept the offer of tenure without promotion, at least he would have the satisfaction of not voluntarily agreeing to it. The university also agreed to abide by the judge's opinion.

At the meeting in his chambers, the judge asked for a status report. The professor's attorney informed the judge that the university was now willing to grant tenure in the department, but that it would be without the normal promotion to associate professor. The university's attorney responded that promotion to associate professor was a matter that should be left to the professor's peers in the department. Besides, the university's attorney continued, the university had already compromised by awarding tenure. It was now time for the professor to compromise by accepting the tenure without the promotion.

The Judge then inquired what proportion of all tenure decisions carried with them promotion to associate professor. The professor's attorney responded that 90 percent of all tenure decisions in the previous five years had included promotion to associate professor. The attorney for the university objected and stated that the figure was too high. The judge asked the university's attorney for the true figure, and he responded that it was approximately 70 to 75 percent. The professor's attorney interjected that the 90 percent figure could be proven if the judge so desired.

The Judge pondered the matter for a moment and then stated that if by the university's own admission, 70 to 75 percent of all tenure decisions included a promotion to associate professor, the figure was still high and that the court could not allow the professor to be treated any differently from the majority of other professors because it would be discriminatory. Promotion to associate professor, therefore, should be granted along with tenure. He stated he would so rule if the matter came formally before the court.

The university's representatives protested the judge's opinion. He was informed that the president was adamant in his position that promotion to associate professor would not be granted. The vigor of their protest prompted the judge to say that if the president was looking for a scapegoat the judge would gladly serve in that capacity, but that the court could not sanction discriminatory behavior on the part of the university.

A few days later, the professor received a letter from the president informing him that he had been awarded tenure and had been promoted to associate professor. The tenure and promotion were made retroactive. The entire process had taken five years.

Discussion

The politics in the department that fueled the tenure dispute were not motivated by prejudice. The professor does not believe that he was singled out for invidious treatment, nor is it possible to argue that he was disliked simply because he was a Chicano. In fact, throughout the tenure dispute the professor maintained friendly and cordial relations with many of his colleagues in the department.

The politics of group interests, and not racial prejudice, were the motivating factors in the dispute. It was a matter of a group of individuals seeking to tenure one of their own. They were motivated because they perceived the female candidate, married to a member of the group, to be in direct competition with the professor for what they perceived to be only one tenure slot. The professor believes that had this not been the case, he would have been reviewed favorably in the initial consideration. The fact that he received a favorable vote on appeal supports this contention.

This is not to say that prejudice does not exist in the university and that it did not enter into the case. The professor does feel that there was prejudice in the dean's office. This prejudice is evidenced by the refusal to accept the department's recommendation to grant tenure and by the manner in which two members of the department were lobbied to reverse their favorable votes following the professor's appeal. Beyond the prejudicial activities of one individual, the professor remains firm in his belief that prejudice was never a significant motivating force throughout his tenure dispute. However, there were institutional discrimination and prejudice.

Evidence of a case of institutional discrimination is clear. This type of discrimination occurs when institutions select Chicano and other minorities for disparate treatment. The joint appointments in Chicano Studies and Black Studies are an example of this. The joint appointments were the primary way in which Chicano faculty could be recruited. There were no other positions available to Chicanos. Conversely, unless one were Chicano, one did not qualify for the joint appointments.

The university expected faculty holding the joint appointment to meet unusual administrative and service obligations. It is reasonable that a department that accepted a joint appointment would not surrender its jurisdiction over tenure. However, by accepting a joint appointment, a department implicitly recognizes the obligations that are unique to the faculty member holding the joint appointment, and thus, in principle, agrees to take these into consideration in tenure decisions.

In the professor's case, not only were his responsibilities to the Chicano Studies Program met, but in the process he established a publication record in his discipline. However, in the tenure evaluation, the publication record was judged insufficient. Yet his obligations to Chicano Studies were not part of the evaluation even though they had been a condition of his employment. This was a classic example of institutional discrimination, and as such it formed the basis of the lawsuit.

The professor's case was strengthened considerably by evidence that revealed that other faculty, non-Chicano and not holding joint appointments, but who had equivalent scholarly records, had been granted tenure. In these cases, service had indeed been included in the evaluation and had been a contributing factor in the granting of tenure.

It should be noted that joint appointments per se were not the issue. They can and do work, as an examination of the university's files revealed. It is only when the joint appointments involved the ethnic studies programs that they became controversial and were doomed to failure. The contrast between joint appointments involving Anglos and those involving minorities was a striking one, and it is here that prejudice and discrimination become impossible to ignore.

The professor's lawsuit might have taken another, completely different direction, had it not been for the role played in it by the federal judge. It might be facile to conclude that the case was won only because the judge and the professor were of the same ethnicity. It is true that legal cases have been decided solely upon racial and ethnic sentiments, but this did not happen in the professor's case. For instance, a review of the judge's record of decisions reveals that he has ruled against Chicanos in a variety of other cases, including some discrimination cases. Ethnic affinity was not, therefore, an absolute factor in obtaining a favorable decision for the professor.

The judge's experience in private practice proved much more helpful in securing his understanding in key areas of the lawsuit. The judge had firsthand knowledge and insight into how institutions practice, conceal, and resist the elimination of discrimination. It is crucial to gain access to information in the institution's possession in order to build a case for discrimination. Had the judge ruled against the professor's having access to the university's tenure files, the professor would not have been able to argue against the university's claim that an insufficient number of publications was the justification for the denial of tenure. The judge's ruling in favor by the professor proved invaluable in striking down a major claim by the university.

Also, it should be noted that the case was narrowly defined and that the judge was not asked to rule upon the quality of the professor's scholarship. Generally when a professor is denied tenure or promotion on the basis of mediocre or inferior scholarship, and the professor challenges the decision in court, the case is almost certain to fail because federal judges have consistently refused to substitute their judgment for that of scholars in the field (Farley 1985).

The role played by the Chicano Legislative Caucus proved to be more than a simple exercise in power. Prior to the caucus members' involving themselves in the professor's tenure dispute, it is extremely doubtful that the university was aware of their significance. However, by the time the issue of the professor's tenure was resolved, it is certain that the university had a clear and vivid image of the Chicano Legislative Caucus.

The caucus proved to the university that they were an important group in the legislature, one with which the university would have to deal. The caucus's active support of the professor, of course, was influenced by the negative perception they had of the president due to his faux pas in calling the professor by the pejorative *Taco*.

The president's blunder, incidentally, is now a part of caucus folklore. Whenever the professor visits the state capital, caucus members continue to ask if the president ever learned to say his name correctly. Or they will jokingly call him "Taco."

The president also erred in underestimating the will of the caucus by refusing to bring the issue to a quick and speedy resolution. Of course, it is not possible for the professor to obtain the president's private thoughts on the entire process. It might be that the president relied on the precedent that the university had not lost a lawsuit in thirteen years. Or it could be attributed to the president's personality and his no-nonsense style of leadership.

Nevertheless, it is safe to assume that the president acted in what he thought to be the best interests of the university. No doubt, too, he received advice and counsel, in general, nonlegal terms, from many quarters of the university. Nevertheless, his actions, it must be stressed, allowed the relationship between the caucus and the university to deteriorate unnecessarily.

Once the lawsuit was fully outlined before the judge, in light of his informal opinion and taking into account a similar assessment by the attorney general's office, it is difficult to understand the president's recalcitrance. The university, from all indications, had little, if any, choice but to settle the case. Given the hardened position of the university, had the case gone to court it is likely that the judge would have taken it as a direct challenge.

Another possibility is that the president truly believed that the professor would accept one of the compromise offers. Whatever the reasons for the delay, it was unnecessary and it serves to illustrate how institutions can become entrenched when the leadership feels threatened, even in the face of an unjust and ultimately lost issue.

A brief word should be said about the tenure process. It is a highly subjective process that unfortunately too often operates under the masquerade of objective evaluation. There is a reluctance on the part of the courts to second-guess professionals in their own field, and thus the tenure process is afforded too much protection and too little scrutiny by the courts.

The subjective aspects of the tenure process allow departmental politics and other factors to enter into the process, and the courts' protection effectively absolves the universities of any responsibility under the guise of educational decisions. This is often detrimental to minorities, as evidenced by the high rate of court cases they lose (La Noue & Lee 1987). Minorities often engage in nontraditional research and must face the enmity of their colleagues. In such cases, the courts must begin to look behind the mask of educational decisions; they must seek to more carefully consider all factors that might impinge upon a particular educational decision. Only in this way is more equity going to be introduced into the system.

We must bear in mind that universities very often hire minorities in part to act as symbols of their commitment to racial equity and fairness. These faculty, once in place, are expected to perform in ethnic and symbolic roles. When the time comes, however, universities seldom recognize these factors and almost never make the appropriate adjustments during the evaluation for promotion and tenure.

An egregious example is illustrated by university officials who repeatedly told the professor that they recognized his worth to the university. This meant an elevated worth regarding purely Chicano issues. For this reason, once he had been denied tenure, they were willing to retain the professor in an administrative capacity as director of Chicano Studies. The professor provided the university with a great deal of credibility in the Chicano community, and it seems obvious that this credibility was of considerable worth. Not enough, though, to warrant the granting of tenure. Implicit in this attitude is institutional prejudice, since the tenure files revealed that the value of the services of other non-Chicano faculty was cited in their reviews.

The professor won an out-of-court settlement that reinstated him as a full-fledged tenured associate professor, thus healing prejudice and discrimination. Unless the issues presented in this discussion are resolved judiciously and in a timely fashion within the universities, the courts could conceivably intervene and in their wisdom impose reforms that extend beyond the narrow limits of the professor's case.

Notes

1. Chair of the Chicano Legislative Caucus, letter to the president, 22 January 1985, university system, author's personal files.

References

Farley, J. (1985). Women versus academe: Who's winning. *Journal of Social Issues, 14*(4), 111–20.

Gray, M. W. (1985). Legal perspectives on sex equity in faculty employment. *Journal of Social Issues, 41*(4), 121–34.

La Noue, G. R., & Lee, B. A. (1987). *Academics in courts: The consequences of faculty discrimination litigation.* Ann Arbor: University of Michigan Press.

Metzger, W. P. (1979). The history of tenure. *Current Issues in Higher Education, 6,* 3–12.

Wessells, F. P. (1980). *The current legal status of tenure in institutions of higher education.* (Eric Document Reproduction Service No. ED 198 771).

CHAPTER 3

Surviving the Journey

MARÍA E. TORRES-GUZMÁN

The Meaning of Tenure

I grew up in a small town in Puerto Rico and in a Detroit ghetto. My father was a steelworker and my mother a seamstress. I did not have models of Latino teachers or academics during my elementary school experience in Detroit; I met the first Puerto Rican teachers when we went back to the island during my junior high school years, but that was after going through the Spaniards and Costa Rican priests and nuns of the first school I attended. Coming to an Ivy League institution as a faculty member from that background was significant enough. I must admit, I was in a place beyond my childhood dreams. There was a point in my life as a graduate where I imagined staying in academia, but as a friend later put it, "the big deal" was being granted tenure at an Ivy League institution. I never doubted my intelligence or my ability, I just did not know much about this world nor did I know what to do about tenure. It seemed an overwhelming task at first, but then things became clearer. I am satisfied with the outcome, but to others I wish a smoother road. As I think about what really seems most important in retrospect, I realize it is not the "club membership" so much as what is learned on the way there.

I will not indulge in a life history because that is not my purpose here. Suffice it to say that not only was I a female from a working-class family and of Puerto Rican background, but I was also a single parent of one growing female child. Given my circumstances, every choice I made, professional, political, and otherwise, was deeply personal. I came to understand that I had to make choices about what I wanted, what I was willing to sacrifice, and what was worth the struggle. I had to come to terms understanding when a task was my sole responsibility and when I could ask others for help; what was institutional and what was individual; and, most importantly, whether I was committed to "going for" tenure and doing what I had to do to obtain it. It was a rocky road, and I know that not all my decisions were the correct ones. I am still in the process of evaluating what occurred, and I am sure that even after this chapter goes into print I will still be rethinking and reevaluating it.

Thinking about Some Important Issues

My first two years were chaotic. First, I arrived as a junior faculty member with a Latina senior faculty member in charge. She first went on sabbatical and then left for a new job. It was an important job and I understood why she left, but within three months I was practically alone, feeling like I had to fend for myself and for the program in unexpected ways. Those months were very difficult. As the power of the program, vested in the senior faculty member, became scarce, all the barracudas of the college popped their heads in to see what they could bite. At least, that was the way it seemed to me. The following year or so was the testing period. I was tested consciously and unconsciously by staff members, by faculty members inside and outside the department, and by the administration. Even students came around insinuating that the level of support they were receiving from my administration did not stand up to the previous level of help. My hands were full; my time was taken over by my desire to be a good teacher, a good mom, a good administrator, a good companion, and so forth. My days began at about 6:30 A.M., and sometimes I was still up at 2:00 A.M.

By the end of my first year, I had written a research proposal that was funded, I had accepted a consulting job of unanticipated enormous proportions, and I had my job as an academic and as an administrator. The second year became what one of the administrators later called "the two years in one." I brought in totally new staff because almost everyone was gone. I started my research, I finished my contract, I oriented my new staff, and I went through my second-year review. I ended up in the hospital by the end of the year.

Going through my third year, I knew I had to do something about how things were going. Living in the city was becoming more tolerable and the staff was not as new, but my writing was thin and so were the prospects of obtaining tenure. I decided to take a good look at my life and to do what was necessary to safeguard my own and my daughter's well-being. I could not do this alone, I needed someone who could help me. So, I started therapy. This I find a very important step because I was brought up in a Catholic household where hard work, self-sacrifice, humility, and a sense of guilt came in a package. Throughout the next few years, I would wade through all of this and more. I am happy I made the commitment to do so.

The result was a lot of rethinking about my past and what I wanted to do in the future. It permitted me to live the present more consciously. Among the most important things I learned was that you don't have to go through this process alone. I had my therapist, my daughter, my family, my friends, my colleagues, and my students. Each, in their own way, gave me strength and kept reminding me of the value and the fragility of life. This helped me put my work toward tenure into perspective. But putting my work into perspective also gave me a different sense of life.

I made some conscious decisions that changed my perspectives, my attitudes, and my behaviors; it was like putting my house in order from then on. First, I sought to balance my personal and professional lives by separating them. In other words, I gave to Caesar what was Caesar's and to God what was hers. In addition, it made me see more clearly what I had to do for what. Second, I took a serious look at the multiple hats I wore at work. My goal was to make the multiple demands on me more manageable. Assessing the value of playing each role, discarding some, keeping some others, and integrating various professional and community projects were ways of uncomplicating my life. And, finally, writing became a priority.

Having taken these postures made me see and think more clearly about my professional life as a minority scholar. The third through the sixth years were still difficult; the program was still a lot of work. I continued to do consulting and many other things, but somehow I had arrived at some wholeness, which I called "inner peace." I started seeing the world through new eyes. I was learning how to balance my life, how to understand my needs, and how to read the institution.

Balancing My Person

Even though from the beginning I tried to stay in touch with my physical and personal needs, thinking about balance led me to better assess how I was taking care of myself and how I was spending time with my daughter. I decided to make a few changes; I began by reclaiming my weekends, my evenings, and as much of my summer as possible. I began separating activities so that when people at work asked me to do something that infringed on my personal life, it was easier for me to say no. Establishing

my home-life routines was important. Balancing my checkbook, difficult
as it was, cooking, grocery shopping, fixing my car, and the like were all
part of the process. Sharing with my daughter, planning play dates with
other children's parents, and sharing with my friends regularly all became
important. In addition, the spiritual journey to reclaim my heart, my soul,
and my inner peace had begun.

Considering Fit and Committing

I was concurrently reconsidering my commitment to pursue tenure. I realized that when I came to the institution, I had made a commitment to
myself, not to the institution. Everyone had given me the institutional
history. Only one Latina had obtained tenure, and she had not entered at a
junior status as I had. I had replaced a Latina who had not been given
tenure. Furthermore, within my first two years at the college, another
Latina was denied tenure. The message was written on the wall: Latinas
rarely make tenure; you have got a struggle on your hands.

When I accepted the job, I had committed myself to being who I
was. I frequently found myself saying things that created discomfort for
others because what I heard angered me. Every time I opened my mouth
I went home feeling I had blown it, but I found comfort in remembering
the spirit of Zapata's words: He would rather die standing than live on
his knees.

I had also committed myself to changing my relationship with writing. I had had some bad experiences with writing, but I also remembered how good I felt about writing my dissertation and other papers. I
wanted to feel good about it more often. As I took a good look at these
premises and more, I realized that I had to seriously consider the possibilities of tenure. Both my daughter and I also longed for some stability.
This is when I took a serious look at "fit."

What does *fit* mean, you may ask. I asked myself the same question.
I had experienced its use on various occasions; at times it meant the
user did not want to recruit an individual into an organization or an
institution, and on other occasions it was the contrary. I came to see it
through questions that I had. Is there space in this institution for me to
do the work that brings me passion? Do I generally feel penalized when
I stand up for what I believe in? When I do the work that I have to do
for the college and the program, do I feel so overwhelmed and angry
that I can not do what I want to do? In other words, do I feel zapped
(violated, crazed, unfulfilled) by the institution? What about my per-

sonal and professional integrity? How do I experience the institutional structure and the people with whom I work?

The responses to these questions became important because I was reading my internal barometer and my desire to stay at the institution. These are not questions I considered once; I was constantly examining them, because my posture was that I always had a choice of staying or leaving. This, though, is only one side of the coin. I tried to read the messages the institution, and the people who make up the institution, were giving me. The questions here were these: What do they say they need in order to grant me tenure? (I mean, beyond the official criteria of tenure documents.) How were they communicating what they needed, and how were they making me feel? Again, these are questions that I considered and reconsidered throughout the years.

My desire to stay, and the institution's capacity to integrate me, could best be described as something that evolved. Initially, I thought I would have the protection of the senior faculty member, and then she left. For a while I received many mixed messages and I experienced ambivalence. Eventually, I made a commitment to go through the process. I could live with myself at the institution and the institution could live with me. I emphasize this mutuality in commitment because I think it is important to be clear how important it is for individuals to exercise the personal power they have to make decisions about their lives. The tenure process is difficult because others are making judgments about the value of one's work (scholarship, collegiality, leadership, etc.) with respect to their collective, institutional interests. In this context, it is easy to assume the role of a victim. I felt that it was important not to be passive; I could eventually have become a victim, but it certainly was not going to be my doing.

Institutional Issues

Couching in a language of tentativeness my strong belief that individuals have a say in the eventual outcome of the tenure process stems from my understanding of power relations. Even when the individual does everything that she or he is supposed to do (I am not here referring to "being in your place" but rather to the professionalization of your work), institutions reject individuals under the rubric of "fit"; they do so based on many different rationalizations, including ideological stances, personality, racism, gender, and language bias. The politics of higher education is filled with such examples, and some historical periods are more intensely committed to the process of "academic cleansing" than others are. It would be naive not to acknowledge how politics plays itself out.

In my case, I am in bilingual/bicultural education, an area of great debate nationwide. Within my institution, individual faculty members would approach me with comments such as "I understand that there is a rift between bilingual education and English as a Second Language," or by making reference to the "lack of pedagogical basis for bilingual education," or simply to "you people." In my courses, no matter which one, invariably someone wanted to know more about the debate. I had a philosophical stance that guided me; if anyone in the courses wanted to debate bilingual/bicultural education, there was a course on contemporary issues where that was covered. Not all the work in bilingual/bicultural education was predicated on the claims of the English-only movement which was opposed to bilingual education in the first place, nor was I going to lose precious teaching time on an individual's whims. The students' desire to understand and work with the language minority populations in our schools was more important. As far as faculty members went, it depended on the context and who was talking. There were moments in which aspects of the debate could be explained despite the hostility I could feel through the language used and the accompanying paralinguistics. Most of the time I asked them to tell me what they meant. I found that when they were asked to define, they themselves realized how ignorant they sounded and would eventually get on to another topic. In other words, I tried not to be egged into a debate nor to waste energy or time on the topic. This attitude was sufficient in situations where I had some control, but the institutional structure and the historically and socially based constructions about bilingual/bicultural education had to be dealt with differently. In addition to dealing with the attitudes, I had to deal with structural issues (e.g., the reliance on federal monies for program development and student grants, the nature of coordination with other fields, and the "minority" nature of the field).

Structural Issues

Tensions emerged between my need to play numerous professional roles and my desire to play them well. While every faculty member must face a similar dilemma, as a minority female in a unique program I found many situations in which decision making could not merely be seen as a matter of setting personal boundaries and priorities. Often I was forced to choose between what was good for the program and what was good for my professional advancement. Unfortunately, the two were not always the same.

With the departure of the then director of the program, I was faced with the transition. I did not feel there was much room to make choices about what I should focus on: The program needed my attention. I had to attend to it with some urgency. Beyond the years of transition, some of the persistent chores related to the program included proposal writing, coordination, and minority issues.

Proposal Writing

Most faculty members in this field understand the necessity of proposal writing. Not only is there a dire need for teachers who understand and know how to work with linguistically different students, the field itself is relatively new and enjoying varying degrees of institutional support. The potential student population has great financial need. Fortunately, Title VII of the Elementary and Secondary Education Act (ESEA) has provided a vehicle for establishing higher education programs that commit themselves to institutionalization and capacity building, while also providing students with scholarships.

My institution is private and expensive. For those students who already possess the language proficiency necessary to work in bilingual classrooms, the financial investment far exceeds the rewards of working in overcrowded, linguistically complex, and inadequately supported school settings. Even when would-be teachers have the commitment to the children, they often do not have the money. The Title VII scholarships not only provide the immediate financial incentive for those who already have the commitment; they also have become a means for recruiting others who would otherwise consider it too costly to enroll in our college to become a bilingual teacher.

What this means for a faculty member like me is that proposal writing for the support of students and the development of the program is part of my agenda. The tension emerged when I had to consider the time I invested in a training grant as opposed to a research grant. The training grants were necessary for program and student survival. I knew that the college would appreciate our program faculty's efforts in this area, but the reality was that, in the hierarchy of academia, research grants were more prestigious. Furthermore, the research grants were more likely to provide the kind of resources that I needed in order to write and publish academic articles.

Coordination

The second structural difficulty, coordination between disciplines and programs, was more institutionally problematic. Historically, the programs in bilingual/bicultural education were set up as specializations within other disciplines, particularly at the doctoral level. The thinking behind this was that professionals prepared in bilingual/bicultural education should be first-rate and should not be ghettoized. Educators would be based in a discipline with a specialization in bilingual/bicultural education. I had gone through such a program and knew that in this model the need to conceptually integrate the two fields was left up to the student. In many colleges and universities, the call for conceptual integration led to new courses and eventually to integrated programs in bilingual/bicultural education. Many have moved in this direction, and others have refused to do so because of their concern for the proliferation of programs. My institution had not completed the process of program integration beyond the M.A. At the level of the professional degree and doctorate, the old model, where bilingual/bicultural education is a specialization, still reigned.

Tensions emerge given the complexity of coordination with a multitude of other academic programs. There is little time to coordinate. Some students who are majoring and minoring in two programs fall through the cracks unless they are assertive. Our program faculty frequently found themselves solving programmatic problems of students who did not major with us, and the bilingual program faculty members were not even getting credit for what they did with these students.

Writing Title VII proposals for anything above the M.A. in elementary education within my institution was frequently the program faculty members' responsibility. We got very little help from other faculty members in the college. Despite this, we knew the field needed these professionals and we needed to continue to write the proposals that would enable our students to go through them. We also felt that the joint program model was a good strategy for getting other faculty members interested in the issues of bilingualism and multiculturalism. More importantly, we began to feel the urgency of creating integrated programs beyond the M.A. Finding ways to do both without overburdening the members of the faculty became a challenge and undoubtedly created new tensions.

These structural issues have yet to be resolved, but throughout the years in question the department and the college faculty responded to them in ways that were encouraging. They acknowledged some of the problems, and responded positively to some by making small but significant changes, but many still remain unresolved. What was most important for me was that the solutions strengthen rather than violate the integrity of the program. I was willing to be assertive and protective in this area; it did not always win me friends.

Minority Education

Bilingual/bicultural education teacher preparation programs have a large number of minority students with all the difficulties, real or imagined, of being so identified. This complicated our work. It required time and a lot of patience. Academically and socially, our program is designed to create support structures that help students to continue through graduation. The experience and knowledge we gained in working with this student population was helpful in responding to individual college faculty members who also were struggling with difficulties and dilemmas, real or imagined, of having minority students in their classes.

In addition, there were many demands from the field. The pool of minority educators is small and is constantly being called on to shed light on bilingual/bicultural and minority education. The requests I received were many and varied. Sometimes they were tangential to my interests, but the plea for a "minority perspective" was very convincing. As the years passed, I began to think more in terms of the value of this work in relation to my goals and the extra work it required.

Whether at the college or in professional organizations, I found that an implicit expectation was that, as a minority, I would serve as the connection to minority networks. When it was time to think about minorities who would be good for this or that, or about a minority candidate for a position, the minorities in the room (sometimes I was the only one there) were assigned the task. This was reasonable at one level, but unreasonable and unfair at another. While minority faculty members tend to know other minorities, it is unreasonable to expect them to know minorities in all fields. It may have been easier for me to find minorities interested in other areas because I already had established professional relationships with minority networks, but I decided that it was more important to develop the institution's or organization's capacity to connect with my own field. Moreover, I felt it was necessary for nonminority faculty members to establish linkages with minority scholars in their fields. I needed to encourage them to do so, otherwise they would never learn how to do it on their own. I also realized that the burden of affirmative action was not on my shoulders, but on the institution's. This was the most difficult lesson to learn.

I noticed another dimension in which minorities were called on somewhat unfairly. We are asked to provide the minority perspective on almost anything. I have been asked both to look at other people's written work and to help locate written work on multicultural education that relates to their area of interest. On the one hand, it is most flattering and signals a high degree of collegiality. In addition, it gave me confidence to go to my colleagues on various occasions and ask them to look at my writing. But I found that it was important to communicate that there were multiple minority perspectives. At most, I would reciprocate in ways I thought appropriate. I was willing to ask colleagues to share what they already had done in an area that I was interested in, but I would never ask them to do a search for me. These values set limits, but time also became a factor. Responding to the requests was time consuming and placed a burden on me. I think that it is important that colleagues search out people with minority perspectives within their own fields; they would be able to discuss the issues of multiculturalism in a way that takes into consideration the subtle issues each field raises. As a bilingual/bicultural educator, I can offer only so much.

Most importantly, there is an urgency in the field of education to do what I think is central to my work: to rethink minority education and to raise concerns about cultural and linguistic diversity in classrooms, about recruitment, and about the preparation of minority teachers. To do this well, while trying to avoid the pitfalls of previous attempts and to overcome the stigma of illegitimacy concerning research on minorities (Garza & Cohen 1988), requires thoughtfulness and deliberation. This kind of work also takes time.

Taking Some Important Steps

Rethinking my institutional and professional positions was critical, but equally critical was finally getting to the point of writing and guarding my writing time. The following are some of the ways in which I made it work for me.

Writing

Much has been written about the process of writing, but we usually consider the literature to be applicable to younger children or beginners. Every time I sat down to write, I found it difficult because I felt that in essence I was bounding my ever-evolving ideas by stagnant linguistic symbols called "words"; they never seem to carry the richness of reality. Writing is a lot of work. Few have accomplished its mastery and most of us are forever in the process. I have learned about writing by reading novels and other texts, by editing my own and other people's work, by having others edit my work, and by reading about writing. Most importantly, I learned by doing. I found no advice better than the actual doing.

I now schedule myself to write as much as I can. A colleague once told me a story about Ruth Benedict. She wrote a certain amount every day, very early in the morning before she started her more public day. A variation on this was another colleague's confession that he wrote three pages a day, no matter what. He felt he could then approach other tasks more positively because he knew he "had cranked out the quota." Pablo Neruda used to sit routinely at his desk, where he would contemplate some yellow roses in a vase and the paper that was about to receive his thoughts. He would stare at them as long as he had to; both were always present. Another colleague told me that the time (one hour, two hours, half a day, an entire day, etc.) she dedicated to writing was solely for that, whether she produced or not. These and other stories gave me a perspective on what I needed to do. Basically, I needed to establish a routine and develop the discipline associated with making it work.

Blocks of time were important to me, although as a single parent I was not able to manage many of them. Every Monday, year round, every summer when my daughter was visiting her father, and those few weeks when my daughter was in school and I was on a break, became sacred. Designating them as reserved and guarding the time were two different things. I still needed to learn how to do the latter.

Guarding My Writing Time

I found a short article on time management that broke down what a minute and an hour of my time cost in dollars and cents (the cost depends on your annual salary). This and many other tidbits about time use helped me to start making decisions consciously about how much time each activity (including phone conversations) were costing me if they were translated into dollars and cents, into the number of pages I could write, or whatever was important to me at the moment. Consequently, I found myself valuing my time.

Decisions about Annual Travel

I decided to be selective. I would participate in consulting and professional presentations only if I could make the travel back and forth within the day. I chose to concentrate on two to three major professional conferences a year. I always went beyond two to three presentations, but I made these choices consciously; the pay was worth it, I enjoyed myself, or I was committed to participating for other reasons. Examples of the latter were the Ethnography Forum, the work with the Colectiva Intercambio, and the Freire Conference in New York. All of these were activities that I enjoyed participating in and were worth it to me. Before I made this conscious choice, I was putting in weeks of approximately ninety hours and the results were not as visible. Every year I update my vitae; I began counting the number of presentations after I made the decision that my professional activities had to become more conscious choices. I came to see how much I really enjoyed what I did—I was now making more presentations than I had previously, with less effort and feeling less burdened by them.

Decisions about Consulting

My decisions about paid work began to change as well. For example, I no longer took on a lot of staff development in school districts; the staff development that I did was concentrated in a few classrooms (longer-term and without pay; this part of my work was integrated with research and writing). The paid work, to the extent possible, was the type I could do in town or at home (as a reader for publishing houses, curriculum development, evaluations, and so forth). Since the consulting work also began to have a written product, writing itself became part of the day's work.

Disconnecting during My Writing Day

Monday was my writing day (I did prewriting, reading, thinking, writing, editing, etc.). I let no one disturb my day! It was sacred, even if I ended up twiddling my thumbs all day. I told my friends, my office, my colleagues, and anyone that tried to interrupt that I would consider any future action of this sort an act of hostility. I stuck to it. Gandhi practiced twenty-four hours of meditation. I felt this to be an equivalent. At first it was hard, but little by little the results were visible, and I became a professional at protecting my writing time.

What's Next?

I started with the idea that I survived the tenure process, but I have arrived at the conclusion that the challenge continues. I have received tenure (and

I was anxious through it all), but I still have the stage of full professor ahead of me. I may have more to say then. What I have learned is that while I have gained personal and professional power, its significance is weakened if I remain the only Latina at this ivory tower. I need colleagues, and the nation needs more diversity.

I wrote this chapter because I felt it was important to share some things. There are many experiences of a sensitive nature that are particular to my case that I still cannot share with ease. However, it is important to remember that the process each individual goes through is very personal. We must all decide on the level of personal integrity that is required to be at peace with ourselves. Furthermore, our circumstances are different, and therefore the issues that are relevant also may differ.

As a bilingual/bicultural educator and a minority woman who believes in social justice, I believe in the need for more collective gains. While I am pleased that at a recent AERA gathering of the Hispanic and Bilingual/Bicultural Education SIGs some of us commented on how many of our group are presently tenured and in institutionally important positions, the situation we face as Latinos is still sad. As of 1987, only 1.9 percent of the Latino population had completed a doctoral degree (De la Rosa & Maw 1990). Not all of these are in academia (Verdugo, this volume); many of them find other areas of work more rewarding, less judgmental, and more appealing. Fewer yet are researchers who are contributing to the creation of knowledge. Furthermore, the trend is that fewer Latinos are in the pipeline and more are dropping out at the junior high and high school levels. Our task is not complete even when we have gone beyond that which we had never dreamt could happen. It is hope that keeps me working to make sure that our children can begin to see beyond the tenement building and the ghetto shacks; it is a hope that more of them will reach the ivory tower and go beyond the survivors' camp.

References

Garza, H., & Cohen, E. (1988). *Minority researchers and minority education.* Special report commissioned by the American Educational Research Association (AERA), Washington, DC.

De la Rosa, D., & Maw, C. E. (1990). *Hispanic education: A statistical portrait.* Washington, DC: National Council of La Raza.

CHAPTER 4

Actuando

ANA M. MARTÍNEZ ALEMÁN

Miami, December 1992

My mother tells our Spanish-speaking Christmas guests to forgive me. She reminds all who have gathered around the *lechón*, the *yuca*, the *frijoles*, and *maduros* that it is too soon in my visit for me to be free of *disparates*, to be free of those errors in Castillian grammar, vocabulary, and syntax that are symptomatic of my exile. I take no offense. Mamy is right. My conversation is rusty from a spring, summer, and winter in the American Midwest; *entorpecido* from two years here, and thirty years away from home. As the conversation continues on without me, my silence once again reminds me that I am becoming an *extranjera*, a foreigner among my own kind. Relegated to the margins of the conversation, I listen as each voice, rich with the rhythm of unfettered expression, moves effortlessly around my silence. Soon their voices are far away from me, far, far out of my present reach. I become painfully aware that this silence, my silence, is exilic. *Mi segundo exilio.*

Do I choose this silence? Do I knowingly walk away from that which originally defined me as *cubana*, as *hija*, as *nieta*, as *hermana*? Do I allow this Euro-American exile to wash over me time and time and time again, leaving me colorless, detached, nicely assimilated? I don't remember actually choosing anything, if truth be told. Not as a six-year-old in Sister Mary Laurentia's first-grade class; not at sixteen among my Jewish and African American public school friends. How did I get here? Who, or what, has tied my tongue?

Iowa, March 1992

Required reading for my course on American educational thought is Richard Rodriguez's (1982) *Hunger of Memory*, an autobiographical account of assimilation. As a Mexican American, Rodriguez finds that his young life is played out within the intimacy of his native language, kept safe by Mexican cultural certainties not yet confused and compromised by Euro-American society. As he makes his way through the mysteries and puzzles of Anglo schooling, he becomes "son," not *hijo*, and a public, individual Richard, not *Ricardo*. As an altar boy in his Catholic church, he hears in Latin the "echoes of Spanish words familiar" (p. 99), often understanding their meanings but rarely trying to do so. Dressed in the sterile black-and-white cassock of an Anglicized ritual, rehearsed in Eurocentric habituations, Richard, né *Ricardo*, the scholarship boy made good, has arrived.

I begin our class meeting asking, "From where has Richard come? What has his life's journey been about? Where is *Ricardo*? ¿*Quién es* Richard? Who is Richard?" Several bright, energetic, and appropriately articulate students acknowledge the questions with confident nods. As they speak, they confirm my suspicion: These intelligent, genuinely politically sensitive, novice scholars will not hold Richard's feet to the fire. The Church, the schools, the government, his American neighbors. His *anglo* teachers and *anglo* friends. His school's anglocentrism. Eurocentric books. Stanford's Eurocentric curriculum. These were responsible for Richard's assimilation into Euro-American culture, for his valuation of *anglo* ways, speech, thinking. "He is a product of Eurocentric socialization!" shouts one Kansan. "He didn't stand a chance!" injects his fellow Plainsman. Quickly, all rally to the cry of unavoidable socialization, of deliberate Americanization, of involuntary and unwitting mutation.

It doesn't seem to occur to my students that perhaps Richard should be held responsible for some of his assimilation. As an adult, could Richard have made the choices that would have distanced him no further from his cultural point of origin? Could he have chosen to maintain his cultural identity, to strengthen his cultural ties, to regain the intimacy of his past? And having freely and intentionally removed himself from that which defined him as *mejicano*, is he guilty of colluding with the oppressor? Is Richard Ricardo's traitorous self?

Accusing Richard of monocultural complicity is a risky and dangerous act for these students. To hold a member of an oppressed group accountable for his assimilated identity smacks of a social conservatism that their liberal politics cannot embrace. To them, an oppressed individual can not defend herself or himself against the forces of assimilation. How can we expect Ricardo to deflect such powerful enculturation? To these students, Ricardo's is a defenseless and pregnable mind. By placing the blame on the oppressed individual, don't we absolve the oppressor of its ethnocentric sins?

Ironically, I tell them, such a position robs Ricardo of the very autonomy that their politics espouse. By failing to hold Richard to the standards of individual choice, autonomy, and independent moral agency, my students have made him an impotent player in his own cultural politics. Richard, I suggest to them, *can* self-direct, *can* self-define, *can* fend off cultural compromise.

It is not that I hold the child Ricardo/Richard responsible for his own seduction. On the contrary, I do not blame the victim-child. It is the adult Richard, the educated and ego-strong man who continues full force on the path of assimilation. I hold the adult Richard culpable for much of his own loss of memory, for much of his continued ethnic transformation. If he hungers for the memory of the lost Chicano world of family and sense of belonging, why doesn't he choose to reenter this world? Why doesn't Richard take his mother's advice and improve his Spanish skills? "Practice it with your dad and me" (Rodriguez 1982, 178), she says to him. But her invitation to regain what was lost or atrophied goes unanswered.

To my mind, what we are and do as children very often has little to do with choice. To suggest that the child Ricardo/Richard fully realizes the implications of his steady movement toward assimilation is to impose adult standards of self-legislative morality on children. Can the child Ricardo/Richard really understand the implications of name changing, for example? If my renaming pleases, if it is what the adults who validate my intelligence (my teachers) wish to call me, and if it soothes the sting of my difference—less teasing from the kids in school, fewer questions from their parents about my parentage—then, why *not* accept it? Why not take the opportunity to become a bigger and bigger part of what appears to be the majority of my world, *lo estimado*, the validated world? The weakening and degeneration of his Chicano ethnicity is not something Ricardo/Richard can predict at a young age. But what of the adult Richard? Can and should he be held culturally accountable?

As adults, those of us who, like Richard, have experienced name changes, who as children have dutifully walked the path of assimilation, are duty-bound to resist further absorption and to impress our ethnic fingerprints on the Euro-American scene. As adults, as thinking, self-governing, experienced women and men, we must critically question the value of assimilation, the emphasis on sameness, the objectives of monoculturalism, and the need for the negation of self. If I am *Ana María*, not Ann, not Anna, not Ann Marie, and if, as an adult, I do not refuse such identity changing, I am guilty of cultural complicity. If I do not make a point of my name—if I don't assist with its pronunciation, if

I do not take the opportunity to explain its construction, it's ethnic etymology—I miss the opportunity to assert my identity, to be counted as a particular individual, and, more importantly, to educate and inform about the existence of others like me. When I do this, when I demand that my name be correct on my office door, in the faculty phone book, and on department letterhead, or when I acquaint students with why my name is what it is, I resist assimilation. When I engage in these small but significant "outrageous acts and everyday rebellions" (Steinem 1983), I take back the power of identity, the power of an existence validated. This is a small component of a strategy to validate cultural identities traditionally excluded or erased by Euro-American schooling and socialization. But it is a way to stay true to myself, true to my cultural character, and, more importantly, to indicate to my students and my colleagues, whether *latinas* or not, that what I am counts and that what I am culturally is of consequence to me *and them*. That I am not assimilation's pseudonym—that I am not Ann Marie, not Anna, not Ann—makes me someone who claims a powerful heritage, and in claiming and asserting such a heritage, I bring it within reach, I make it available, I verify its significance.

These everyday rebellions may seem burdensome, too much to ask of an individual. Why should I constantly act as cultural educator? Why should I always have to make a point of making the cultural point? Why do I need to point out the cultural deficiencies of my department's curriculum? Why must I be the one at a faculty meeting to address the issue of ethnic student recruitment? My answer to these questions relies on the obvious: *¿Quién hablará por nosotros si no yo?* If not me, who? I don't see anyone like me at these faculty meetings; there are no other *latinas* or *latinos* in my department, and there are very, very few Latin American faces among the students I teach at this midwestern American college. Who else is here to take action? At the faculty's seminar on feminist theory, who is there to critically challenge the dominant Euro-American perspective on identity politics? Who is there to submit, in that polite, intellectual Euro-American way, the perspective from the margin? Who is there to challenge the ethnocentric, European-elitist literary opinion of Cisneros's (1989) *The House on Mango Street*? Who is there to call colleagues to task for not bothering to translate the introductory Spanish prose in Lugónes and Spelman's (1983) "Have We Got a Theory for You! Feminist Theory, Cultural Imperialism and the Demand for 'The Woman's Voice' "? The circumstances of our Latina lives require us to take action, require us to take on the burden of making our presence known, of making our presence felt, of having us count. As individuals present in realities that dismiss us, ignore us, forget us, and are indifferent toward us, our choice is either to keep quiet and live professionally as affirmative action statistics, or to speak, to make ourselves heard, to *act* affirmatively. For me, it seems that to choose silence is to embrace cultural complacency.

Iowa, September 1991

The first box full of canned *frijoles negros, café Pilón, plátanos verdes* and packets of *comino* arrived just a day after I had unloaded, unpacked, and arranged my possessions in the white prairie farmhouse I keep from calling "home." Most of my friends sent plants or cards to welcome me to Iowa, to urge me on in this last stage of the doctoral process. Mamy sends me a box of assurances, a box full of cultural therapy. Her gesture's significance will initially elude me.

Mamy's care package seemed like just another episode in a relationship marked by punch lines and psychic distance. We had joked about Iowa when I announced that I had received a fellowship to finish my dissertation in a small college in this rural midwestern state. Would I be picking corn on my days off? Would I finally get to answer firsthand Shoeless Joe's timeless question, "Is this heaven?" But like a joke that hits too hard, like the punch line that hits your most vulnerable nerve, I grew more uneasy and afraid with each can of black beans I removed.

Why would she think that these things were so necessary? I don't need to eat Cuban food all the time. Why can't I drink coffee instead of *café*? Eat a baked potato instead of *arroz con frijoles*? I've lived in this country most of my life. What's so different now? Do I really need these things or are they just cultural amenities? Just how much of my cultural identity comes in a can of black beans ready-to-serve? Why did she send these things? *¿Qué piensa? ¿Qué sabe Mamy?* What does Mamy know? Days after I had finished my last can of *frijoles*, I began to understand what Mamy had perhaps known instinctively, or most probably had learned from her own life in exile: For a *cubana*, places like Iowa cannot be heaven.

In places like Iowa, I imagined my mother thinking, I would struggle to find the familiar. I wouldn't hear the comforting sound of Spanish spoken thick with the nuances of Latina context calling me home. There would be no *salsa* on the radio, no news of Cuba on TV. No statues of *Santa Bárbara*. No chivalrous men in *guayaberas*, no heavily perfumed, high-heeled women with the fancy gold chains around their necks. No white-haired *viejítos retirados* playing dominoes in the park. No *abuelitas* reciting *redondillas* and *los versos sencillos de Martí* by heart. No dark-haired baby girls with pierced earlobes and chubby, chubby legs. No birthday parties with *piñatas*, no *tías*, no *primas*. *Nadie*. No one. I called Mamy and humbly asked her to send another box.

Living so far from the familiar has made me painfully aware that I am a cultural *mestiza* in crisis. Somehow the move to the rural American Midwest, to a college where cultural sameness seems unusually durable, has become the turning point, for better or worse, in this fever of assimilation. The absence of the culturally familiar suddenly brings all of my Anglo habituations into sharp focus, signaling a decisive moment in my exile. How will my *cubana* self survive this cultural loneliness? Will it atrophy, wither, and eventually be consumed by Velveeta, Garth Brooks, and postmodern feminism and deconstructionist theory? Will I turn a deaf ear to *Celia Cruz*, a blind eye to *Cristina García* dreaming in Cuban? How is it possible for a *cubana* in *exilio* to affirm a determined grip on her cultural lifeline? Will Mamy's care packages be enough? *Creo que no*. I don't think so. I need to take some decisive action. I need a cultural booster shot.

How will I inoculate myself against further assimilation? On the surface, the prairie's Cuban pickins' seem slim. ¡*Adelante!* Take action! Submit papers to conferences scheduled to meet in Latin America; engage in joint research projects with other Latina faculty at other institutions; make a point of getting to know the few Latina/o students on campus; use that computing network to exchange information with other Latina/o academics; make sure that your syllabi include works by *latinas/os*; take the opportunity to mentor a Latina student; take the opportunity to teach a first-year tutorial on Latina fiction; join your discipline's Latina/o caucus; teach a semester in your college's Latin American semester abroad program; submit the names of Latina/o scholars to your college's lecture series and speaker's bureau; suggest Latin American movies to the film society; add *El Nuevo Herald* to the library's collection. *Los que no se muevan, se quedan*. Move, or get left behind.

Wisconsin, October 1992

The Associated Colleges of the Midwest sponsors minority students and academic careers workshops for its member colleges. The goal of this program is to encourage and support minority student interest in graduate school through summer independent research grants and faculty mentoring.

A clear and spoken objective is to arouse or stimulate interest in the academic life, in particular the liberal arts college professoriat.

I attend the weekend workshop with four students, having served as a faculty mentor to a Chicana student studying the construction of self in feminist Chicana fiction. Throughout the proceedings I wonder whether anyone will address the perils of being a minority in academia; whether someone will talk about the risks involved: Co-optation, losing touch with the realities of our peoples; would "talking and walking" like an Anglo become second nature? Would we forget to take care of our own? What are the contradictions of being an "Other" in the academic professions? But all anyone seems to talk about are the legitimately pragmatic concerns of graduate school applications, financing graduate education, and the academic demands of doctoral scholarship. Luckily, none of the pale, white-bearded, more-than-middle-aged tenured types pontificated about the merits and magnificence of a life dedicated to inquiry and the pursuit of ideas. Instead, they maintain a safe, detached, and uninvolved distance from these young faces, who watch them with knowing skepticism and disarming envy.

Our recruits are tempted but cynical; naive but already tested. They live dark-skinned lives, speak in accented working-class voices, prove themselves exceptions to rules, endure the constant self-inflicted assessment of their market value—Is it me they want or just one of my kind?—and worry that they, too, will become pale, white-bearded, more-than-middle-aged tenured types. What advice can I give them? What lessons have I learned? What are the "minority" professor's hoops to jump, obstacles to scale, precedents to set, and principles to compromise? What is being a role model, a mentor, all about?

On the long ride back to our campus in Iowa these questions continue to disturb me. I am annoyed by them. They disturb my concentration; they are *molestias*, stubborn, unyielding irritants fixed on getting my undivided attention. I grow more and more *incómoda* as each question repeats itself again and again. *¡Qué jeringue!* I want them to leave me alone, to be gone, be off to some other consciousness. But soon I realize that I will not be free of them until I have answered them, until I understand the source of the *molestia*, until I do what I ask my students to do—until I investigate the source of my cultural discomfort.

As a woman in what has been traditionally a man's profession, I am very well aware of the discomfort of being a woman in a man's world. I am conscious of what Martin (1991) calls my "contradictory status." I am asked to be educated—to be rational, self-governing, independent, and capable of engaging in sophisticated abstract analytical thinking. As a woman in the professoriat, I must be distant, objective and efficient, traits typically antithetical to the feminine socialization norm. These professorial qualities, masculine constructions of androcentric thinking, are required features of my essential professorial personality. The contradiction, of course, is that as a woman I am socialized against these very qualities, and, more importantly, that my expression of these traits appears contradictory. Women professors, then, are caught in a cultural perplexity, a perplexity of gender. To be womanly is to be unprofessorial; to be professorial is to be manly. A woman wishing to dedicate her professional life to teaching undergraduate or graduate students must appropriate these masculine qualities, must make the masculine her own, must conform to, and accommodate, cultural values outside of her gender role. What results, according to Martin, is a class of women speaking a language often foreign to their experiences; a class of women securing unfamiliar values and behaviors in order to successfully navigate professional waters. Moreover, due to her status as academic immigrant, the woman professor has the potential to become a "disturbing element" (Martin 1991, 7) in the professional world. Never really fully assimilated, never completely absorbed by the culture, she might create disturbances that change the character and disposition of academic conventions; she might question the validity of established ways of thinking, acting, and relating to others; she might challenge dominant perspectives and ideologies.

As I negotiate the dark rural roads, I ask myself if this is so different from what happens to me as a Latina in the Euro-American professorial world? Is such cultural "otherness," like sex and gender, a contradictory phenomenon? ¡Cómo no! Of course it is! Though I speak their languages and know their secret handshakes, sing their ceremonial hymns, and worship their academic gods, I cannot fully be one of them. I am a convert, baptized by academic missionaries who have shown me the way into the promised professional land. Dressed in academic regalia and fluent in its discourse, I can only masquerade as one of them, never truly *be* them. I am born outside the boundaries of the pedigree, born into another neighborhood. Moving into my faculty office, taking my seat at the faculty meeting or at commencement, sampling the hors d'oeuvres at the president's holiday bash, I am struck by my lived contradiction: To be a professor is to be an *anglo*; to be a *latina* is not to be an *anglo*. So how can I be both a Latina and a professor? To be a Latina professor, I conclude, means to be unlike *and* like me. ¡Qué *locura*! What madness!

As Latina/o professors, we are newcomers to a world defined and controlled by discourses that do not address our realities, that do not affirm our intellectual contributions, that do not seriously examine our worlds. Can I be both Latina and professor without compromise? If I take on the Anglo professor's posture of distance and informed detachment, if my focus is solely on noncontextual theory, if I reinforce the master's house with the master's tools (Lorde 1984), have I surrendered parts of my cultural identity? If, instead, I practice a pedagogy that relies on reality as text, where cultural lenses provide the perspectives for critical examination, and in which knowledge is characterized politically, do I maintain cultural integrity? And, in disturbing the Eurocentric professorial way-of-being, have I resisted assimilation?

To be a disturbing cultural element requires that I take action. I can inject Spanish into my classroom conversations. Students begin to hear the sound of another culture's thinking, the sound of another experience that welcomes them, invites them to feel at home. This is a subtle point, but it seems to me an important one. Euro-American students often remark that my use of Spanish in the classroom thickens the context of the work but, more importantly, invites them, the cultural strangers, to connect with the material in a different way. It is the welcoming sound of difference that they hear inviting them to consider a new and different dimension. For Latina/o students, the use of Spanish in the classroom signals the opportunity for intellectual intimacy. Spanish speakers often feel that they will be understood, that in this classroom, speaking up is not a risk. Like the sign outside the shop window, "*Aquí se habla español,*" weaving Spanish throughout the content of a course tells the student that she is welcomed, that she will be recognized, that she will be respected. In turn, for any student who considers herself on the academic margins, who perceives course work to be outside of her cultural frame of reference—lesbian and gay students, African American, Native American, and Asian American students—the sound of difference in the classroom vindicates them, if only in a modest way.

When I explain myself, explain my Latina context in the classroom, I extend the invitation to engage in a particular critical consideration of text or theory or practice. Such cultural positioning enables students, the inquirers, to deepen the complexity of the query, confirming the holographic character of knowledge and the myth of value-free, neutral scholarship. More important to me, however, is the fact that when I explain my cultural self, I am no longer perceived as distant and as dominating. The fact that when I situate myself culturally, and thus politically, I step outside the tradition of the unapproachable, knowledge/power-broker professor. Like bell hooks, I am convinced that by positioning myself culturally/politically, I challenge the "traditional ways of teaching that reinforce domination" (hooks 1989, 52).

As I watch the last of the young scholars hop off the van, I vow to resist paleness, white-beardedness, the effects of being more-than-middle-aged, and make a mental note to push toward tenure.

Miami, December 1992

My tongue has been tied by years of Euro-American schooling, years spent with the Bradys, the Waltons, Ed Sullivan, and the Cartwrights; years spent unraveling John Dewey, reading Emerson, Hutchins, and Twain. To loosen these knots takes courage, takes purposeful, decisive, and unsentimental action. Just inviting memory of my unassimilated past is not enough. If I hunger for inclusion, I cannot worry about *disparates*; I cannot culturally paralyze my self. To hunger for memory seems *inútil*, a worthless endeavor, when what I hunger for is still within reach. I can leave the margins of the conversation. I can work my way to the middle, where *tías* and *primas, mi hermana* and *Mamy* undo the last of the knots. It is here, in the center of the conversation, where I will speak. It is from here that I will be heard. But I shouldn't wait for the invitation to practice my Spanish, to exercise my cultural self. Waiting for such invitations leads to cultural complacency. Cultural complacency leads to cultural rigor mortis.

Mamy is right. I *am* culturally rusty but need not stay that way. To mourn cultural loss ultimately *tiene pocos resultados*, serves little purpose. Our culture is alive all around me. I must seek it out. Find it. Embrace it. Speak it. Share it. Live it. Own it. Even in Iowa. Especially in Iowa.

References

Cisneros, S. (1989). *The house on Mango Street*. New York: Vintage.

hooks, b. (1989). *Talking back: Thinking feminist, thinking Black*. Boston: South End Press.

Lorde, A. (1984). *Sister outsider*. New York: Crossing Press.

Lugónes, M., & Spelman, E. V. (1983). Have we got a theory for you! Feminist theory, cultural imperialism and the demand for "the woman's voice." *Women's International Forum, 6*(6), 573–81.

Martin, J. R. (1991). The contradiction and the challenge of the educated woman. *Women's Studies Quarterly, 19,* 6–27.

Rodriguez, R. (1982). *Hunger of memory: The education of Richard Rodriguez*. New York: Bantam.

Steinem, G. (1983). *Outrageous acts and everyday rebellions*. New York: Holt, Rinehart & Winston.

CHAPTER 5

In Search of the Voice
I Always Had

MARÍA CRISTINA GONZÁLEZ

"*¿Que haces, mijita?*"

The words disrupted me as I sat sprawled on the dusty backroom floor of my grandparents' house. All around me were sheets of ivory-colored paper from the Pecos County State Bank, covered with line after line of pencil scribbling. I still clutched a pencil in my right hand as I looked up toward the doorway where my Papa M. R. stood. He held his grey felt cowboy hat in one hand, just having come in from the *Rancho Grande*, and I could smell the familiar scent of hot summer sun, perspiration, and the *tierra* that still reminds me of those days.

He wanted to know what I was doing. I was about four years old, and I answered him proudly, "Writing."

Papa M. R. chuckled in the way he always did when one of his grandchildren said something that amused him. His eyes twinkled behind his glasses, and he shuffled his ranchworn cowboy boots over to where I was.

"*¿Y que dice?*"

What does it *say?* I was stumped for a moment, on the verge of one of those experiences that create childhood shame, thinking I might have done something "wrong" in writing. I loosened the grip on my pencil and waited, as he reached down, squatting on the floor beside me, about to teach me something. He told me I could write as much as I wanted, but that I should always have something to say. I looked at him, not fully understanding what he meant. To write with nothing to say was wasteful, he went on, gesturing at all the paper around me. He then drew a picture that to this day remains indelibly etched in my mind, and he told me a story about a lazy farmer who wasn't watching his watermelon patch and was robbed by some guys who were passing by while he was busy sleeping in his house. While he talked, he drew

77

lines on the paper until the story was finished, holding my attention as I watched the lines slowly become the picture of a bird!

El Cuento de Las Sandías
(The Story of the Watermelons)

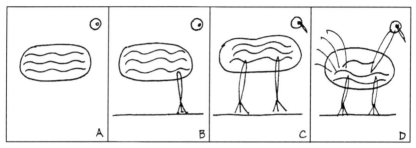

Fig. 5.1 *El cuento de las sandías.*

Once upon a time, there was a man who had a watermelon patch. He lived in a house off to the side. Every day, he planted the watermelons in rows and watered them and worked very hard to take care of them [see frame A of fig. 5.1]. But then, he got lazy and went to his house and fell asleep. While he was sleeping, three men were walking by on the road that went by the watermelon patch. They saw that no one was taking care of the watermelons. "*¡Ay, vamos a llevarnos unas sandías!*" they said to each other. So, they went into the patch and took a bunch of watermelons and went on their way [see frame B of fig. 5.1].

Later, when the man went to his garden, he saw that some watermelons were missing. But he was still lazy, and he went back to his house and fell asleep. That day, three more men came. They saw the watermelon patch and decided to take some watermelons too. They went into the patch, picked some watermelons, and went on their way [see frame C of fig. 5.1].

That day, the man became very angry. "*¡Esos ladrones! ¡Ahora ya no voy a dormir!*" He decided to catch them. He went into his house, but he kept watch from the little window he had. This day, the same men came again. "*Ese tonto—siempre está durmiendo. ¡Vamos a robarnos otras sandías!*" When the three men came by, he looked out his window, saw them in the patch, and he ran from the house to catch them. The three men saw him, and they went running out the other end of the patch, telling everyone, "*¡Ya no se pueden robar sandías de* *ese jardín!"* and the man went back to his house to have dinner [see frame D of fig. 5.1].

Papa M. R. finished telling the story and looked over at me until I took my eyes off the picture of the bird. *"Así, mija, tienes algo que guardar; si haces esto, puedes usar todo el papel que quieres."*

I could use all the paper I wanted if I did what he just did! I was fascinated!— but not just because I could use lots of paper. Papa M. R. had shown me how to do magic. Ever since before I walked, my mother had read stories to me, but until Papa M. R. told me this story, I had not realized that writing was the way these stories came into existence. Learning through stories was a large part of the way I was raised. It is the way I learned the principles that guided me throughout my life.

It would be easy to criticize what I have just presented as unrealistically sentimental and idealistically nostalgic. In fact, often when I hear these kinds of stories among Chicanos and Chicanas and Native Americans, they do seem to provide an opportunity for their tellers and *oyentes* to sigh heavily and lament the demise of tradition, the travesties of modern society, especially that driven by "white" Anglo-Saxon, Germanic U.S. cultural values. Often when I hear this kind of story shared, it helps create a shared sense of in-group suffering, longing for what was, trying to finds ways to recreate it.

I have often participated in this type of group bonding. However, that is not what I wish to highlight with the present sharing of the little tale of my Papa M. R. and my early experiences at writing. Rather, I wish to highlight one of the ways in which character built in traditional narrative might be formed. I believe that this type of learning forges a significantly more resistant type of character. It is resistant, because it is not explicitly learned. Rather, it is learned through the holistic experience of narrative context. I think this type of character is similar to what is acknowledged by Native Americans as "spirit." It is the sense of knowing one's ontology subjectively, in direct response to specific experience. It is not something that can be readily verbalized without considerable introspection and practice. We incorporate these lessons of character through indirect narrative experience, such as mine, when my *abuelito* strongly shaped me through his stories.

When Papa M. R. told me about *las sandías*, he was concerned about a few of the things he observed in his little granddaughter's afternoon activity of "writing." I was using a lot of paper in a way that guaranteed that it would not be usable again, and although I had a reasonable explanation for the activity and was enjoying myself and amusing him, when it came right down to it, I had no idea what writing was all about. In time, I would probably grow bored with it, as with any other childhood diversion, and leave it behind with the wastepaper. Papa M. R. could have done a couple of things. He could have played the strict disciplinarian (and in his ranching business, he rarely refrained from *that* role with my uncles and father). He could have told me to pick up that paper and quit wasting it. He could have told me that I didn't know how to write, and that what I was doing was scribbling and wasteful. He could have told me to go help my grandmother in the kitchen. I would have obeyed. I would have remembered some rules for the future. I would have learned very little, in the sense that my character would have remained unchanged.

More implicit in his story, and in his *way* of telling me the story, were lessons that were as powerful as, or even more powerful than, the explicit moral of the tale. Through a childhood story, Papa M. R., in the way of thousands of other elders throughout the ages, taught me some fairly "obvious" lessons. When we read fairy tales, fables, and traditional legends, it is fairly easy to pick out the "morals" they teach. In the *cuento de las sandías*, a simple tale of how a man lost the watermelons from his fields, the surface-level moral is relatively easy to discern: If you are lazy, the fruits of your labor can be taken away from you. This was definitely a family theme that I grew up with. It is a lesson explicitly taught throughout U.S. culture as well.

But Papa M. R. did not tell me this story because I was being lazy, or because someone was taking something from me. There was more involved in the telling of the story than the story itself, and often when we study our traditional tales and narrative traditions, we get caught up in what was said and not in the context of the telling. Yes, our people have learned through the narrative traditions of our elders, but not just because the stories had morals. We are missing very, very much if we choose to stick to content and thematic analysis of text. Papa M. R., a man who never had more than a few years of childhood formal education himself, taught me some principles that would shape a character motivated to perform in school. He clearly framed the task of writing for me as a creative task, one that produced results that taught lessons and could be preserved. (I treasured that little stick figure of a bird, and for years I told the story to my sister and anyone else who would listen. Even today, I have told it to my nephew.)

Of course, Papa M. R. never *said* all these things to me; at least he did not say them with the words he used. But his indirect, implicit presentation of wisdom was one of the keys to my future success throughout school. I am convinced that had he tried to teach me explicit principles, they would have simply gone down in a mental book of rules, external guides to monitor behavior. Writing would have been something I "had to learn," and I would have not had the self-realization that I could use pencil and paper to tell stories and make pictures. In addition, Papa M. R. told me I could do this as much as I wanted; it was not wasteful to use paper in *that* way. He was truly a wise man.

When it came to writing, this little storytelling sequence in my early childhood taught me things I'm sure that as a child I would not have been able to formulate in ways that would allow a modern-day researcher to recognize as the learning of principles. I could not have told anyone that I had just learned that one shouldn't write if she doesn't have anything to say. I could not have verbalized that writing for the sake of writing was wasteful of resources. Neither could I have expressed intelligibly that writing with a purpose was an enterprise worthy of resources otherwise rationed. I'm sure that I could have told someone, and did, that lazy farmers lose their watermelons. But that was not what I *learned;* there was no true insight in that logical deduction. And it is what I *learned* that remained with me as part of my character, part of who I was becoming. The rules I etched into memory through the years were much more predictive of how I would *behave* in the future: In my family we repeatedly were taught the rule to not be lazy, to not neglect our labor (and we are happily a family of workaholics). Our shared identity is much deeper, however, and it is much more tied to our character, to those things we learned implicitly. Today, we can verbalize some of those attributes of character after serious self-reflection. Formal education facilitates such verbalizing. For others, it might be far more difficult to express explicitly what was learned implicitly in early years. But for all of us, it remains rock-solid ontology that rears its (beautiful) face each time the vehicles of progress attempt to move over it.

My Papa M. R. never went to high school, much less college. He was *puro indio,* as my family would always say, and he was consequently a man of the land. But very early in my life, before I even knew what a professor or scholarship was, he had already taught me the most important lessons I would ever learn about writing. He also taught me lessons that would cast me in major conflict with the lessons of socialization into the social science professoriat in graduate school and thereafter.

The traditional indigenous, earth-based way of teaching that my grandfather used allowed me to learn principles implicitly, etching them indelibly into my character. Therefore, when I was confronted with new sets of "rules for being" in graduate school, the essence of the identity with which I was familiar, even if I was not conscious of it, was challenged.

It was January 1979 when I took my first stab at graduate school socialization. I had enrolled at North Texas State University to study organizational communication, having been encouraged by two of my best professors (who, incidentally, were not part of the graduate faculty that would "socialize" me). I had graduated in December, so I had about three weeks between my graduation and my return to school as a teaching fellow and master's-degree student. The role shifts were to be the least of my troubles. I remember sitting in my first seminar and listening to the doctoral students avidly discussing communication behaviors. This one word kept popping up, and it had the most uncanny ability to stump people and make them agree with the critic, even when their own comments had been intuitively true and sound. The word? *Empirical.* It was amazing! All someone had to do was ask, "What *empirical* basis do you have for that?" and people would readily concede. What in the world did *empirical* mean? It was definitely backed by a great persuasive force. I didn't know what it was on that first class night, but I rapidly found out. The word *empirical* meant far more than the word simply defined. Simply defined, it meant that something was based on experience. Academically applied, it meant "scientific" experience; it meant it had been demonstrated with research accepted by a scholarly community. I kept my observations to myself, but all this seemed very strange to me. This unbending focus on empirical experience thus defined somehow lacked wisdom, lacked a connection to the world of *lived experience.*

Still, I had little trouble doing well in that first class. Our initial assignment was the classic review of literature. As a habitual workaholic, I easily read everything available in 1978 on doctor-patient communication, even traveling to a medical school in Dallas to find additional sources. Growing up Mexican American in a racist environment, I had been raised as a critical thinker, and, like many of my current students of color, I had no trouble seeing gaps and inconsistencies in what was presented as "fact." Seeing trends and speculating on possible avenues to explore was a bit more challenging, but still not impossible. I surprised everyone, including myself, by getting a higher mark than even the continuing doctoral students on that assignment. I was perceived as perhaps "better than them"?

What they didn't realize is that my zeal for my work is what made my utilization of habitual skills possible. And that zeal was driven by my character—a character based on a sense of deep obligation to one's friends and family. I had chosen the topic of medical education on doctor-patient communication because of a personal friend who was having severe social troubles in medical school. The need to understand his experience drove my curiosity—How was it that an institution such as medicine could hurt the social skills of a warm, energetic, and talented individual? (Little did I realize I was studying the same sort of process into which I was just entering.)

The second assignment was to actually conduct some training for an organization. I did some very basic team-building training for the leaders of campus organizations. I soon learned I was naive to subtitle the paper "An Effective Team-Building Workshop." My professor laughed as he presented me in our mock convention panel format the night of our presentations: "This paper should be interesting—it is about an *effective* workshop, because she *says* it was effective." I was rapidly learning what all successful graduate students in my field had to learn in studying positivist methods of research. I was learning that my expression was constrained by the rules of inquiry. Sometime before finals that semester, I had a dream that greatly disturbed me. In that dream, I was required to sleep, and have sex, with all the male professors and students in my graduate program. In the dream, I was then obliged to complete a set of Likert-type scales about the experience in order to report what I felt about it! I was not consciously aware of what was happening to me during that first semester of graduate school. However, at the subconscious level I was already aware that even those things most intimate and sacred in my life were becoming objectified, and my expressions limited to forms acceptable to social science.

One of the skills that I think many of us learn as we grow up as members of the nonmajority culture is the "presentation of self as other." From very early in our lives, we learned that there were certain "faces" that were not appropriate when in the presence of dominant Anglo society. Suppressing our primary expressive impulses is a taken-for-granted aspect of our participation in social life. I believe that, for many minorities in our society, open expression can therefore be a casualty of socialization into "mainstream" society. If this sort of socialization is a transgenerational experience in a family, repressed expression can come to be seen as indigenous to the culture, rather than as the reaction to one's environment. In other words, the experience of openly or publicly expressing oneself is seemingly alien, and therefore associated as something "they" do, rather than being the legacy of humans in general.

Papa M. R. gave me the gift of this legacy. I was fortunate to have excellent writing teachers throughout elementary and secondary school, as well as my undergraduate days; they encouraged me to express myself creatively. It was not until I was in graduate school that my creative voice began to be silenced in favor of orthodox modes and messages.

Many might claim that this is common to many graduate students, and not just to *latinos*, not just to minorities. I would agree. The socialization process into any form of organization will require that there be some sacrifice of creativity, some constraint of one's individual impulses. It is not this universal socialization experience that I discuss now, however. The experience I am describing is based on the fact that the ways in which I saw the processes and implications of human communication were inherently different from those in the popular dogma in my chosen field of communication.

I was rewarded for pure memorization. Even in my history classes in college, I would freely embellish the "facts" with my observations. I found in my graduate education that my observations were often termed "bizarre," "unfounded," or "unrelated" to those things we studied. In a small-group communication seminar, my focusing on the dialectic tension that I observed between group membership and individuality earned me a B, while a presentation in which I handed out cookies and merely parroted the theories of another scholar was rewarded with an A. In a relational communication seminar, I was chastised in the margins of a paper for assigning a positive value to relationships that work out. The in-vogue "theory" posited in the field was that all relationships *end*.

By the time I was to write my dissertation, I was aware of the fact that the goal was not self-expression; it was task accomplishment. (Some might respond, "But of course! You shouldn't take it so seriously—it is a rite of passage!" It is this very kind of uncritical acceptance of repressive norms that I challenge.) So, for the first time in my entire life, I suffered from writer's block.

The possible reasons for my inability to put words onto paper overflowed: fear of success, socialization of women to fail, fear of failure, fear of evaluation, procrastination, burnout, some traumatic childhood event . . . I talked to counselors, professors, fellow students, and even went to a hypnotist! Yes, all these possible explanations were just that: possible. But they were not probable. They did not fit me. And over the years, even after the dissertation was completed, as writer's block soon became my frequent companion, I sought and sought for the answer to "why I can't seem to write anymore."

Then I went to Mexico.

While at Rutgers, getting really frustrated with my reactions to academia, I had applied for a Fulbright Professorship to Mexico. From my descriptions of my teaching, and my ability to teach qualitative research methods, I was named a Fulbright Scholar to Mexico, and taught at the Facultad de Psicología, A.C., a part of the Universidad Autónoma de Chihuahua. It was one of those times to which the term "blessing" could be appropriately applied. It had been years since I had been to Chihuahua. Throughout junior high, high school, and my undergraduate years, I had traveled frequently to Chihuahua. I had stayed there over holidays and summer vacations, and had always dreaded my returns to the fast-paced, mechanical lifestyles of the United States. But with graduate school and increasing demands on my time, I had gradually just stopped going. By the time I arrived in Chihuahua for my Fulbright, it had been ten years since the last time I had been there. And when I arrived, I was in shock.

Of course there was some culture shock. But that was not the greatest shock for me. Chihuahua had been "Americanized." The *maquiladoras* had arrived, the city had doubled in size, and there was even a new colonia whose streets were named after the fifty United States of America! I was saddened but, more than anything, fascinated by how the talk of the town was "becoming modern." In no time at all (relatively speaking, of course—Mexico had not become *that* modern), I had organized student focus groups and community interviews, and developed a large set of questionnaire items to determine some of the things that were happening to Mexican identity as traditional or modern. I sat and wrote for hours and hours, by hand, and in Spanish! And I realized that the question of a writer's block had not even crossed my mind. Instead, my mind was full of things I wanted to write, ideas I wanted to pursue. If anything, I had *too much* I wanted to write! I organized a panel for an international convention in San Francisco, and students and faculty from Texas and Mexico that I had invited to work with me on this project presented their work. I was inspired.

And then I returned to the United States. And my writer's block eventually returned. I was perplexed, but with my knowledge of my Mexican experience in hand, I set out to discover why I could not seem to bring myself to write easily. If only I'd had explicit awareness of the lessons Papa M. R. had taught me. The answers were always within me. I could not write easily because I did not feel I had anything to say to the academic community that demanded my productivity. I could not write easily because it seemed wasteful to dedicate so much time and resources to work that would be seen by so few people, and by people who would use it to build their careers rather than to contribute to society. I could not write easily because the praise I received for productivity was praise for *productivity*, not acknowledgment of my message. I was being asked to scribble on sheets of paper to see how many I could fill up. In this academic world, Papa M. R. was wrong. But because of the way Papa M. R. had taught me, I *was* Papa M. R. The lessons were not separate from me. They had become my character, and they were the reason I suffered.

That is the way culture works. And the more implicitly we learn our culture (some would call it "high context"), as with traditional narratives, the less we are aware of the whys and wherewithal of our actions and reactions, of why certain things motivate us and others simply bore us. There is nothing "wrong" with this. But I think it explains the pain of much experience of those of us "traditionals" who find ourselves in this leaning ivory tower. We simply don't know at first, or even second or third, glance why we are so unhappy. That which makes us happy was not explicitly stated to us; the markers were not highlighted for us. In many ways it makes that core self very stable and resistant to change. But the irony of it is that because we are so blind to that stable self, we can spend our time running back and forth into this wall and that wall, again and again and again, creating the semblance of instability with the variety of public selves we learn to perform on call.

My experience had to do with writing. It didn't *have* to be writing. For others it is discomfort in unfamiliar social situations, politicking in an impersonal bureaucracy, or living away from home. The real stresses of being Chicana in academia are not about whether one can get *pan dulce* or *menudo* in one's university community, or whether or not we can engage in bawdy Spanish-language jokes. These things may bring us the comfort of familiarity, but there are more painful stresses that come from those things that our growing up Chicana or Chicano made *implicit* in the way we react to the circumstances in our lives so that we do not see them readily. These stresses come from those things we can not see without careful, thorough scrutiny of our characters, so that we might understand better what it is about our work in "the academy" that moves us to lean in one direction or the other. The irony of it is that when we see more clearly the sources of distress, it does not necessarily mean the distress diminishes. Not as long as we still try to stand straight in a tower that leans.

I had thought very little about the metaphor of a "leaning ivory tower" when I first sat down to write this essay. I wrote an essay in a way that Papa M. R. would have said was wasteful. It was an assignment, a publication opportunity. I had sections and subsections of factors that contributed to my experiences in academia. There were a lot of words, but I had said nothing—María Cristina González had not expressed herself. I threw it away and I sat back, reconsidering the metaphor and its implications. A *leaning* ivory tower. What would I do if I found myself in a tower that was leaning? What would any sane person do if he or she found him/herself in a leaning tower? I would imagine—get out!

So why do I stay? Why, despite the real pain and distress that is so frequent an experience in this ivory tower, have I chosen to stay? Maybe it is because I believe that by having found that voice in me that was silenced by the protocol of academia, I might be able to contribute to that which will right it. Maybe that is too lofty a goal. Perhaps I am not even interested in making the tower stand erect; perhaps, instead, I just do not want to be mistaken any longer as part of the weighty voices that make it lean. I want my screams to be heard—screams that cry that I *see* that the tower is leaning. I want students like me to recognize in me that their perceptions are valid; that there isn't anything wrong with their sense of balance; that the floors *are* slanted. Perhaps then they can be spared the pain of naïveté, although I seriously doubt we can ever be spared all pain.

Maybe it is stretching the metaphor a little too far, but I have never heard of a tower that was leaning that was not ultimately abandoned before too much damage was done. Maybe academia will be different. Maybe as we acquire the courage to be ourselves and adapt the academy to reflect those things with which we are comfortable both practically and intuitively, it will somehow begin to right itself. I don't know. What I do know is that in order to gain the courage to begin voicing myself the way in which I have begun doing in the last few years, I had to have several things happen and exist.

First, I needed to take a long, hard look at my own misery. I had to look at my behaviors. I had to see honestly those masks I had put on in order to "fit in": the expressed valuing of objectivity over subjectivity, the desanctification and transformation of family and relationships into life "issues" and "factors," the teaching of a narrow band of literature so culturally biased that teaching it did not even *require* my voice. There were many more. Having identified and acknowledged the process of accommodation to which I had succumbed, I had to make the slow and arduous journey "back" to the place where my voice was waiting for me, waiting to make a noise, having been silenced for so long.

The decision to "make a noise" required that I seriously consider what my profession meant to me. I had to realize that I chose to be a professor that I might be able to *profess*. The experience of being without my voice throughout graduate school and the first years of my time as an assistant professor was lonely. Although I want to profess, I do not want to do so in isolation.

I needed voices around me that did not judge me for not thinking like the majority, voices that did not silence me when I openly stated things that struck at the foundation of the ivory tower. As difficult as it would be to find, I needed to be near a significant community of fellow minority faculty. For me, that has been provided through my alliances with Chicano and Native American faculty.

Next, I had to assess how I was contributing (or failing to contribute) to the socialization of my graduate students into the academy. We cannot continue treating the ivory tower as if it were sacrosanct simply because we have been granted office space and a title. I needed the freedom to teach graduate students in ways that I never experienced in graduate school, and to voice things that do not come "from the literature." I needed the freedom to formally respect and value traditional wisdom. If we continue to teach our graduate students in ways that perpetuate the systems that have contributed to our personal infernos, then we can never expect to remedy the problems we so eloquently and frequently lament. For me, being Chicana brings with it the cultural legacy of an awareness of the interconnectedness of generations. That applies to academia as well. We suppress our voices through conformity, through mindless repetition of scripts, through the indirect devaluing of that which is important to us each time we give in to the aspects of academia that force us to compromise our core values.

It is important that we be allowed to determine who we are, rather than having our identities designated by others. This seems self-evident and simplistic at first, but it is actually much more complex than a basic platitude. I believe that many times, in addition to the professional socialization experience, we have bought into the definitions of our ethnic groups popularized by outside stereotyping. This includes an emphasis on our shortcomings, our sufferings, our obstacles, to the exclusion of our strengths and achievements. A culture with dignity sees its potential with as much clarity as it sees its history of oppression.

For members of cultural minorities in the United States who have histories of oppression in its many forms, I agree that it is necessary to acknowledge the wounds of history and society and the effects those wounds have had on us. But if we focus almost exclusively on "righting wounds," and rarely on acknowledging strengths and our culturally natural ways of experiencing life, we lean too far to one side. We buy into a politically correct model that the voice of the minority is the voice of the slighted soul, displaying her or his wounds for society to observe. We learn well how to construct a rhetoric of the oppressed, but we do not learn how to construct our own rhetorics of strength and dignity.

When we glorify the oppressive experiences as those that characterize us as Chicanas and Chicanos, we do not allow for the possibility of transcending oppression without losing our cultural membership. It is time to look for unifying strengths that characterize us across social and economic strata. For those of us who were born into barrios with no paved roads, whose grandmothers practiced adaptations of *curandería*, who were migrant farmers, who were punished violently for speaking Spanish, who took drugs along with the precursors of today's gangs— my advice is to not see these experiences as those that qualify us as Chicanos and Chicanas. We buy into our own stereotypes. Our children, our *sobrinos* and *sobrinas*, are not being raised in those realities. Their parents, *tíos,* and *tías,* are university professors! If we identify our ethnicity with our oppression, then we deny our progeny the right to be Chicana or Chicano when we provide them with a "better" life.

We will not learn how to present our dignity by dwelling on those situations in which we have been treated without it. Rather, I believe we will begin presenting ourselves as dignified when we balance the picture by searching our own experiences for those occasions and themes that gave us experiences of dignity and a sense of *ubicación* in the social world.

I look back over my life and can remember being told we could not speak Spanish in school, being accused of not paying for something when I had, being placed in the lowest-level classes in junior high simply because I was Mexican and had gone to school in Latin America. Those memories give me the basis for knowing that there must be changes. But others give me the basis for knowing I am a human being with worth and a sense of self. There might have been dysfunction in the family unit, but it is not the dysfunction that characterized it as Chicana. It is the endurance and resilience, the maintenance of contact, the extended network of social obligation that transcends negative history. That is where my voice comes from. Its volume might come from the anger of injustice, but its essence comes from those instances that built the strengths of my character.

I have had to develop a resolve to enable me to deal with the fact that, despite the support I have received from colleagues and fellow Chicanas and Chicanos, despite the recognition of what I think makes the tower lean, and despite believing without a doubt that I have "found"

my voice, it is not going to get any easier. The tower is leaning because
of years of bad architecture and poor construction. Whether we aban-
don it altogether or try to salvage it, we are unfortunately in the midst
of a time of great need for institutional reflection and revision. So I have
found that it helps to recognize that I am not solely responsible for the
tower's leaning, nor for its salvation. But I can contribute to either, and
it is my choice to determine which it will be, recognizing that both
alternatives will likely be painful. The major accomplishment is that I
no longer believe that my voice is something to be found "out there" in
"the world of success." It is something that was given to me early in
life, as a function of the identity to which I was born.

Papa M. R. did not teach me about this with *el cuento de las
sandías*. But before he ever told me about the watermelons, he had
taught me something else. When I was about three years old, I asked
him one day why women had to wear false teeth when they got older,
and men didn't. You see, both of my *abuelitas*, Mama Fina and Mama
Carmelita, wore false teeth. Both of my *abuelitos*, Papa M. R. and Papa
Cosme, did not. In his typical way, Papa M. R. chuckled and asked me
why I wanted to know that. I explained to him my three-year-old's
process of logical deduction. He told me that I was wrong. That it was
not true. That *he* had false teeth, and he was a man! I did not believe
him, and I shook my head, saying I didn't think that was true. He
answered me, "*Mira, no tengo fuerza,*" trying to convince me that he
had no strength to his teeth by feebly biting with his teeth as if he were
very weak. I hesitated, but then persisted in saying that he was lying.
Papa M. R. then took two of his fingers and bit down on them, telling
me to notice that he could not even hurt his own fingers. I was slowly
being convinced. Sensing my lingering doubt, however, he offered to
demonstrate with my own fingers. I let him take my index finger, and he
bit it sharply, causing me to jerk it away, yelling in pain! I felt so
betrayed! He laughed.

"*Para que veas . . . para que veas . . . que cuando sabes algo, nunca
debes dejarte . . .*" I should be aware, he said, that when I know something, I should never let myself be taken advantage of—"*¡porque duele!*"
because it hurts.

Although it might be painful to be in this leaning ivory tower, I am
convinced that it would be far more painful if I were to let myself be
taken advantage of, if I were to give in to the realities that are not valid
for me. I have no desire to put my fingers in anybody else's mouth. I
have found my voice, and I will speak what I know. What else can
anybody offer me to beat that?

CHAPTER 6

Struggling with the Labels
That Mark My Ethnic Identity

DULCE M. CRUZ

When I was doing my master's degree, I taught at a university in New York City, where I grew up. Back then I did not think too much about my ethnic identity. But when I was completing my doctorate and teaching at a predominantly white institution in the Midwest, everything changed, mainly because I was one of the very few Latinas on campus. In 1992, for example, of a student population of 35,489, only 544 were Hispanics, mostly Mexican Americans; 1,371 were African American. Hispanic and Black representation among faculty and staff was, and still is, even smaller. Of the 1,484 faculty, administrators, and lecturers, only 58 are Hispanic or Black; of the 4,842 nonacademic employees, only 118 are Hispanic or Black. And that is including Latin Americans. Otherwise the numbers would be lower.

Throughout my six-year stay I was the only Latina—the only Dominican American—in the department of English. In such an environment there is just no denying that I have been the "Other" and that as a result I had to confront life-changing circumstances. Now as I get ready to start a tenure-line assistant professorship in the mid-Atlantic region I cannot avoid stepping back and examining what I have learned—how, for example, being "different," the "only," and the "Other" has prompted a struggle with the labels that mark my ethnic identity.

When I arrived at the midwestern university, I was assigned to teach composition to "foreign" students. Although no one ever said it directly or explicitly (and even though I enjoyed the students tremendously), I soon realized that no one else wanted to teach those sections. I heard through the grapevine that the courses were assigned to me because *I* was "foreign." I suppose it did not matter that I was raised and socialized in the States and that my dominant language is English. And so right from the beginning I felt "different"—in a negative way. The first day of class my own "foreign" students looked at my black hair and asked if I "really" knew English well enough to teach it. One immediately dropped the course because he wanted to be taught by "a real American." Later my white students in "regular" composition and literature courses asked similar questions: "Where are you from? Where did you learn to speak English so well? But you're Hispanic, how come you like Katherine Mansfield? You know, I have a friend who knows a Hispanic and she's Black but you're not?"

Faculty and other graduate students also emphasized my ethnicity, my "difference." One professor habitually turned to me whenever she needed someone to explain "the plight of the marginalized." She designated me, without asking my permission, as the spokesperson for all Hispanics and Blacks. When the term ended, she thanked me for "giving voice to the oppressed." But I did not feel she was thankful (nor did I want her thanks); she was congratulating herself for being liberal enough to "empower" me—as if power can or should be given! Consequently, I often felt like the token most people in the department thought I was. And those feelings were not just in my mind. Once I overheard a colleague complaining that I received a teaching fellowship, and she did not, because I am Latina. Of course, she did not bother to mention that I am a summa cum laude who had solid teaching experience prior to my arrival.

Usually faculty and other graduate students were stunned when I said I was pursuing nineteenth-century British literature. "Aren't you interested in the literature of your people," a few asked. My people! When did knowledge and literature become the property of a specific group, I often thought but rarely had the nerve to say. The worst part was that at conferences when I met other Latinos they too would question me. "There is so much need in our own community. Why don't you do a doctorate in Caribbean literature?" Well, I did change my field, not because I felt pressured, but because I found literacy theory more interesting and challenging. But even then there were incidents. Once I attended a breakfast for a committee I belonged to. There were several state politicians and important university officials. One of them was seated on my left. In the course of conversation he asked what my dissertation was about. When I explained that I had done research on highly literate Dominican Americans, his immediate response was, "Oh, so you must be a Dominican American yourself." "Yes I am," I answered, and by the end of the conversation I was angry: It is a no-win situation. Had I done research on a typical mainstream subject, my right and ability would have been questioned. When I do research on my own community, I am considered suspect, narrow, ethnocentric, and incapable of being objective.

And it was not just strangers who made such comments. Even my friends made me feel different. When I began a job search, they were very reassuring: "You'll definitely find a position. You have it made. You're a Latina and English departments are desperate to fill their quotas." They could not emphasize my research or my vita. To them my asset is my ethnic identity. Needless to say, those experiences have been painful—but I have no regrets. During those six years I also encountered very supportive people. And even if I had not, I firmly believe that the extra burden of being different, the "only," and the "Other" has helped to shape me into a stronger and wiser woman, Latina, Dominican American, and scholar. That is not to say that I welcome the anguish, or that I think nothing should be done about such attitudes. I just refuse to let it stop me from growing.

It was not simply that my colleagues and students made me feel different; it was that my difference was equated with inferiority. One of the painful results of feeling inferior was that I was compelled to revise my identity. (Truthfully, there were times when I wished I could slip out of who I am.) That redefinition hurt because inherent in the process there was a devaluing of my heritage. I know that process is unavoidable; it is the result of two cultures' meeting and clashing. And indeed, other immigrants experience it too. For example, the words of a Korean American could very well be mine:

> One day you raise the right hand and you are American. They give you an American Passport. The United States of America. Somewhere someone has taken my identity and replaced it with their photograph. The other one. Their signature their seals. Their own image. And you learn the executive branch the legislative branch and the third. Justice. Judicial branch. It makes the difference. The rest is past. (Cha 1982, 56)

So could the words of a Puerto Rican:

> I forgot   I forgot the other heritage   the other strain refrain   the silverthread thru my sound   the ebony sheen to my life   to the look of things to the sound of how I grew up which was in Harlem right down in Spanish Harlem El Barrio . . . . What I didn't forget was the look of Ithaca Rochester Minneapolis and Salt Lake   bleached bleeded and bleached . . . . I forgot this heritage. . . .   I know why I forgot   I'm not supposed to remember   what I do remember is to walk in straight and white. (Morales 1983, 107–8)

I also know that many other people in my situation believe that the hurt is necessary. In *The Hunger of Memory* (1982), for instance,

Richard Rodriguez insists that the forging he personifies *is* painful, but that it produced "a public identity" that allows him to be an active participant in society (p. 19). In other words, "while one suffers a diminished sense of private individuality by becoming assimilated into public society, such assimilation makes possible the achievement of public individuality" (p. 26). According to Rodriguez, the hurt of subsumption is less than the pain caused when marginalization is perpetuated by, for example, speaking Spanish in school. For him personally, using Spanish was a constant reminder of his "separateness from *los otros, los gringos in power*" (p. 16). But I think Rodriguez fails to really understand that shedding our culture (and thereby attempting to erase our ethnicity) is not the only factor that creates a public self: gender, race, class, and level of formal education are just as significant. And in any case, regardless of how hard we try to reshape our identity so that it is more acceptable to the mainstream, we simply can never be fully "American," at least not by the mythical definition of American. No matter what we do (get a Ph.D., become wealthy, move out of the neighborhood), we are still separated and boxed into categories like "ethnic" and "minority."[1] As a Vietnamese American explains, the message we get from mainstream society is mixed:

> From "forget who you are and forget me not" to "know who you are and copy me not," the point of view is the same: "Be like *us* . . ." Don't be us, this self-explanatory motto warns. Just be "like" and bear the chameleon's fate, never infecting *us* but only yourself, spending your days muting, putting on/taking off glasses, trying to please all and always at odds with myself who is no self at all. (Trinh 1989, 52)

This is the confusion (anger and pain) I confronted because my colleagues and students made me feel different, only, Other. As a result I have thought a great deal about the labels that are assigned to me and that I identify with.[2] To begin with, I learned that I am not just a Latina; I am not simply that nebulous monolith. I share linguistic and some cultural similarities with other Latinos, but that is about it. Certainly there are vast differences among us. Latinos are a composite of various races and nationalities, each with its own unique historical, economic, educational, political, and social characteristics. Mexican Americans, for instance, are a conquered people. Many have been in the United States since before the founding of Jamestown. I know of some in the Southwest who believe they live in occupied Mexico. Puerto Ricans are a colonized people with American citizenship who have been displaced by the United States' attempt to industrialize the island. Cubans are political refugees. Dominicans, for the most part, are economic emigrants. Those differences are significant and must be acknowledged, because they have repercussions for the way each group functions in United States society.

For example, Cubans and Dominicans began to arrive at about the same time,[3] and today each group's population in the States numbers approximately one million, and yet Dominicans remain subsumed in the "Latino/Hispanic" monolith. Cubans have been extricated from the monolith—they have a visibly distinct identity—perhaps because they have become substantially more successful economically and educationally. It is important to note that their success is, I believe, directly related to their unique history and circumstances. The first wave of Cuban immigrants was predominantly white, upper-class, and highly educated; subsequent waves come from a revolutionary Cuba where society has been transformed so that people—women in particular—participate more fully in higher education, employment, and politics.[4] Cubans enter the States as political refugees. There are programs to help their transition, and mainstream America is less resistant to them. That is not the case with Dominicans. Most Dominicans are dark-skinned "economic refugees" that mainstream American society disdains.

And so I think that it is important for me to recognize that I am also Dominican, not just a Latina. Initially I believed that calling myself Dominican was a less complicated matter, but I was wrong. I perpetuated many myths and pretended that my Dominican identity was not a questionable issue at all.[5] Like other Dominicans, I systematically denied my mulatta condition.[6] Even right now as I write this it is difficult to acknowledge that indeed Dominicans are a mixture of Europeans (mainly Spaniards) and Africans. There may be a few "pure" whites, and maybe even fewer mestizos (a mixture of European and Indian),[7] but overwhelmingly we are mulatto. Yet we look exclusively to the "Madre Patria," Spain, for our roots. Although there is a myriad of shades representing "an extensive and rich process of contributions and cultural assimilations drawn from an extremely varied gamut of ethnic groups," we—I—insist on considering ourselves white or mestizo (del Castillo & Murphy, 1987, 50).[8] We persist in using endless euphemisms to disguise the color of our skin and other traits of the African.

When I was a child it was important that I be called *indiecita*, rather than *morena*, particularly when people fussed over my cousins' blond hair and blue eyes. And when people called me *indiecita*, they would qualify it, as if to make up for the insult, by saying, "Don't worry, you have beautiful *pelo bueno.*" Thus, like other Dominicans I came to the States with very intricate beliefs about the labels used to describe who I am. I emigrated with an incredible internalized and unspoken turmoil, and then that complexity was magnified by uniquely American definitions of race, color, ethnicity, and cultural allegiance, so that the task of figuring out what to call myself was doubled. It was disturbing that in the States I was not even *indiecita* anymore. On the island I was *blanca* or *india*, but in the States there was no end to what I was/am called: Hispanic, Hispanic American, Hispanic Caribbean, Latin American, Latina, Spanish, Dominican American, nonwhite, person of color, minority, Third World woman, ethnic, Other, pariah, the inevitable "spic," and on and on. At least, I figured as a teenager, I did not become "Black" the way darker-skinned Dominicans were labeled. It was worse for them, because, in being "Black," by default they were "African American."

And then as an adult I had to decide if I wanted to call myself Hispanic or Latina. I was and still am uncomfortable about using *Hispanic,* since it is a sanitized Anglo word imposed by the United States Census Bureau. It implies an attempt to pass. And it belies the influence African and native Indians had on my language, religion, music, architecture, agriculture, philosophy, art, and culture. The term *Hispanic* denies that Spaniards themselves were influenced by Gypsies, Sephardic Jews, Moors, and other North African Arabic cultures. Some Dominicans (and other Latinos) are not direct descendants of Spaniards, they do not have Hispanic names, and now some in the States do not even speak Spanish. So the label is not quite accurate, and I feel a bit uneasy using it. The term *Latina/o* is equally problematic, since it too denies the African influence, and its direct reference to Latin America is reductionist. *Latina/o* does not really include or describe my Dominican island experience.

I think that both *Hispanic* and *Latina* are confusing misnomers that perpetuate subsumption into a monolith. But I have decided to use them because in some circumstances it is valuable to have a collective identity. Either term helps to create a "supraethnic identity that has the power to mobilize" us (Sommers 1991, 34). Either term helps to coalesce us into an imagined community that can then work together to acquire power and adequate representation, something all Latinos desperately need in order to secure our fair share of the political and economic strength we have been denied. (For the same reason, I think it is also very useful to appropriate a "Dominican" collective identity.) I prefer the label *Latina,* though, because it resonates with political consciousness, and because, unlike the English word *Hispanic, Latina/o* has gender.

I would like to be identified as a woman and an educator, but since it is not that simple, I have settled on the term *Dominican American*. I realize that label refers more to a national identity than to an ethnic one, but of the options available I believe it more or less describes my tripartite heritage. I am not just Dominican. I no longer have the majority of characteristics attributed to people socialized on the island. I have absorbed a lot of mainstream America's ethos. But neither am I just an American. I have too many memories and traits that mark me. I am not just a Latina either. My history and experiences are definitely different from those of other Latinas. I feel closer to Latinas than I do to other people in our society, but my circumstances are unique.

I like to think of myself as the "spaces" between the Dominican, Latina, and American worlds. That is how Juan Bruce-Novoa describes Mexican Americans:

> the space (not the hyphen) between the two, the intercultural nothing of that space. We are continually expanding that space, pushing the two out and apart as we build our own separate reality, while at the same time creating strong bonds of interlocking tension that hold the two in relationship. (Cited in Sandoval Sánchez 1992, 32)

I am something new, as Aurora Levins Morales and Rosario Morales say of Puerto Ricans:

> I am a child of the Americas . . .
> a child of many diaspora, born into
> this continent at a crossroads . . .
> I am new. History made me. My
> first language was spanglish.
> I was born at the crossroads
> and I am whole.
> (Sandoval Sánchez 1992, 38)

The estrangement my colleagues, students, and friends at the midwestern university forced on me caused me pain, but it also prompted much introspection, which, I believe, has been fruitful. I wish that such impositions did not exist. Latinos (or anybody) should not have to deal with the extra burden. But since they do exist, I decided to use them, to make them work for my growth, for my benefit. In doing so I circumvented the very real possibility that I might have hated myself and my heritage. That is what happens to many Latina/os, as Cherrié Moraga (1983) notes:

It is frightening to acknowledge that I have internalized a racism and classism, where the object of oppression is not only someone *outside* my skin, but the someone *inside* my skin. In fact, to a large degree, the real battle with such oppression, for all of us, begins under the skin. (p. 54)

Had I not been introspective, I would have believed that I am inferior. Instead, I think I have a deeper understanding of the power structures, the historical and psychological forces, that subordinate my heritage and shape my anguish. In examining these labels, I also gained strength to create a firm voice for myself and others. I became more empowered and determined to fight back. And undoubtedly, fighting back is a role—a responsibility—that I must assume, if for no other reason than the fact that in relation to the population there are too few Dominican American professors. Higher education—and everyone—needs to be reminded that Dominicans are here, and that we will not be shut out regardless of the circumstances.

Notes

1. C. Nelson and M. Tienda (The Structuring of Hispanic Ethnicity: Historical and Contemporary Perspectives," *Ethnic and Racial Studies,* 8, no. 1 [1985]: 49–74) explain the difference between being considered an ethnic and being considered a minority: A minority "is a group whose members are subjected to unequal treatment through prejudice and discrimination by a dominant group. Ethnic groups, on the other hand, are a collectivity sharing common cultural norms, values, identities and behaviors, and who both recognize themselves, and are recognized by others as being ethnic. The extent to which ethnicity is a matter of individual choice depends on the group's access (or lack thereof) to the reward system of a dominant society" (p. 53). This difference is clearly illustrated by African Americans and Jews. They are both "ethnic" groups, but African Americans are more of a minority (in the stigmatizing sense) than Jews are. That is why Cubans are rarely identified as a minority group, but Mexicans, Puerto Ricans, and Dominicans usually are. The reason, Nelson and Tienda maintain, "has to do with their very different modes of incorporation and socioeconomic integration experiences" (p. 53).

2. Similarly, Gloria Anzaldúa (*Borderlands La Frontera: The New Mestiza* [San Francisco: Spinsters/Aunt Lute, 1987), one of the loudest voices speaking for Latinas, particularly Chicanas, writes about her struggle with the labels imposed upon her by mainstream society. She writes: "As a culture, we call ourselves Spanish when referring to ourselves as a linguistic group and when copping out. It is then we forget our predominant Indian genes. We are 70–80%

Indian. We call ourselves Hispanic or Spanish-American or Latin American or Latin when linking ourselves to other Spanish-speaking peoples of the Western hemisphere and when copping out. We call ourselves Mexican-American to signify we are neither Mexican nor American, but more the noun 'American' than the adjective 'Mexican' (and when copping out)" (p. 63).

3. Before Trujillo's assassination in 1961 only members of the elite and political exiles were allowed to leave the Dominican Republic. But after his death there were two major waves of immigrants: the first in the mid 1960s, the second in the mid 1970s.

4. Muriel Nazzari (" 'The Woman Question' in Cuba: An Analysis of Material Constraints on Its Solution," *Signs: Journal of Women in Culture and Society,* 9, no. 2 [1983]: 246–63), for example, argues that this transformation has also perpetuated "women's inequality in the home and in the work force," but I maintain that, however hegemonic the conditions in Castro's Cuba, women have more opportunities to become highly literate and politically involved, and therefore they are better prepared to fit into United States' society. Also see Larguia, I., and Dumoulin, J., "Women's Equality and the Cuban Revolution, " in J. Nash and H. Safa (Eds.), *Women and Change in Latin America,* pp. 344–68. (Granby, MA: Bergin & Garvey, 1985).

5. Similarly, Sandoval Sánchez (1992) writes that Puerto Ricans on the island do not find it "necessary to question what Puertorriqueño is, because ultimately everyone is Puertorriqueño and lives in a place called Puerto Rico which is theirs; here [in the States] the Boricua is called Spic, and is outside his home. There it was no great bout to be more or less dark skinned; here they find themselves with a new definition of race which divides them from their brothers: White, Black, Puerto Rican, puts them in the middle of a battle between the dominant white society and the Afro-American nation" (p. 34, my translation).

6. Blacks from various English, French, and Danish colonies, Africa, and Haiti have been a constant presence in the Dominican Republic. But mass mulattoization did not start until the end of the eighteenth century, because the discovery (in 1519) of the riches of Mexico and Peru diminished interest in the island. By 1540, economic decline was widespread, and by 1605 most of the sugar plantations were abandoned. Therefore, there was no need to import slaves. When the French saw the island's potential for growing coffee, they began mass importation of African slaves. The boom lasted from 1740 to about 1790, when the slave trade reached its highest level. During that time the Spanish, French, Portuguese, and German colonist population grew from 6,000 to almost 150,000. Moya Pons (1983) writes that because there were virtually no white women, "the plantation owners were obliged to use the most attractive of the female slaves in order to fulfill their natural impulses" (p. 164, my translation). As a result, between 1780 and 1789, for example, the mulatto population increased from 12,000 to 28,000 (Moya Pons 1983, 164).

7. Taínos did not survive the Spanish conquest. The combination of hard physical labor and new diseases decimated them within thirty years of the Spaniards' arrival. When Columbus "discovered" the island in 1492, there were

approximately 400,000 Taínos, and by 1508 there were only 60,000 (Moya Pons 1983, 26).

8. This is not often recognized, but a diverse group of immigrants have shaped the Dominican identity. Del Castillo and Murphy (1987) explain that in the past 150 years there has been an active influx of Cuban, Puerto Rican, German, Italian, Sephardic Jewish, and Arabic immigrants. Cubans and Puerto Ricans contributed to education; Germans traded tobacco; Italians established commerce; Sephardic Jews were involved in financial and commercial activities; Arabs (Syrians, Lebanese, and Palestinians) contributed to the retail trade; and Chinese set up laundries, restaurants, and cafes (p. 55). Most recently, Chinese from Taiwan and Hong Kong have established supermarkets, motels, luxury hotels, and manufacturing enterprises. In fact, second to Haitians, Chinese are the fastest growing immigrant group on the island (p. 56).

References

Cha, T. H. K. (1982). *Dictee*. New York: Tanam Press.

del Castillo, J., & Murphy, M. F. (1987). Migration, national identity and cultural policy in the Dominican Republic. *Journal of Ethnic Studies, 15*, 49–69.

Moraga, C. (1983). *Loving in the war years: Lo que nunca pasó por sus labios*. Boston: South End Press.

Morales, R. (1983). The other heritage. In G. Anzaldúa & C. Moraga (Eds.), *This bridge called my back: Writings by radical women of color* (pp. 107–8). Latham, NY: Kitchen Table, Women of Color Press.

Moya Pons, F. (1983). *Manual de historia dominicana* (7th ed.). Santiago, Dominican Republic: Universidad Católica Madre y Maestra.

Rodriguez, R. (1982). *The Hunger of memory: The education of Richard Rodriguez, an autobiography*. Boston: D. R. Godine.

Sandoval Sánchez, A. (1992). La identidad especular del allá y del acá: Nuestra propia imagen puertorriqueña en cuestión. *Bulletin Centro de Estudios Puertorriqueños, 4*(2), 28–43.

Sommers, L. K. (1991). Inventing Latinismo: The creation of "Hispanic" panethnicity in the United States. *Journal of American Folklore, 104*(411), 32–53.

Trinh, M. T. (1989). *Woman native other*. Bloomington: Indiana University Press.

CHAPTER 7

The Segregated Citadel:
Some Personal Observations
on the Academic Career Not Offered

RICHARD R. VERDUGO

In the fall of 1980, as I neared completion of my doctoral dissertation, the prospect of accepting a teaching position at a reputable research-oriented university was not only personally satisfying but would have been the culmination of seven years of grinding graduate study.[1] Since my first love was research, early on I had decided not to apply for academic positions at teaching institutions. My goal was to develop into a first-rate scholar. My prospects, so I thought, looked good. In fact, a number of other graduate students continually reinforced this belief by informing me that I would "have no problem" landing a position at a first-rate research university. Interestingly, I later realized that such comments were made simply because I was a Chicano and had little to do with my academic accomplishments. Today the perception remains that minorities who achieve success do so because of affirmative action policies rather than their own accomplishments.

I completed the dissertation in the winter of 1981, and as I sit at my desk writing these lines, in the spring of 1993, I have yet to hold a teaching position at any institution of higher education. Though I have managed to craft a satisfying career in public policy at the national level, it is somewhat irritating that I have not held a professorship at a reputable research university. In this essay I would like to describe what I believe were the main reasons for my not having a career as an academic, both early and later in my career. Before proceeding I should point out that I am not alone in this experience. I believe that we (Chicanos) have a fairly large cadre of individuals who earned doctorates in the late 1970s and early 1980s yet for one reason or another have failed to obtain academic positions.

101

Background: Racial Stratification
in Higher Education—the Segregated Citadel

Higher education is a highly stratified institution. Ethnicity, race, and gender are factors on which such stratification is based. I have elsewhere discussed how higher education is racially stratified.[2] In this section I would like to briefly draw out the rudiments of my earlier writings.

Racial stratification appears to affect Hispanic faculty in two ways. First, racial stratification uses an elaborate ideological mechanism that assumes that subordinate ethnic/racial groups are both biologically and culturally inferior to superordinate ethnic/racial groups. Such an ideology encourages the negative stereotyping of minorities and influences how faculty and school personnel interact with and evaluate minority faculty; it also leads to negative stereotyping of "minority" research as inferior research. A second factor is segregation. Aside from its distributional functions, segregation reinforces stereotypes and reduces self-esteem among ethnic/racial minorities.

Stratification systems are complex social structures that maintain social order. They are "a way of classifying people and their functions, of prescribing which sorts of people should do what sort of things" (Hodges 1964, 84).[3] The mechanisms by which stratification systems are maintained vary by society, but two seem to be quite common: *ideological* and *spatial*.

Stratification systems are elaborate ideological schemes that justify the existence of a given social order through group ideas that explain important aspects of life. Ideological schemes have ranged, for example, from such justifications as the "will of God" to those alleging biological superiority. Bierstedt (1963) has noted: "an ideology is an idea supported by a norm" (p. 171). [4] Ideologies, then, encompass norms, mores, folkways, values, and theories. Thus, ideologies provide explanations for the order of things. But more importantly, ideologies are rooted in group interests (Mannheim 1936).[5]

In addition to the ideological component, stratification systems are characterized by spatial mechanisms. Such mechanisms as isolation, segregation, and discrimination may be indices of spatial forms of stratification.

Both of these forces, ideological and spatial, reinforce one another and serve to both justify and maintain social order. Ideology is used to justify differential treatment or spatial separation, which in turn is used to perpetuate a given ideology. For instance, productivity in one's scholarly field is the most important criterion used in promoting faculty to tenured positions. Since a large proportion of minority faculty are not tenured, there is the commonly held notion that they have failed to meet certain standards of scholarship.

Racial stratification in higher education has negative effects on the status of Hispanic faculty. Ideologically, there is the pervasive belief that Hispanic faculty lack the necessary academic skills that would allow them to flourish in academe, that there is a lack of objectivity in their research, and that the topics with which they deal are irrelevant or only marginally important. Spatially, Hispanic faculty are concentrated in less prestigious institutions, in several academic disciplines, and are given only committee assignments that concern minorities.[6] Another spatiality-related issue is the role the few Hispanic faculty have as mentors to Hispanic students. This and related outreach activities place great demands on the time of Hispanic faculty and divert them from activities more likely to be rewarded by their institutions, such as publishing.

My own experience has been not as an academic but in attempting to gain entry to academe. These experiences are well explained by a racial stratification framework because such a system works effectively as a screening device by limiting the number of ethnic/racial minorities entering the academic profession. It is to these experiences that I now turn.

The Path Not Offered: A Racial Stratification Issue

Before describing my experiences from a racial stratification perspective, I think it is important that I briefly describe the demographic situation in higher education as I was completing my dissertation. Certain facts exacerbated my situation and made it doubly difficult to obtain a position at a university.

The Demography of Higher Education

During the time I was completing my dissertation, academe was undergoing several crises that worked against all newly minted Ph.D.'s hampering their efforts to attain academic positions. Outsiders, such as women and ethnic/racial minorities, were especially hurt by these trends. The facts were these: (1) An aging baby-boom cohort meant an oversupply of new Ph.D.s, concomitant with a decline in the student population, and (2) tuition costs were rising.

Data from the U.S. Department of Education (Snyder 1991) indicate that the academic labor market rose steadily until about 1977 and has remained somewhat stable since then. This leveling off of faculty can be attributed to several phenomena. Certainly, one of the more important is the declining need for additional faculty because of the decrease in the rate of total enrollment in higher education. For example, from 1970 to 1975 enrollment increased by over 30 percent, by 8 percent between 1975 and 1980, by only 1 percent between 1980 and 1985, and by nearly 10 percent from 1985 to 1989. So although enrollment has been increasing, it was doing so at a decreasing rate.

A second explanation has to do with the increased cost of a college education. This cost has risen by 58 percent from 1980 to 1985 and by 28 percent from 1985 to 1989. From 1980 to 1989, tuition increased by 102 percent (Snyder 1991).[7] Finally, given the economic recession experienced since the 1980s, college-age youth and their parents carefully weigh decisions about investing heavily in college.

As a result of these trends, I was competing in a tight labor market that had less demand for my services. It was, by all accounts, a buyer's market. Nonetheless, it was also a period in which there was a desperate need for Hispanic faculty. Hispanics as a percentage of total full-time faculty increased by only 0.5 percent between 1980 and 1990 (Carter & Wilson 1988). In contrast, the percent of Hispanic students enrolled in higher education as a percent of total enrollment increased from 3.9 percent to 5.5 percent between 1980 and 1990. Though I had prepared myself for an academic position, and there was a clear need for someone with my skills and training, an academic offer never materialized.

Ideology: Skills and Research Interests

In academe, the most important index of productivity, and of one's status within the academy, is publishing. As I entered the academic labor market in the early 1980s, I was without a single journal publication but had presented twelve scholarly papers at national and international meetings. In years past, my productivity would have been enough to land me a teaching position at a fine research university. But in a tight labor market, these accomplishments were not enough.

Recently, the issue of publications arose again. Since 1984 I have averaged at least two refereed publications a year. In 1993, I was lucky enough to have five papers accepted for publication. Apparently, this is not enough for some institutions. Indeed, recently I had an experience that highlights this factor. An individual from the department of sociology at the University of California at Irvine scrutinized every one of my publications and subjectively ranked the prestige of each journal in which I had published. This person was also concerned because I have been publishing in economics journals! A professor at UCLA wondered if I had enough publications, and "Gee, wouldn't it be great if I could finish the book I've been working on." These individuals fail to place my productivity within the context of my work life—that I have a demanding job and all my scholarly efforts occur in the early hours of the morning.

The issue of my research interests was raised not only by Anglo and Black scholars (mostly Anglo, though) with whom I interacted, but also by several Chicano scholars. I particularly remember several Chicano scholars who were concerned that my research was not "Hispanic" enough. The criticism was that I tended to focus on mainstream issues and methods, especially the status attainment framework. Indeed, my training was within the status attainment framework. However, my interest was in applying the attainment framework to minority populations, especially the Hispanic population. In any event, I truly felt between a rock and a hard place: For Anglos I was a "minority scholar," and to Chicano scholars I was really not in their camp.

Another issue that arises is my lack of teaching experience other than teaching assistant positions. Interestingly, well-intentioned friends or acquaintances continually advise me to take a part-time teaching position if I am serious about landing a full-time teaching position. I have several colleagues who have taken this path, and I can honestly say that they have been exploited for the time and effort they have put into their teaching, as they have not been given tenure-track academic positions. This simply isn't an effective way to get one's foot in the door; I see no merit in taking a part-time teaching position when in my spare time I would rather be conducting my research.

In the past four to five years I have undergone a rather dramatic transition about my desire to obtain an academic position. I'm no longer in a hurry to land an academic position, and should I do so it will be mainly because of my scholarly output. I believe there are two reasons for this change in my attitude. First, quite naturally I have become very frustrated with academe. In my research and in my own personal experiences, I have come to realize that merit has little to do with obtaining either a quality academic position or promotion within academe. Academe is not unlike any other labor market, where both ascription and achievement are important influences on one's attainment. My own sense is that ascription plays a heavier role than most are willing to admit. Second, in the past five years I have enjoyed my work, and my career has been moving along extremely well. For me, academe no longer holds the allure that it once did.

Spatial Issues: Potential, Lack of Fit, and Mentoring

Racial stratification uses spatial mechanisms to maintain order. In higher education, spatial mechanisms are used to distribute Hispanic faculty in less prestigious institutions, funneling them into certain kinds of academic disciplines, and so on. In my case, I experienced three kinds of phenomena that I would call spatial. First, I was particularly incensed at one rejection for a postdoctoral position from the University of Texas at Austin. The rejection letter from the chair of the search committee stated something to the effect that they were interested in "actual accomplishments rather than potential for scholarly activity." What then is the purpose of postdoctoral work if not to develop and provide opportunities for scholarly activity?

Another set of reasons for my not being offered an academic position was "your areas of expertise do not fit our current needs." What I found truly astounding about these reasons was that I applied for positions that announced teaching positions in my areas or positions that were open to all areas of expertise.

Finally rejections of my applications were at times based on a whole host of "other" reasons. For example, that I didn't have enough teaching experience, that I hadn't experienced teaching at a small, liberal arts college, which, by the way, would exclude about 99 percent of all minority scholars.

Mentoring is an important aspect of one's graduate career. An excellent mentor, especially one well connected in one's discipline, can almost guarantee a graduate student's landing an academic position. My mentor turned out to be a superb friend and mentor, but he always felt he "got to me too late." That is, in his view he had little to do in shaping my approach to conducting sociological research. Indeed, we were only together for two years. The fact that my mentor had this opinion could be gleaned from the letters of recommendation he wrote on my behalf. These letters tended to be courteous and brief, and never said anything negative, but, again, they never expressed any sense that I would be a productive scholar.

Nevertheless, he did reveal certain biases about minority scholars in general and about me in particular. His letters of recommendation always contained the phrase "the best minority student" or "will be one of the truly fine minority scholars." I was always ambivalent about such phrasing when I read my letters of recommendation, but in later years I became both very disappointed and angry with him for writing about me and a whole category of scholars in such a limiting fashion. In fact, when I complained about the language and perceptions that his letters were conveying to others, he dropped the term minority altogether. These letters, as I soon came to realize, spoke more about him and other nonminority faculty than about me or other minorities.

Conclusion

I have both positive and negative feelings about not ever having had the opportunity to become an academic. On the negative side, academe is something I had wanted to do since my early twenties, so never having had the chance means that I have this unfulfilled yearning, something that I should have had the opportunity to experience. Not ever having achieved that goal makes the investment of time, effort, and money I put into my graduate training somewhat questionable.

Other negatives include having to work twelve months a year rather than spending my summers traveling or pursuing my research interests. Finally, having worked in a policy environment throughout my career, I have managed to produce a fairly large body of published research, but most of this scholarly productivity has been opportunistic rather than something I would have pursued on my own. As an academic I would have had the luxury to spend time on topics of my own choosing, not merely those that dovetailed with my "daytime job."

There are at least three positive aspects of having a nonacademic position. First, there is the matter of my salary. I now earn a salary commensurate with that of a full professor. I doubt that I would have commanded such a salary in academe because of the fiscal and racial problems that seem endemic to higher education. Second, my career path is not tied to my scholarly output. I can pursue my scholarly activities without the "publish or perish" norm. Finally, from a sociology of knowledge perspective, I have not been pressured to accept the views held in academe about certain research areas in which I am interested. As an outsider I see things slightly different from how academics see them.

In conclusion, the path not offered has been bumpy but exhilarating. It is a path I believe a large proportion of Chicanos earning Ph.D.'s in the late 1970s and early 1980s have traveled and have had to deal with in their own ways. Sadly, I believe higher education, and society itself, has suffered the most from denying that generation access to teaching positions in its institutions. And, I don't foresee any major improvements in the situation in the years to come. In my own case, I have continued to pursue my own research interests and carve out a satisfying career in public policy. Life outside academe, life in the real world, might after all be the best perch from which to observe and study real-world problems.

Notes

1. This paper benefited greatly from the comments made by Naomi Verdugo, Raymond V. Padilla and Rudolfo Chávez. I am however responsible for any errors in the manuscript.
2. See Verdugo 1986, 1992b. Also, I use the term racial stratification to denote both ethnic and racial stratification.
3. See, for example, Hodges 1964.
4. See Bierstedt 1963.
5. See Mannheim 1936.
6. There is an emerging literature on the status of Hispanic faculty. I would recommend the following studies: Olivas 1988, de la Luz Reyes & Halcón 1988, Garza 1988, Uribe & Verdugo 1990, and Verdugo 1992a.
7. Data refer to all colleges and universities. It should also be pointed out that the cost of operating a college also increased. The best way to make this assessment is by examining the Higher Education Price Index (HEPI). Changes in the HEPI are exhibited below:

Year	% Change
1975–80	43.5
1980–85	44.6
1985–89	20.2
1975–89	149.3

References

Bierstedt, R. (1963). *The social order: An introduction to sociology* (2d ed.). New York: McGraw-Hill.

Carter, D. J., & Wilson, R. (1988). *Minorities in higher education.* Washington, DC: American Council on Education.

de la Luz Reyes, M., & Halcón, J. J. (1988). Racism in academia: The old wolf revisited. *Harvard Educational Review, 58,* 299–314.

Garza, H. (1988). The barrioization of Hispanic faculty. *Educational Record*, *68*, 122–24.

Hodges, H. M. (1964). *Social stratification: Class in America*. Cambridge, MA: Schenkman.

Mannheim, K. (1936). *Ideology and utopia*. New York: Harcourt, Brace & World.

Olivas, M. A. (1988). Latino faculty at the border. *Change*, *20*, 6–8.

Snyder, T. D. (1991). *The digest of education statistics, 1991*. Washington, DC: U.S. Government Printing Office.

Uribe, O., Jr., & Verdugo, R. R. (1990). *A research note on the status and working conditions of Hispanic faculty*. Paper presented at the annual American Education Research Association meetings, Boston.

Verdugo, R. R. (1986). Educational stratification and Hispanics. In M. Olivas (Ed.), *Latino college students*. New York: Teachers College Press.

Verdugo, R. R. (1992a). Analysis of tenure among Hispanic higher education faculty. *Journal of the Association of Mexican American Educators*, 23–30.

Verdugo, R. R. (1992b). *Racial stratification and Hispanic faculty in higher education*. Paper presented at the sixth annual meeting of the Hispanic Association of Colleges and Universities, Washington, DC.

CHAPTER 8

The Odyssey of a Chicano Academic

A. REYNALDO CONTRERAS

Growing Up in the Shadow of the Ivory Tower

My voyage began in a poor, traditional family. I arrived to a humble couple raising a brood of eight girls and two boys. My mother devoted herself to raising a family. My father, who could barely read, struggled to keep us fed and clothed. We lived in the "East Barrio" of Claremont. The neighborhood was near the campus of a cluster of small liberal arts colleges and a graduate school. My parents were proud owners of their own home.

I grew up in a traditional community. For me and my younger brother the yard was our first playground. It was enough space to explore and enjoy our many imaginary worlds. Soon, however, we moved beyond our yard, visiting other homes full of children who were also curious about what lay beyond their homes and yards. This led to many neighborhood games and play. The "East Barrio" became a safe haven for us to explore and to pretend and to play in. It was an extended family where everyone knew everyone else, adults acted as surrogate parents of others' children, and everyone made sure children were safely off the streets at sunset.

The community had its own Catholic church, a pool hall, and family-owned grocery stores. Many of the families were related to each other. Life had a rhythm. During the week, everyone was busy going to school or work. The weekends were full of church activities. Men of all ages went to the pool hall. They went to unwind from the long week of hard work, drinking, playing pool, singing, telling tall tales, and infrequently getting into a brawl. The women gathered at church activities or visited each other at home. Occasionally there was a social event that drew the neighborhood together: a baptism, a wedding, a wake, or a

111

"Jamaica." The neighborhood provided me with my values, first aspirations, and self-identity. It was a place where I went to catechism ("La doctrina") every Saturday, where I learned to play baseball.

I joined in the rites of passage from boyhood to young adolescence in the "street corner" society, where boys learned the rules of being "brave": learning the vulgar language of men, learning to "drink," and boasting of minor conquests of the opposite sex. This all happened in the name of becoming "men."

We attended "school" outside of the neighborhood. Schoolbuses to the various elementary and high schools that served the "East Barrio" came by to take us to and return us from our schools. The neighborhood was divided by two counties (San Bernardino and Los Angeles), three cities (Claremont, Upland, and Ontario), and, therefore, three school districts. My family lived on the Claremont side of the "East Barrio." Therefore, I attended the Claremont schools. Claremont is a conservative college town. A handful of Latino students and occasionally an African American student attended the school, which had just recently been desegregated. Mexicans were allowed to attend, but Mexican children were discouraged from congregating together or speaking Spanish. We were sent to the office for misbehaving, while the non-Mexican kids were verbally reprimanded by the teacher but stayed in class. In spite of these difficulties, going to school was fun. I made new friends and shared in doing many things.

Throughout my years in high school I lived in two worlds—the world of the "East Barrio" and its street-corner society, and the world of "school" and its related class and athletic activities. I had two circles of friends and engaged comfortably with them, but in different places. I spent weekends with my barrio friends and the school week with my school friends.

I was an average student. My grades were adequate to help me gain admission into California State Polytechnic College, a local California State University campus. However, I gave little attention to attending college until my junior year in high school. Until then, I gave little attention to the future. I lived each day one at a time, enjoying my time with my friends and doing just well enough to achieve passing grades. It was in the eleventh grade when a counselor informed me that I did exceedingly well on a standardized test and suggested I take the SAT examination. At the time, I had no idea what the SAT was or the implications of taking the test. I took the examination. When the results returned, the same counselor asked me if I had given any thought to attending college. I had not. I thought college was where rich kids or children of professors went after high school. Many of my neighborhood acquaintances or friends of my sisters talked of the local junior colleges. My friends talked of joining the Army or Navy or getting a job. Few, if any, mentioned going to college. I knew little of what it entailed. I had no concrete sense of what higher education was about.

I made my decision to attend college in the fall of my senior year. I gave no thought to applying to the local colleges in Claremont because my grades were only average and those schools were too expensive. I decided to take seriously the challenge of "going to college" and applied to Cal-Poly, Pomona. The college had a small campus located not far from my home in Claremont.

In the spring of my senior year I knew I was going to college the following year. I settled down to doing well in school, maybe to see if I could "cut the mustard" as a student. During "senior week" and the graduation party, classmates shared plans. Many were going to UCLA, Smith, Michigan, and San Diego State. Other classmates were attending a local junior college. I found myself sharing that I would be off to Cal-Poly, Pomona.

I worked for the Claremont Parks and Recreation Department during the summer as a recreation leader in the "East Barrio," earning my first money for college and preparing to leave the "East Barrio." The summer went by quickly, and by the end I began receiving literature and registration materials beckoning me to the Cal-Poly campus.

I arrived at Cal-Poly along with several hundred new freshmen discovering a new reality—being a college student. This included attending large lecture classes, studying at the library, and having to be responsible for oneself in a sea of anonymity. Overwhelmed by this new adventure, I set my mind to taking each day at a time and hoping for the best. I moved into a dormitory room on campus. Shortly thereafter I experienced "culture shock" from moving into "public living quarters." Students were up all hours of the day and night and partied all weekend. I shared a room with someone I had never met before and who was not Hispanic. It was an initial step in diversifying my personal space. We shared alternative perspectives about life in college—the many trials and tribulations of living in a campus community. I lived in the dormitory for two quarters. I felt guilty about living so well compared to my parents and siblings still at home, who lived in less than adequate circumstances. I returned home, paid my parents room and board, and commuted to college. The change drew me away from the mainstream of social life on campus, but my decision alleviated my guilt and motivated me to take seriously my responsibility for my academic performance. I began working part-time on campus to pay for my college expenses. During holidays and vacations I worked for the Claremont Parks and Recreation Department. Thus, time for studying became scarce. Getting top grades became important to me. Every quarter, getting on the dean's list became my primary motivation. Going to college became a four-year process with an established rhythm of going to class, going to the library to study, going to work, and doing studying until the early hours of the morning.

The Activist Sixties

A major experience in my undergraduate career was becoming a community leader. As a consequence of moving back to my parents' home in the "East Barrio," I became involved in developing an evening tutorial program and a youth center. These programs provided white upper middle class students from the Associated Colleges of Claremont opportunities to become involved in community activities. I helped in the tutorial program for high school students as a resource person. The first year of the program worked out well, but as the academic year ended for the college students, the tutorial program drew to an end. This created a social vacuum for many of the kids who had participated in the program. I went to the Claremont Parks and Recreation Department, my summer employer, and asked for an assignment to the "East Barrio" neighborhood. At the time, I did not realize what I had gotten myself into. My scope of responsibilities mushroomed from supervising youth recreational programs to conducting community activities for preschool children to young adults. I retained contact with most of the youth who had been involved in the tutorial program. As the college students returned, I found they were without their program coordinator. The program was rudderless. As a result, by default I assumed leadership of the tutorial program. The program quickly evolved from helping kids with their homework to include youth counseling. My life as a college student became extremely complicated. I carried my full load of classes, continued working part-time on campus, and supervised each evening of the week the expanded tutorial program.

The summer after my sophomore year found me establishing a community center to house expanded tutorial program and summer youth programs. This led me into the world of the "war on poverty" politics of the sixties. The Los Angeles County Human Relations Commission was the new political arena. The commission was disbursing federal and private funds to youth and young-adult leadership initiatives throughout Los Angeles County. I became acquainted with community development politics. The experience taught me skills of networking, lobbying, bargaining, and compromising. I acquainted myself with the leaders of community organizations throughout the county and the city of Los Angeles. They were a sophisticated group. Aggressively, they wheeled and dealt for available funds. They were masters of urban politics. With their encouragement and sponsorship, I obtained funding by the end of the summer to establish a "Teen-Post" program.

With the new funding, I employed youth from the neighborhood to supervise activities for young children and adolescents. Students from the Claremont Associated Colleges and Cal-Poly, Pomona, became involved in tutoring and taking youth out on a variety of field trips. Meanwhile, I struggled to stay up with my classes and work part-time. This was the era when student activism began to escalate on many campuses. Student activists "visited" the center to "discuss" the social issues of the time with high school students. The situation became uneasy for several months, but the student activists eventually decided to move on. The kids were unharmed by the experience. We spent the following year maintaining the programs as I completed my undergraduate requirements. Many students from the Claremont Colleges came and left. They befriended many of the kids, impressed the kids of the "East Barrio," and, I suspect, left impressed by the youth they shared time with.

The sunset of my tenure as a volunteer director of the community center rapidly approached. I was graduating in the spring without any clear idea about what I would be doing after graduation. At the time, I did not see myself going on academically beyond an undergraduate program. I saw my options as pursuing a career in recreation administration or teaching at the high school level. After a period of indecision, application deadlines forced me to decide. I chose to become a high school teacher and applied to a "fifth-year program" for teacher certification at Cal-Poly. I retreated into a role as member of a community center advisory committee. The advisory committee employed a director for the community center. I was again looking at leaving the "East Barrio" the following year. I would be a graduate student at Cal-Poly preparing to become a high school teacher.

My graduation from college surprised my family. I had been busy so much of my time throughout my college years that the only time my family saw me was late in the evenings when I was completing assignments due the next day or "cramming" for an examination. Thus, I gradually distanced myself from my family even though I was living with my parents and several siblings. So, when I announced the impending graduation and the additional year of graduate work, they were surprised. In their view, I could now go out and get a job and enjoy life with the family.

My year of teacher preparation was not any less intense than the previous four years were, but the focus of this intensity was my involvement in schools, observing teachers, talking to students, doing curricular planning, and teaching lessons—all those things that were expected to make me a good teacher. However, one thing I did not anticipate encountering was the culture of the teachers. I perceived the teachers' culture to be authoritarian. Those in authority talked down to students. The primary objective was to control kids by "keeping them at their desks" and keeping them "busy" with paper-and-pencil exercises. Teachers knew who would succeed and who would fail. It was a culture shock when I saw teachers tending to be direct, terse, and to the point in disciplining students to the extent that many students felt either humiliated or rejected. Teaching only happened between 8:00 A.M. and 2:30 P.M. I was not prepared for the culture. But I was not ready to reject teaching as a career. My experiences led me to conclude that I needed to grow up a bit more before I became a teacher. I began looking around for something else to do. President Kennedy's Peace Corps caught my attention. I requested information, applied, and immersed myself in completing my student teaching.

The Peace Corps

"Big Dave" Carrasco from El Paso, Texas, introduced me to the Peace Corps. He was assembling a group of volunteers that would be establishing a sport development project in Ecuador. He was in the area interviewing potential candidates for his project, and he came by to interview me. I was impressed by "Big Dave." He was the first Mexican American professional I had met who expressed interest in me, in what I wanted to do, and in what I wanted to become. We had a good meeting. He left encouraging me to pursue my own goals and with the possibility that I might be a member of his project group. I anticipated some follow-up for several weeks, but nothing happened. Then one morning at the end of the semester I received a call from Washington, D.C., inquiring if I could fly to Ohio for Peace Corps training within five days. When I said yes, they indicated I would be receiving my airplane ticket within a day for travel to Ohio. I was left stunned. All of a sudden things were escalating for me. I was not only announcing to my family that I was joining the Peace Corps and leaving in a few days, but also helping them to accept the fact that I was leaving. I arrived in Columbus, Ohio, and was taken to Dennison University, a small liberal arts college located in Granville, Ohio. We were a group of thirty-six, four women and thirty-two men, from different parts of the country. Some came from major universities, including Stanford, Yale, Harvard, Notre Dame, and Michigan. Others came from smaller universities, like Ohio Wesleyan, UC-Riverside, Ball State, American University, and Cal-Poly, Pomona.

The Peace Corps has been perceived as a paternalistic endeavor, and the volunteer training did much to reinforce such a perception. We were prepared in the international relations, history, and culture of Ecuador from a United States perspective. Several returning volunteers assisted us in the use of Spanish in coaching and teaching sports training techniques popular in collegiate athletics. The highly structured training lasted four weeks, at the end of which we were ready to test our new wings. We traveled to San Juan, Puerto Rico, via New York, for two weeks of "field training."

We arrived into hot and humid San Juan in the middle of the night. The next morning, a Sunday, we met with the director of Peace Corps training in Puerto Rico and received our assignments to small communities in the rural region of the Island. We were to return in exactly fourteen days.

Having a volunteer live in your community was a novelty in many Puerto Rican communities. But in my community my ethnic identity was an additional matter of interest to many of the Puerto Ricans I met. I was perceived in Puerto Rico to be a "Mejicano," and usually I was asked from what part of Mexico I came. While I was not offended by their perceptions, it did take a number of conversations to clarify my family roots and my identity as "Mexican American." These conversations revealed strongly held stereotypes of what a "gringo" is. The resentment held by many in the community against gringos was rooted in the adverse experiences of many people of the community who had immigrated to the mainland and returned to the island. Those who considered me a "Mejicano" buffered me from any potential antagonism someone in the community might want to project upon me. It was a concrete prelude of the "anti-gringoism" that I experienced in Ecuador.

The two weeks in Puerto Rico went by too rapidly. I said good-bye to my adopted community, my colleagues at the high school, and the kids. I felt ready to respond to the uncertain times I was to experience in Ecuador. I found my way back to San Juan happy to return from a severe test of cultural immersion. We were given airplane tickets to our homes and instructed to be at the airport in Miami, Florida, in two weeks. I flew back to Los Angeles and spent my home leave with my parents, excited about going off on my Peace Corps service. The two weeks went by quickly. After emotional good-byes I flew to Miami, where I met the rest of my volunteer group. From Miami we flew to Quito, Ecuador. We arrived at the Andean city as dawn broke the next morning.

I went with twelve other volunteers to the coastal region of Ecuador. We lived in the port city of Guayaquil while working with the local teacher training institute ("Escuela Normal") and the provincial sports federation. We were assisting in demonstrating coaching skills in basketball, baseball, wrestling, and track and field. We traveled throughout the coastal towns and villages, giving clinics as well as helping coach in various sports clubs in Guayaquil. After we'd spent several months settling into our new assignments, "Big Dave" came by to review our progress. To my surprise he asked me to take on the responsibility of being a "volunteer leader" and to work as his liaison to the local sports federation. This new role drew me into the midst of local sports politics and severely tested the political skills I developed in the "East Barrio." I spent days on the road visiting towns and villages requesting assistance from the Peace Corps. I also worked with volunteers in implementing new projects by facilitating communication with host country agencies. By the end of my first year I had teamed up with another volunteer and developed a boys' and girls' junior track team, trained them, and challenged the local clubs. We competed against the local clubs who had the star athletes and decided to challenge the junior athletes of Quito. Through the competitive contests we demonstrated how kids with average abilities could be prepared to compete. The local sports officials, embarrassed by our success, banished the other volunteer and me from coaching in the coast. I went to Quito to assist in placing a new group of volunteers. I spent several months on this assignment. Then I went to the "Oriente," the Amazon jungle region of Ecuador, to help in organizing camps for young children of Quito. After six months in the "Oriente" I returned to Quito to help draw to an end the activities of volunteers from my project who were due to leave Ecuador. I also was recruited to help a team of evaluators from Washington, D.C., evaluate Peace Corps projects in South America. This new assignment extended my Peace Corps service another half year. By the end of my Peace Corps service I was ready to leave. I had found my experiences as a Peace Corps volunteer rewarding, but I discovered how complicated it is to bring about social change. While volunteers were trained and directed to be social missionaries, many of us realized how impotent we were as change agents in a society where at best we were seen as guests. This predicament left me feeling antagonistic toward those I had tried to "help." I needed to move on and deal with my own life.

During my last year in Ecuador, I gave thought to life after the Peace Corps. I felt uncertain about what I would be doing. I was ambivalent about going into teaching. One evening while I was talking to my project director about returning to California, he suggested I think of attending Stanford. He felt I would have no problem completing a master's program. This suggestion startled me. I had never aspired to go beyond a B.S. degree. Even becoming certified as a teacher was going beyond my expectations. Now being told I could succeed in completing a master's degree program was intriguing. I had no idea what Stanford was like or where it was located. However, being adventurous, I said, "Why not!" and wrote to Stanford requesting an admissions application. I applied for admission and took the necessary TESOL and GRE tests and three months later received notice of my admission to the Stanford School of Education's master's degree program. Yet Stanford University and attending Stanford University were abstract notions to me; there was still a very real possibility that I would become a high school teacher. However, the event was significant. A window into graduate education opened for me, and I was undecided about whether I was going to jump through it. After I returned to California, though, I discovered that I could not get a job as a teacher, so I opted to go to Stanford.

Getting "Stanfordized"

I arrived at "the Farm," as Stanford is called, in January 1969. I went to the School of Education and, like any confident ex–Peace Corps volunteer, announced my arrival. A secretary cordially instructed me to meet with an advisor, who would introduce me to the university. My advisor greeted me. He informed me that he had graduated from Pomona College, one of the Associated Colleges of Claremont, and we spent a large part of our first meeting reminiscing about life in Claremont. Little did I realize how important an influence he would have on my academic career at Stanford. He spent an extraordinary amount of time in my first year at Stanford helping me adjust. I learned to be an "independent learner" and established rapport with members of the faculty. I discovered that learning at the graduate level happened beyond the class meetings and required reading lists. This was a major shift from the learning style I developed as an undergraduate student. Mentoring was essential to survival at Stanford. Informal relations were important safety nets for coping with the overwhelming stress and psychological fatigue that occurred as one battled the anxieties resulting from the uncertainties about what one was learning. My advisor was there whenever I felt I was hitting a wall.

Another dimension of getting Stanfordized was becoming part of informal networks with other students throughout the campus community and learning from these relationships. For example, I moved into a dormitory that housed the law students. My roommate, a law student, was a former Air Force officer. He had lived in Japan and acquired many Japanese customs. I lived with him for only a quarter, but during that quarter we spent time comparing intercultural experiences, his in Japan and mine in South America. We explored how these experiences influenced our response to the elitist culture of Stanford. While we came to no clear answers, it seemed like we drifted to a consensus that we had become more open and cosmopolitan, probably more respecting of others and more appreciative of how others could enrich our lives, whether at Stanford, East Palo Alto, or Oakland. This was an optimistic attitude to share, especially on a campus like Stanford where it seemed like faculty and students alike were self-driven.

My first quarter found me intimidated by my perceptions of the academic performance expected at Stanford. As a result I fell into a very rigid routine of studying and going to class, and I spent little time socializing outside of class or hours at the library. It was during this time that one of my Peace Corps volunteer friends, a Stanford graduate, came to visit the campus. He gave me a grand tour of the campus and introduced me to many of his acquaintances in the Stanford community. In particular, he introduced me to the dean of students and his wife, a teacher at a local high school. They also were resident advisors of a fraternity cluster. Through my ex-volunteer friend I got to know the couple and became part of their circle of student friends. At the end of the winter quarter the dean of students invited me to move into their fraternity cluster, which I did, and I thereby became part of the more intimate Stanford community and involved myself in campus activities other than going to class and studying. These events drew me out of an isolating student lifestyle. I gained a support system I leaned on in sorting out experiences I encountered as I lived at Stanford. Similarly, I became a resource to others who were part of the social network.

One of my important involvements at Stanford was being part of a Mexican American group that, like many student groups in other universities, was seeking recognition and programs of activities as support systems. It was through this group that I became acquainted with many Mexican Americans (then) and Chicanos (now) who were students in other departments and professional schools or on the staff and faculty.

The group evolved at a time when there was a great deal of unrest on campus. We were having sit-ins and public debates about the Vietnam War and other social issues while police patrolled the campus dressed in riot suits. It was a time when Mexican American students established alliances with student groups at other universities to advance and reinforce the presence of Latinos in higher education. Several of us attended a conference held in Santa Barbara that gave birth to MECHA: El Movimiento Estudiantil Chicano de Aztlan. MECHA emerged as an alliance of student groups that became visible and provided generations of students with an organization for affiliation. At Stanford, MECHA became an impetus for the university to develop programs that enhanced the presence and success of Chicano students, faculty, and staff on campus. It was a fulfilling experience working with Chicano students, faculty, and staff establishing programs and seeing more Chicanos arriving on campus from throughout the country. It became a support structure but of a special kind. It supported a dialogue about one's presence and legitimacy in the academy. It provided a means by which students could reach out to Latino communities in affirming ourselves as Latinos while we grew as professionals. Moreover, it provided for a cohesive alumni group that is bonded by the Stanford experience and continues to reinforce the Latino presence at "the farm" and in various professional arenas.

In returning to Stanford as a full-time student I needed to work part-time to pay my expenses. I worked as a student teaching supervisor in my first year, helping teach a problems seminar with two other supervisors and providing a series of workshops for supervisors on teaching minority youth (in addition to supervising student teachers). The next year I was employed as an assistant to the dean of the School of Education, where I worked on the recruitment, admission, and financial support of minority graduate students. In the third year, I worked as director of visitor and guide services for the university's Office of Governmental Relations. My part-time employment gave me flexibility to work on my dissertation proposal.

I consider writing my dissertation to have been an important experience. It was a severe test of discipline and perseverance. The road from crystallizing a research problem and research design to completing the study was turbulent and uncertain. I spent two years at Stanford developing the research proposal for studying decision-making behavior of Latino executive administrators of precollegiate and collegiate educational organizations in California. While traveling throughout California collecting my data, I received news that one of my sisters, a year older than I, was seriously ill with cancer.

The news about my sister devastated me. I realized that family was a value I strongly held. There was no question in my mind. I had to help her. My research project went to the "back burner." I took leave from the university and flew to her home in Eugene, Oregon, to see how I could help her and her husband. She decided to return to California for treatment and to be closer to her family. This was costing money they did not have, so I decided to get a job to help her settle down in California and, in essence, live out the rest of her life comfortably. I took a position at San Diego State University. The position allowed me to visit my sister and her sons and to see that her needs were met. At San Diego State, I was employed as one of the several administrators of a program of federal technical assistance and as a faculty member in a new multicultural education department. I lived a very hectic life, working in San Diego during the week and visiting my family in Los Angeles during the weekends. My sister lived for only another six months.

After my sister's death, I stayed in San Diego and returned to completing my dissertation while continuing to work at San Diego State. I took two years to complete the study—two years longer than if I had stayed at Stanford. However, I do not regret the delay. I fulfilled an obligation I felt to my sister and family that was more important at the time. What became important to me after my sister's death was to complete my study. I successfully presented the research to my committee. I was free!

Inside the Ivory Tower

I continued to work at San Diego State for a year after completing my dissertation. I hoped to move into a tenure-track position in educational administration. This proved to be fruitless for at least two reasons. First, the faculty of educational administration were former practitioners not receptive to employing a social scientist with little or no practical experience. Second, they seemed to indicate they already had their minority faculty, a Latino with experience as a principal. The dean of the College of

Education, a Latino, did not seem to be in a position to help me move into the department. Therefore, in spite of the dean's optimism and promises, I began to search in California for a faculty position in educational administration and policy. There did not seem to be anything available for a Chicano with a Ph.D. from Stanford. The only Latino with a social science background and a faculty position in educational administration in California was a woman at one of the University of California campuses. Thus, the odds of getting a faculty position in California were not good. Therefore, I expanded my search to other states.

I accepted a faculty position at California State University at Los Angeles (CSULA). Though it was not in educational administration, the position allowed me to work with educational administrators through the Desegregation Institute. It also allowed me to stay in California, close to my family. My loyalty to my family continued to be strong. Moreover, my sense of obligation to my parents gained additional significance. Shortly after my sister passed away my parents asked me to become responsible for their affairs. They were elderly and in poor health, and were finding it increasingly difficult to keep up with their affairs. Somehow I had earned their respect. I suppose the way I responded to my dying sister's circumstances earned their trust and confidence in my ability to help them in their personal affairs. Moreover, I was without major obligations. This was significant because one of my older siblings could have assumed this obligation. I was chosen. Thus, I became more central in the affairs of my family in advising my parents and mediating family conflicts. Therefore, moving out of California would have been difficult at the time.

I was at CSULA for three years, but in the second year, I realized that I wanted to go to a research-oriented university. The University of California was not recruiting minority faculty in departments of educational leadership, so I applied to universities throughout the Midwest and the Southwest. Meanwhile, my wife, whom I had just married, was accepted to a doctoral program at the University of Massachusetts. I took leave from my position to accompany her to Amherst and to conduct postdoctoral research at the Center for Desegregation Research.

In the summer before we left for the University of Massachusetts, Indiana University called and invited me to the campus for an interview. I accepted the invitation, motivated by my curiosity to see a midwestern university. Whether I would consider a position was not certain. I visited Bloomington, a small college town in southern Indiana, where Indiana University is located. IU is a traditional midwestern university that spawned famous educational leaders of the West including David

Starr Jordan and Ellwood P. Cubberley. I was impressed by the campus, with its rich foliage and its resources for conducting research. After two full days of interviews, I left Bloomington having enjoyed the visit but not optimistic or enthusiastic about the possibility of returning.

We left California in the last week of August 1979, off to the University of Massachusetts, expecting to return to California the following summer. We arrived at Amherst after a long drive across the United States. My wife began her classes while I began exploring the archives of the Center for Desegregation Research and auditing seminars on economic history and economic policy taught by Herb Gintis and Sam Bowles, who had written a popular book on education as a social reproduction process. We lived a typical graduate student lifestyle throughout the fall. Somewhere midsemester, I received a call from Indiana University and was offered a faculty position beginning the following spring semester. I was surprised, to say the least, and was not prepared to make the decision. I asked for time to consider the offer. Though traveling to and living in Massachusetts had been adventurous, the thought of moving to and living in southern Indiana for an extended period of time was a serious personal and professional decision. My wife and I are very close to our siblings and parents, and moving away a long distance would certainly distance us from our families. Professionally, it was an opportunity to move to a research-oriented university where I could develop my research and scholarship capabilities. After discussing the decision with my wife, I accepted the position with the objective of seeing how well I did in three years and evaluating the possibility of returning to a research-oriented university in California.

After a Christmas holiday visit with our families in California, where I informed our families that we would be moving to Indiana, I flew to Indiana while my wife stayed in Massachusetts to complete her course work. She would join me after her spring semester. I arrived in Bloomington in the dead of winter with snow on the ground and a cold wind cutting like a knife. The first winter in Bloomington was a cultural shock. I was not prepared for it and had to learn very quickly how to survive in a cold, damp environment.

Just as cold, I discovered, was the social ambiance of the School of Education. After settling in I went to the campus and discovered that no one was expecting me. I had no office space nor any assignment for the semester. I quickly discovered that little was expected of me. I would be marginally involved in the core curriculum of my department. I was to be shared with various programs in addressing multicultural issues. Thus, becoming a member of the department's core faculty was not an immediate concern. They provided me an office one floor above the floor where the department suite was located. I was "given" the responsibility for a floundering bilingual education doctoral fellowship program and assigned to teach a multicultural education course on the campus in Indianapolis. I quickly became involved in my responsibilities. During my first semester, I discovered that I had walked into a politicized situation. Essentially, I had been recruited into the School of Education as a symbolic gesture. The gesture signified to external agencies that the university was taking affirmative steps to deal with cultural pluralism. My recruitment was a consequence of pressure brought to bear on the school by Latino students and the dean of the School of Education. The dean went against the wishes of the Department of Administration and Administrative Studies and African American administrators and faculty who wanted an African American to be recruited. After finding my department cool toward my presence, I requested and had a meeting with the dean and my department chair to clarify my situation. While I did not see much resolved in the meeting with the dean, he was quite blunt in telling me that in spite of the unreceptive situation I would need to take the initiative, establish myself in the department. It would not be easy.

The dean was right! It took me twelve years to establish myself in the department. Twelve years of changes in the department's faculty and a change in the mission of the department. The dean who recruited me resigned the semester after I arrived. He had made too many changes and, as a result, a very dissatisfied faculty dethroned him. The new dean, a member of the social studies faculty, was employed. He quickly moved to refocus the mission of the school to a more entrepreneurial one. His goal was to transform the School of Education into a "center of excellence," and he downsized the school by encouraging faculty to retire and/or leave and to selectively recruit new faculty for the new School of Education mission. This new direction divided the faculty more than usual. It became difficult to sustain any sense of "affirmative action" in the recruitment and retention of minority faculty. In downsizing the school, the dean did not recruit new minority faculty. One African American did not receive tenure, and another one left the university. Bilingual education courses were eliminated, and minority student enrollment declined. Multicultural education had been transformed from promotion of ethnic/racial diversity through integration by means of affirmative action practices to ethnic studies in social studies.

The change of organizational climate could not have occurred at a more difficult time for me. I was reviewed for tenure and promotion

and experienced an unusual process of being reviewed by two departments because I had taught in both departments. Each department was
split in their vote for my tenure. The School of Education Tenure and
Promotion Committee, representing all departments, unanimously supported my case for tenure and promotion. I never knew how the dean
voted. He might have provided little support. I concluded this after I
received a request from the dean of faculties for additional documenta-
tion on my research activities and research agenda. I could only suspect
that this had something to do with the dean's efforts to redirect the
faculty to his research mission. The university's Tenure and Promotion
Committee recommended me for tenure and promotion. After I obtained
tenure, my office was relocated to my department's suite and I received
committee assignments and was invited to chair dissertation committees.

I settled into my new "legitimacy," yet the struggle continued. I
sought alternative ways of self-actualizing as a professional, including
networking with other Latino faculty in universities throughout the
Midwest. I joined a group that called itself the Midwest Council for
Latinos in Higher Education (MCLHE). We met every few months and
annually organized a conference. The group lasted four to five years.
Several years later another group emerged. The Midwest Consortium
for Latino Research (MCLR) was a more focused group of Latino and
Latina scholars. The group established a long-term mission and has
gained financial support from various universities for establishing an
administrative office and a program of activities to support the development of Latino faculty and students. With the support of MCLR, I
brought together a group of Latino students and faculty on the
Bloomington campus and linked the group to the consortium.

I also networked with other minority professors of educational administration affiliated with such organizations as the University Council
for Educational Administration (UCEA) and the American Educational
Research Association (AERA). There are only a handful of Latino professors of educational administration, and we were all looking for each
other. This is not to say that other professors were less interesting. Each
year at annual meetings of professional groups I find the company of
my Latino colleagues refreshing and stimulating.

Being a member of the faculty at Indiana University was both difficult and challenging during the eighties. The difficulties came from
changes in the School of Education that retrenched the school into a
conservative culture that expected greater accountability. At the same
time my department changed through attrition and new faculty recruitment from a practitioner-oriented program to a social science, scholar-

ship driven program. Accompanying the curricular shift was pressure from the dean of education for us to establish innovative leadership preparation programs that were in line with the dean's new mission. This created a great deal of tension between our department and the dean's staff.

The new curricular emphasis made Indiana University more cosmopolitan and, thereby, more receptive to such concepts as "diversity," "multiculturalism," and "equity." The shift of program emphasis allowed me to establish an educational policy role as part of the core faculty. The new role definition was further enhanced as senior faculty retired or left. As a result of the attrition, I became a senior member of the department's faculty.

However, the exclusiveness of the academy persisted. I was still seen as a minority faculty. I never became part of the informal leadership network in the School of Education, nor was I allowed opportunity to provide formal leadership at the departmental or school levels. This was also true of other minority faculty. It became evident that although employment in a midwestern research-oriented university was beneficial in developing as a professional, it was less beneficial in developing as an institutional leader. The only avenues to formal leadership experiences or opportunities were nontraditional. The opportunities often presented themselves through ethnic studies programs or through programs for interns for potential administrators, which only recently have become accessible to minority faculty.

I became involved in institutional leadership by going outside of the School of Education. Jointly with the dean of Latino Affairs and the vice president for the Bloomington campus we established a programmatic relationship with the Midwest Consortium for Latino Research (MCLR). In pursuing this initiative, I worked in the Office of the Vice President for Research and the Graduate School. The assignment gave me the opportunity to interact with administrators throughout the campus. The interactions with the administrators provided me an intimate perspective on the campus as an enterprise. I represented the university at a number of national higher education meetings and made presentations at midwestern regional meetings on Latino participation in higher education. Through these activities I established myself as a resource to the campus administration. This would not have occurred through conventional means. The traditional leadership infrastructure continues to have a boundary of low permeability.

At the end of my ninth year at Indiana University, I gave thought to asking for review for promotion to full professor. This became a grave career decision for me. Promotion to full professor at Indiana University would probably lock me into staying in Indiana for the rest of my career, because it would be difficult to move to another university at a full rank. I was not comfortable with that possibility. I am from California and wanted to return to the Southwest, if not to California, and end my career there. Thus, I decided to search for a faculty position in the Southwest. There were very few opportunities available, especially at an advanced rank level, as a result of the economic crisis California was experiencing. I considered several opportunities throughout the Southwest, but the positions were canceled or went to junior faculty who were practitioner-oriented. California was no different. The emphasis in educational administration was on "training for the principalship," and I was not a good fit since I was seen as an "educational policy" type. However, I was invited to apply for a faculty position at San Francisco State University. They were looking to develop a joint doctoral program with the University of California in educational leadership and wanted to recruit faculty who would provide the leadership.

I applied to San Francisco State University with the idea that San Francisco would provide me a good field setting for exploring a major interest of mine—educational leadership and policy development in a highly diverse context. In addition, I could provide institutional leadership in developing a preparation program in educational leadership for diverse settings. I saw an opportunity to grow further as a professional and to help guide innovative institutional change in a state that is growing rapidly and becoming more ethnically diverse. It would be a great place to complete my career. I accepted a full professor position with tenure.

Journey to a New California

I arrived at San Francisco State University in the summer of 1992 ready to move in and join the flow of organizing for the new academic year. To my surprise, I discovered no one was around except secretaries, who were not advised of my expected arrival. I had no office space assigned, nor did anyone have any idea where I would be located. It was unclear what courses I would be teaching, in spite of the teaching assignment I received prior to my departure from Bloomington. At that point I thought : "Déjà vu"! I recalled arriving at Indiana University in the winter of 1980 and similarly discovering that I was not expected. There, too, I had no office space assigned nor was it clear in the department what my role was to be.

I had to wait patiently until the administration discovered I had arrived. Should I return to my comfortable office in Bloomington? No! The romantic past is always remembered! Apparently I had arrived too early. I would be making adjustments and changing in many ways while I established myself. Whatever San Francisco State University was as an institution, I would not let it get me down, just as I did not let Indiana University get me down! The odyssey would continue.

CHAPTER 9

MEMOrabilia from
an Academic Life

RAYMOND V. PADILLA

I have spent most of my adult life in American universities. Since the day
after Labor Day in 1964, when I became a freshman at Oakland
University in Rochester, Michigan, there have been only two brief inter-
ludes during my career in which I was not in academia. One two-year
period I spent in the military during the Vietnam War. Later I spent
the first two years after graduate school working for the Michigan
Department of Education (California, where I did my graduate work, was
apparently short on jobs for Chicanos with a Ph.D.). Other than that,
my entire adult life has been devoted to the academic life—as a student,
professor, researcher, and administrator. Also as a Chicano academic
activist.

As a university administrator, I learned to document all important
administrative actions (even some that were not so important but seemed
so at the time). This habit transferred to my activist life, so that over the
years I have accumulated numerous boxes of old documents that testify
to the many issues and problems attendant to life as a Chicano academic. Most of these papers are little more than the academic detritus
of a late-twentieth-century academic, but some of them touch upon the
issues that have been raised in this volume, especially gaining tenure
and promotion, legitimizing Chicano research, networking, and generally "talking back" to an institution that is very open and very closed at
the same time. Following is a brief sampler of memos and letters that I
wrote between 1983 and 1991. They have to do mostly with my promotion to professor, hiring decisions, arguments with journal editors,
and trying to help others get tenured and promoted. These selected
memos are portholes that allow outsiders a fleeting glimpse inside the
leaning ivory tower that is American higher education.

Testing the Turbulent Waters of Early Promotion . . .

DATE: October 7, 1983
TO: [Department Chair]
FROM: Raymond V. Padilla
RE: Application for Promotion to Professor

Enclosed please find my application and supporting portfolio for promotion to professor. When you receive the letters from external evaluators, please insert them in the section marked "Letters from External Evaluators." We have mutually agreed on the following external evaluators: A. A., R. D., R. J., and D. S. I understand that A. A. agreed to serve on a provisional basis, depending upon whether or not, after receipt of my materials, he considers himself qualified to review them. You have also informed me that on your own you have asked R. B. to serve as an external evaluator. As I indicated to you, while Professor R. B. does enjoy recognition in the general field of higher education, he has no particular visibility in my specialization. On this basis, I demurred on his appointment as an external evaluator. On the other hand, I recognize your desire to include external evaluators who "represent the kind of institution that [our institution] aspires to become." My rejoinder was that they should also be expert in my specialization, which essentially is Chicano education. Thus our professional networks, while they may overlap, do not necessarily coincide.

As we agreed, it is appropriate to ask Dr. E. G. to comment on my application for promotion. When his letter arrives, please insert it in the section marked "Other Letters." Dr. E. G.'s letter should be the first one in that section. I appreciate very much your assistance in facilitating the review process.

DATE: October 28, 1983
TO: [Department Chair]
FROM: Raymond V. Padilla
RE: My Application for Promotion to Professor

I appreciate very much the time that you took on Thursday to discuss with me the status of my application for promotion to full professor. As I understand the situation now, the Department Personnel Committee has reviewed my portfolio and declined to recommend a positive action on my application. The immediate question that you posed is whether I wish to

proceed with further reviews by college and university evaluation committees or rescind my application. My decision is to proceed with the application review process. In reaching this decision, I have carefully considered
the adequacy of the departmental review process and the validity of the
nonsupportive decision reached by the committee.

From our extended discussion, I understand that the committee
perceives two inadequacies in my application. First, they are concerned
about how much time I have (not) spent in rank as an Associate Professor; secondly, they are questioning my research productivity (and it is
unclear whether or not there is a connection between the two). Regarding the longevity issue, I understand that it is university policy not to
consider longevity or time in rank as the deciding criterion in promotion decisions. This seems to me to be a reasonable policy because the
principal issue in promotion decisions should be productivity and
effectiveness, not merely how long one has been hired. In any event, I
have held the rank of Associate Professor for one year at [a midwestern
university] and for almost two years at [our university]. During this
time, I have been a productive scholar and academician as evidenced in
my portfolio. On this basis, I regard the Personnel Committee's emphasis on time in rank as misplaced, and reject their decision of nonsupport
for my promotion.

The Personnel Committee's second concern—scholarly productivity—is more serious, though not necessarily better founded than the first
one. I have been an active scholar in the area of Chicano education for
the last twelve or thirteen years. My work is nationally recognized for
its insights, innovativeness, and contributions to the field. The scholarly
volumes that I have produced have been used as textbooks by some two
dozen universities that range from the University of California to
Harvard. I have received awards for my work by numerous organizations, including the American Educational Research Association.
During the past two years that I have worked at [our university], I have
published two edited volumes (both refereed) to which I contributed
three articles. A fourth article is in press at the Bilingual Review Press.
At the same time, I have received one research and one research and
development contract to investigate, respectively, Chicano persistence at
[our university] and microcomputer applications in training limited
English speaking youth and adults. I am the principal investigator of
these two projects and direct the work of nine faculty and graduate
student researchers. Concurrent with these activities, I have produced or
contributed to the production of several major research reports and
feasibility studies, including a bilingual policy paper for the [state]

Department of Education, a feasibility study for the Vice President for Academic Affairs regarding the establishment of a Chicano Research Center, and several evaluative studies for local school districts and community colleges. Moreover, my research interests have led me to create a new course in the department (the qualitative research methodology of Paulo Freire) and to install the only computer programs on campus that can be used in qualitative data analysis.

My research work has been noticed by any number of investigators in my field. Consequently, since arriving at [our university], I have been commissioned to produce contracted research by the National Center for Bilingual Research and to publish a research volume by the National Clearinghouse for Bilingual Education. I have been appointed Associate Editor of the Journal of the National Association for Bilingual Education, the major research journal for bilingual education in the nation. Individual researchers are also interested in my work. For example, the paper that I presented in Montreal last spring at the annual conference of AERA has been requested, and is still being requested, by various researchers. This very month I received a request for a copy of the paper from Jennifer L. Hochschild from the Woodrow Wilson school of Public and International Affairs at Princeton University. Similarly, this month I received a call from a faculty member at the John F. Kennedy School of Public Affairs at Harvard because he is interested in using my bilingual policy volume for one of his classes next spring. As you indicated during our conversation, none of the three external evaluations received so far are negative. Considering that the external evaluators most knowledgeable about my work represent institutions such as the University of Texas and Cornell University, the Personnel Committee's negative conclusion seems incongruous. Part of the incongruity may be explained by the membership of the committee itself. As I mentioned to you on one or two occasions, the membership of the committee consists of two associate professors and only one full professor. I question the adequacy of a review process that includes individuals who do not possess the rank to which the applicant seeks promotion. It seems problematic to accept the negative opinions of the associate professors over the positive opinions of the knowledgeable outside full professors from noted institutions. Moreover, if one looks closely at the background of the two associate professors sitting on the committee, one just recently was promoted to that rank (one year in rank excluding a sabbatical year) and the other (the committee chair) has increasingly less responsibility for directing doctoral level students. On the other hand, the full professor sitting on the committee has no recognition whatsoever in the field of Chicano education. Considering these deficiencies in the Personnel Committee, I find it puzzling that the committee chose not to augment its expertise by inviting a full professor with expertise in my field to sit on the committee. This omission calls attention to itself in a special way because I am officially released one quarter time for three years to the Center for Bilingual Education.

In view of these considerations, I am not persuaded that the committee's opinion about my scholarly productivity is at all reliable. Hence, my decision to continue with the review process. In doing so, I hope that I can receive some support from you, although I recognize that you are reluctant to render an opinion (whether positive or negative) that is inconsistent with the recommendation of the Personnel Committee.

Finally, given the Personnel Committee's nonsupport of my promotion application, please include a copy of this memorandum in my portfolio so that other reviewers may have access to these comments.

Again, I appreciate the attention that you have given to my application.

c: [College Dean]

DATE: April 12, 1984
TO: Vice President for Academic Affairs
FROM: Raymond V. Padilla
        Associate Professor
RE: Promotion to Professor

I have received your letter of April 2, 1984 in which you inform me that you have recommended that I not be promoted to Professor. I have to confess that I am somewhat disappointed in this action. You also advised me that if I have specific questions concerning areas in which I might concentrate my future efforts to discuss this matter with my Chair and Dean. I appreciate this suggestion and have taken steps to implement it forthwith.

In particular I have asked my Chair and Dean to advise me as to specific activities that I need to accomplish, in addition to what I have already accomplished during the last two and a half years, that would justify my promotion to Professor. I have asked them to be specific because I need to know as clearly as possible the specific behaviors that need to be exhibited in terms of their type, duration, quantity, and quality. I understand that university policy specifies that time in rank is not an issue in promotion decisions. Therefore, the substantive issue has to do with what is to be done and how it is to be documented. At senior levels of the academic hierarchy there is very little room for generality.

So far, my Chair is in the process of responding to my request. I have not yet heard from the Dean, but expect to do so in due course. I am now taking the opportunity to request your assistance, as the chief academic officer of the university, in providing me your best advice on specific actions that I need to take to justify promotion to Professor in the future. Your advice, and the advice of the other line officers, will be very helpful to me in planning my academic work for the next three to five years. In fact, my activities and productivity as a scholar and teacher will be greatly influenced by your advice and actions.

With respect to your recommendation not to support promotion, I should like to know how this recommendation will be processed from here on out. I do hope that your report to the President and the Regents will include the names of all applicants for promotion, even those for whom you are not recommending promotion. I believe that it is important for the President and the Regents to know not only who is to be promoted, but also who has asked to be promoted.

Finally, I must add that, having been a participant observer, I have learned a great deal about the promotion review process at [our university]. The process is not altogether rational and does suffer from ambiguity and procedural quirks. Some of my reservations are already part of the record and I assume that you have read those remarks. Should you desire to know more about my observations, I would be more than happy to share them.

DATE: June 24, 1984
TO: Vice President for Academic Affairs
FROM: Raymond V. Padilla
          Associate Professor
RE: Observations on the Promotion Review Process

In response to your memo of June 15, I am taking this opportunity to provide you and [the Assistant Vice President] with a few observations about the promotion review process as I have experienced it at [our university]. I recognize that an N of one is not an overly large sample, but on the other hand case studies do have their place in field observations.

I do not mean to belabor the point, but since tenure and promotion decisions are central to the institutional health of the university, a few moments of reflection are not an unnecessarily extravagant use of time. By the way, I tend to agree with you that departmental evaluations should be central to the promotion review process. Where we may differ is in our opinions about the ability of [our university], at its current state of development as an institution, to carry out such a process fairly and effectively. In my particular case, I believe that the latter did not occur.

The chief points that I would like to call to your attention are these:

1. Do departments really have clearly stated policies for promotion? Are these policies followed?

2. Are promotion criteria stated explicitly? How does one know when to apply for promotion, i.e. when have the criteria been met?

3. What is the relationship between promotion policies as issued by (a) the regents, (b) the university, (c) the college, and (d) the individual department? Is there an increase in specificity as one descends through the organizational structure? How well articulated are the policies as one moves from one institutional level to the next? My conclusion is that specificity of criteria is sorely lacking from the regents on down to the departmental level.

4. The selection of external reviewers needs improvement. Why should the department chair unilaterally appoint outside reviewers, especially when he/she has no substantive expertise in the candidate's field of specialization?

5. How does the multilayered review process guard against an unfair or incompetent review at the department level? Too often a type I or type II error can be propagated through the system simply because there is no workable mechanism for challenging the departmental review without at the same time (a) aborting the bid for promotion and/ or (b) causing prejudice in the collegiate and university level reviews.

I hope that these observations are helpful to you. While I do not believe that our goal is to develop a perfect system of promotion, surely there is much to be done to make it possible for [the University] to bid for the distinction of calling itself a first class university. Institutional quality and excellence are really not possible when the core of the university, its faculty, are not totally convinced that faculty reviews are conducted fairly and with very high levels of competence.

c: [President of the University]

Suffering Your Embarrassment . . .

April 9, 1985

Dear [Vice President for Academic Affairs]:

As you may recall, several months ago I mentioned that you should look
into the candidacy of Dr. M. who applied last spring for a faculty position
in the Department of Elementary Education. Recently, Dr. M. called me —
somewhat distressed — to communicate what he considered as unprofes-
sional treatment of him by the university. Apparently, he has not yet
received an official notice from the university informing him of the
decision on his candidacy. At the same time, he recently was sent a
position announcement that describes a position almost identical to the
one for which he applied last year. He finds the procedure peculiar, to say
the least, and is upset that the university should be so cavalier to applicants for employment.

    I have no formal connection with the search process related to Dr.
M.'s candidacy, except that I sat at the open interviews for the three
finalists. However, I know — and am known to — most researchers in
the field of bilingual education and matters of this type inevitably are
brought to my attention. I regret that our institutional reputation has
been somewhat tarnished by this incident. Further, I am a bit chagrined
that this kind of institutional behavior will inevitably reflect negatively
on me professionally as colleagues in the field hear about "how [the
university] behaves." I have tried very hard to establish respect for [our
university] among researchers in bilingual education and other areas.
Unfortunately, institutional behavior of this type has a corrosive
influence on these positive efforts and is highly counter productive. I
have no idea what went wrong with the search process or who is
ultimately responsible for this situation, but I feel it necessary to apprise
you of the concrete results.

    I feel very proud of the fact that a number of very positive things
have occurred at [our university] in the past several years that create a
positive impression in my profession about what [the university]
represents as an institution. Unfortunately, the incident with Dr. M. was
of the opposite character. I hope that something can be done to repair
the damage, or at least to ensure that future searches can be conducted
in such a way that all candidates are treated with the respect that they
deserve and expect as professionals. Otherwise, our many efforts to
build a great reputation for [our university] among researchers will be

frustrated. Needless to say, I do not believe that any of us desires this result.

Cordially,

Ray Padilla

c: [University President]

P.S. If Dr. M.'s assertions are factually correct, we should at least apologize to him and indicate to him that those are not our routine and customary procedures.

Promotion Round 2: A Deal I Must Refuse . . .

DATE: July 7, 1986
TO: [College Dean]
FROM: Raymond V. Padilla
RE: Promotion to Professor

I have received your memorandum dated July 2, 1986 regarding my promotion to professor. I recognize that you have only recently joined [the university], and that you were not personally involved in the rather protracted search for the Director['s position that I now hold]. Thus, I would like to take this opportunity to present to you the facts of the case as I see them and to make clear what my understanding is about the decisions that are still pending regarding my recent appointment as Director.

The Director's Position

[Enclosed] is a copy of the official [university] announcement of vacancy for the Director . . . This announcement was made in the context of a national search in pursuit of an extraordinarily qualified individual to head the Center. The committee that was constituted to carry out this search consisted of faculty from diverse colleges in the university and represented a wide variety of interests and viewpoints.

The Search Process

The announcement of vacancy was circulated widely to academic and relevant nonacademic institutions throughout the U.S. Committee members actively recruited candidates through a variety of professional networks and associations. I turned over to the committee a list of over five hundred individuals and organizations that we had canvassed the previous year when I chaired the first search committee. This list was further augmented by the chair and members of the second search committee. As a result of this extensive effort, a strong pool of extraordinarily well qualified candidates was created.

Following ordinary administrative procedures, the pool of candidates was reduced to a list of finalists by the university wide faculty search committee. The finalists were then interviewed. The interview process included the following:

1. A two hour interview with the search committee.

2. A one and a half hour interview with the Dean of the College of Liberal Arts and Sciences.

3. A luncheon with Hispanic faculty.

4. A seminar open to the university community in which the candidate presented a professional paper.

5. Dinner with representatives of the search committee and interested persons from the community at large.

6. An interview with [my department] Chair.

7. A two hour open meeting with members of the Hispanic [faculty organization].

8. Lunch with Hispanic faculty.

All candidates followed a similar pattern, with appropriate changes in departmental interviews.

In addition, each candidate prepared and submitted to the search committee a portfolio of documents that showed evidence of the candidate's accomplishments in administration, teaching, and research. Moreover, each candidate's credentials were examined by at least three, and usually more, external reviewers who submitted independent reviews and recommendations to the search committee.

As you can see, this is a very thorough and robust procedure intended to identify the very best candidate. It represents participation by the entire university community, the diverse levels of the university hierarchy, and even professionals from the surrounding community. It further presumes that the search committee is deciding about both an administrative appointment and an academic appointment with tenure.

The Offer of the Directorship

The directorship was offered to me at about the beginning of March of this year. In the negotiations that followed, I asked that the appointment be made at the professor level because:

1. This is exactly the same posture that I had taken as chair of the first search committee. (And, in fact, the one offer that was made during the first round to an associate professor included an appointment at the professor level.)

2. The insistence on that particular level of appointment was premised on the desire to bring to the Center a certain level of prestige and national prominence. But, more importantly, it was thought necessary to protect the director from having to make organizational decisions in the context of potentially conflicting personal goals. I believe that the second search committee had a similar point of view and that it conducted its search accordingly.

As the negotiations proceeded, it became clear that there were some institutional reservations about granting the professorship as part of the directorship appointment. Under the circumstances, the agreement that was reached is that the professorship appointment would be made contingent upon an off cycle [promotion] review process. I was, and still remain, skeptical about the appropriateness of such a review. My reservations arise from the following considerations:

1. To my knowledge, the decision to require an off cycle promotion review was *ad hoc* and not based on established university policy. Such a policy, if it existed, would stipulate that internal candidates who participate in a national competition for a position which might entail a promotion in rank would be required to submit to an internal review for promotion in addition to the regular search process that is applied to external candidates. Note that if such a policy were indeed operational, external candidates would be excused from such a review

2. I see an off cycle promotion review as essentially redundant to the work of the university wide faculty search committee. Throughout its work and deliberations, the committee was fully aware that the appointment could well be made at the professor level. If they had any reservations on this score, I am sure that they would have noted them to the Dean in their report. The fact of the matter is that a university-wide search committee process is precisely an off-cycle review for promotion

when the appointment of a particular individual would result in an upgrading in rank. One of the reasons that external candidates are attracted to new positions is that they may gain a promotion by obtaining a new post. Since it would not be feasible for a university to use the regular promotion review process for these individuals, the search process is designed to include the functional counterpart of a regular promotion review.

3. The entire College of Education was in a process of transition and reorganization: An acting dean was in charge of the college, the departments were being reorganized into divisions, and it was very unclear as to which personnel committees would be convened to consider the case. As an act of professional courtesy, I had advised my faculty colleagues in the Department of Higher and Adult Education that I was applying for the directorship and that I would be asking for a promotion in rank if offered the position. I got overwhelming support from my faculty colleagues and department chair. I therefore proceeded under the assumption that if asked about my promotion they would be supportive. Of course, the department has since been reorganized into the new divisional structure of the college, and the former chair has tendered his resignation from the university.

In spite of these reservations, I acquiesced to the off-cycle review because:

1. I felt, and still do, that the appointment of director had to be made quickly or the viability of the Center might by jeopardized. The search process was already into its second year and there was little to be gained, from an organizational point of view, by prolonging the process.

2. The review was to be conducted immediately so that the institutional concerns that gave rise to it might be resolved. As you can see from the [Liberal Arts] Dean's memorandum of March 12, there was at least one attempt to carry out the review in a timely way.

The Outcomes

Very simply, the off cycle review for promotion was not conducted within the time frame that was expected. Once this occurred, it became very awkward, from an organizational point of view, to argue for the reasonableness of an off cycle review because one quickly falls into the regular cycle of reviews. And it is clearly absurd to conduct an off cycle review when the regular cycle is available. But to undergo a regular cycle promotion review in the context of the hiring decision outlined above is clearly an administrative absurdity. If this were indeed the policy, it would imply that hiring decisions would have to remain suspended for a year or more until the promotion issue could be settled (I am sure that not all faculty are willing to contain personal objectives for the sake of organizational objectives).

Further, it should be noted that the promotion issue is related to base salary. The agreement made includes the provision that a promotion in rank would carry the customary increment in salary. Hence, the final salary determination for the directorship is contingent on the question of promotion.

Reaching a Conclusion

Given the facts of the case as I have outlined them above, the following summary of issues and resolutions can be made

1. Two items were left pending in my appointment to the Center directorship:

• Promotion to professor
• The salary adjustment resulting from the first item

2. There was an institutional decision to require an off cycle review for promotion. I acquiesced to this.

3. The institution was unable to carry out the off cycle review.

4. I have further stated in this memorandum why I believe that such a review is in fact unnecessary, and perhaps administratively improper; and surely it is organizationally unwise.

Therefore, my own conclusion and recommendation is that the proper administrative authority (perhaps the Dean of Liberal Arts and Sciences, the Vice President for Academic Affairs, or even the President who has ultimate authority over these matters) should now bring this matter to a close. The recommendation for promotion can be made directly by any one of these individuals on the basis of a very robust search process. Only an individual quite naive about university processes could argue that there has been insufficient review: Surely a review process for a nationally advertised position is at least as rigorous, if not more so, than a promotion review process in which one essentially competes against himself. And, in any event, the institution did not avail itself of the off cycle review process that it could have initiated. I think that a sense of even handedness, a professional regard for organizational rationality, and the need to keep things administratively tidy now argue for a careful reconsideration of this issue.

For my part, I am thoroughly committed to directing the Center and making it function effectively.

c: [The President
   The Vice President for Academic Affairs
   The Dean of Liberal Arts and Sciences]

The Fish in the Editorial Eye . . .

June 26, 1989

Dear [Editor]:

My, oh my! How the review process goes on! Thanks for the time that you and the reviewers took to look once again at my paper. Unfortunately, the feedback this time is strong but misdirected. I cannot possibly accept the idea that data can be peripheral to any research effort and that tossing out the data somehow strengthens the research! One problem with qualitative research is that so many stories can be told from the same data and in so many different ways. This leads to the problem of reviews in which the reviewer tries to get the author to write a different paper, but not necessarily a better one.

I think that the paper as it now stands has been considerably strengthened (and for this I am grateful to the earlier reviews). As such, the paper now requires a very knowledgeable reviewer who has in-depth knowledge of both qualitative methods and the literature on Hispanic higher education. Unfortunately, the present reviewer didn't quite measure up. S/he, for example, misunderstood the graphic display of typologies as attempts at quantification, rather than as the innovation that it is in terms of strengthening the validity of the work. You may remember the debate held this year at AERA (Erickson, Berliner, etc.) in which the validity of qualitative data analysis was discussed. One important point is that the reader needs to know how much evidence supports a particular claim or conclusion. The idea of giving the number of exemplars that support each category is one possible solution to the problem. Of course, it is ludicrous to confuse this solution with "attempts to quantify." This conclusion totally misses the point that is being addressed.

The reviewer also fails to see a connection between Freire and the research design. I have read every major piece by Freire over the past 18 years in three languages: English, Spanish, and Portuguese; also a good number of books about Freire in several languages. The reviewer obviously has very little understanding about Freire because s/he didn't link the matrix technique to Freire's projective techniques in literacy. Now I do admit that I do not go into much detail about method because the previous reviewers wanted the entire design and methodology to be dealt with in one page! The present reviewer wants to eliminate design altogether! (Thinking, undoubtedly, that design is unnecessary for qualitative research.) I could say similar things about the other cited authors whom the reviewer claims were "shoe horned" into the paper. But since their work is better known in the U.S., I won't say more on this point.

The reviewer also wishes that the paper integrated more of L.'s work. Well, I co-directed L.'s dissertation and am quite familiar with what is in it. While an admirable piece of work, L.'s ideas are only marginally applicable to the paper. L.'s basic analysis centers around the concept of "getting in" and not necessarily around successful students. A more recent doctoral dissertation by one of my other students comes up with the concept of "getting out," which is just as interesting and revealing as L.'s idea of "getting in." The work cited by Arce is quite old. In fact, Arce has acknowledged that my early work on Chicano higher education (dubbed "Transformational Education") is one of several alternative models for Chicano higher education. I don't see the point in citing a work that is eleven years old and that does not reflect the current research on Chicanos in higher education. (My work that Arce cites was written in the mid seventies.) It seems to me quite inappropriate to measure my work, which looks forward, both methodologically and substantively, from the point of view of fairly traditional works that do not break as much new ground.

The reviewer grossly misconstrues the meaning of the political decision made at Campus B not to consider barriers as impinging differentially on students of different ethnic backgrounds. The reviewer considers the inclusion of this point as laughable, and fails entirely to see the significance of this finding. The point is that participants in a research project can affect the data that can be gathered. Secondly, their actions in themselves have meaning. The graphic that shows the participant's political decision is needed precisely to show the reader how that decision may be masking real differences (as demonstrated by Campus A). The fact that the action of these participants makes the analysis less neat is just a fact of life. There is no reason to hide this from the reader and the real point, at any rate, is about informant behavior and its consequences for the research.

Also, both reviewers tended to see the data as if the two campuses were being compared. This is accurate in part, but mostly misleading. The two campuses were used to provide a broader slice of data (than is possible with one campus) that would contain more information and thus increase the validity of the conclusions. It is important to contrast the two campuses, but that is not the main point. The main point is developing the categories and typologies from the aggregate data

Given these and many other points of confusion by the reviewer, it hardly surprises me that s/he wants to punt the whole thing and do a different paper. If the paper had as many shortcomings as the reviewer erroneously perceives, I would be tempted to reach the same conclusion. But the problem is largely with the reviewer and not the paper. Thus, I have to conclude that it is the reviewer's erroneous views that should be discarded

Well, where are we now? I surely can make minor changes having to do with typos and such, and perhaps clarify things here and there. But at this point, I cannot see how the paper can be substantially improved from the comments that I received. I'm sure that if a new set of reviewers were brought into the picture, suggestions would emerge for still a different paper. I don't think that the issue is writing a different paper. There seems to be agreement that the paper makes some original contributions. Its format and content have been influenced by earlier reviews as well as contemporary issues in qualitative research. It presents much that is original, and perhaps even provocative. Maybe that is all that can be expected. What do you think?

Sincerely,
Raymond V. Padilla, Ph.D.

Lending a Professorial Hand . . .

October 26, 1991

Dear [Department Chair]:

As you requested, I am forwarding my review of Professor M. who is a candidate for tenure at your institution. My remarks are based on careful review of the following items: A curriculum vitae, a five year plan, and three manuscripts of works, or portions of works, that have been authored or co-authored by Professor M. In addition, I have relied on personal knowledge that I have about Professor M. whom I have observed for at least ten years at professional meetings and conferences. In your second letter to me, you asked that I specifically address questions related to the scholarly and research work that Professor M. has accomplished. I shall therefore focus my review along those lines.

Focus of the research. I judge Professor M.'s research to focus primarily on issues related to language, culture, and learning. These issues are framed within the context of bilingual, bicultural, and multicultural education in the U.S. She uses a qualitative approach that draws most heavily from ethnography, critical theory, and cultural studies. The assessment of this work, which follows, takes into account my knowledge of the current research in the field, and the review of numerous candidates for appointment, tenure, and promotion in diverse academic institutions throughout the U.S.

Knowledge of the field. The works that I have reviewed demonstrate that Professor M. has command of the relevant research literature in her field. She is up to date and comprehensive. She demonstrates the ability to apply facts, concepts, and theories that she has internalized from her immersion in the research literature. But she does not appear to me to be a mere storehouse and conveyor of information. She challenges the knowledge that has been generated by others as she tries to apply it in specific, and often problematic, settings. This process of challenge through both action and reflection will almost certainly lead to the refinement of accumulated knowledge and the expansion and/or reconstruction of the current knowledge base.

Research methods. Professor M. demonstrates in her work that she has taken hold of a specific methodology and applied it to the many issues confronting bilingual and multicultural pedagogy. She is well versed in the principles of ethnography which she combines with a critical theory perspective to get at the reality of Latino communities and their struggle for survival and achievement. In recent years, ethnography in general has found wider acceptance as a legitimate form of inquiry in education. It also has been used by some researchers to explore issues in bilingual education. Here the work of Henry Trueba, Courtney Cazden, Fred Ericson, etc. stands out. Given the recency of research in bilingual education and the use of ethnographic techniques to study schooling, I believe that there is a good opportunity for Professor M. to make significant contributions to bilingual education research using these methods.

While there are good models for bilingual research using ethnographic techniques, the same cannot be said for the use of critical

theory. Critical theory methods have only recently gained recognition in
the U.S. and their application to education is still novel. The same is not
necessarily true outside of the U.S., as exemplified by the work of Paulo
Freire and others. A few researchers can be identified in this area of
critical theory and bilingual education. They include Donaldo Macedo
at the University of Massachusetts, Antonio Simões at NYU, and,
increasingly, Jim Cummins at OISE. Thus, in using critical theory in
bilingual education research, Professor M. is attempting to break new
ground. I find her work in this area very interesting and quite promising. It is certainly at the forefront of methodological innovation in
bilingual research. I expect that we will hear much more about this
approach in the future as research such as that of Professor M. matures
and gains a wider audience.

   Overall assessment. The strengths of scholarship and methodological sophistication are evident in Professor M.'s research. There is much
promise in her research. But in a sense, to assess her work, and particularly her productivity (as opposed to quality), is to assess both her as
an individual and her situation within the institution. I certainly was
impressed by the section of the academic plan that provides a self-
assessment of what has helped and hindered her productivity as a
scholar. She writes with clarity, force, and intelligence. She is well
centered in the sense that she knows what decisions she has made and
why. It is obvious to me that in deciding what her career is about she
has consistently favored institutional goals over personal ones, that she
has supported colleagues over her own self-interest, that she has tried
very hard to give a full measure to her students, and that she has an
abiding commitment to the larger community outside the university
campus.

   On top of all these things, she is deeply engaged intellectually in
designing and maintaining instructional programs, developing alternative educational institutions, and prosecuting a research agenda that
requires top level scholarship and methodological inventiveness. Clearly,
such an ambitious academic life will require a longer time frame than
normal to reach full flower. But my conclusion is that Professor M. is
making significant intellectual contributions to your institution and the
field on many levels.

   Over the last three years, I have been involved in attracting top
Latino researchers to my own institution. We recruited somewhere
around 30–35 professors, some young, some in mid-career, and some
quite mature. I've learned to look at these hirings as institutional

investments. So one way of looking at Professor M. is to ask: "Is she a good investment?" My answer: "You bet!"

Sincerely,
Raymond V. Padilla, Ph.D.

CHAPTER 10

Toward a Postview of the Chicano Community in Higher Education

HERMÁN S. GARCÍA

The Chicano academic community has been left to fend for itself at the same time that it struggles against a Eurocentric social science that has produced historical and social analyses that are devoid of the Chicano experience in education. Robert Alvarez, Jr. (1986) provides a prime example of such historical neglect of the Chicano experience in his account of the Lemon Grove Incident in California during the 1930s. Lemon Grove was a small farming community just north of San Diego. There, a group of Chicano parents organized against the Lemon Grove school board to prevent their children from being segregated. This occurred during a time when the California legislature attempted to reclassify Chicanos as Indians so that they could be legally segregated in the schools. The Lemon Grove Incident occurred twenty-five years before the *Brown v. Board of Education* decision, yet one cannot find it in the segregation literature.

Neglectful historical accounts can create a sense of nonexistence. Adrienne Rich (1984), in her poetic *Invisibility in Academe*, captures the feelings one experiences when excluded even though present:

> When those who have power to name and to socially construct reality choose not to see you or hear you, whether you are dark-skinned, old, disabled, female, or speak with a different accent or dialect than theirs, when someone with the authority of a teacher, say, describes the world and you are not in it, there is a moment of psychic disequilibrium, as if you looked into the mirror and saw nothing. (p. 199)

Fortunately, there are now Chicanos and Chicanas documenting our experiences in ways that reflect new truths about the legacy of the Chicano community in the United States. This narrative is intended as a contribution, however modest, to that effort of self-inclusion. My story

151

portrays the challenges, opportunities, and advancements that I have experienced in higher education. But it also serves as a "dangerous narrative" about the struggles that I have endured along with other Chicanos across the generations.

¿Quién soy yo?

I am Hermán S. García, narrator of this manuscript, which locates and chronicles my coming of age within American higher education. All along the lengthy and sometimes narrow path that I have traveled, I have consistently wanted to practice democracy. This has meant expending much effort to help colleges and universities provide access to a broader representation of otherwise underrepresented and subordinated communities in the United States, among them the Chicano community. Within higher education, I have made an effort to practice the values and beliefs of my Chicano community as I know them. In maintaining my personhood in academia, several issues central to my career have taken center stage: Promotion, tenure, mainstream journal publishing, the quality of my teaching, research, and service, and other academic obligations that often have become daunting bones of contention. I will use various critical pedagogy discourses to inform my views regarding the issues presented here.

Schooling and the Chicano Community

Cultural Capital

Bourdieu and Passerson (1977) coined the term *cultural capital* in an effort to explain differentiation between and among social classes. They noted that the cultural boundaries within which the various classes are located ordain power and privilege that is used to oppress the disenfranchised. Language, social status inheritance, and other familial tokens and dispositions become the "cultural cash" with which people map their way to life and meaning. Cultural cash thus distinguishes the dominant from the subordinate, the powerful from the powerless. Cultural capital serves to legitimate dominant class norms, values, personal and social competencies, the everyday workings of mainstream edification, and the hegemonies of delegitimation of subordinate-group cultures (Giroux 1983).

Although Chicanos have struggled to acquire the dominant cultural capital, the forces that control it have not been willing to share it readily. Yet Chicanos should focus not simply on acquiring dominant cultural capital, but on the resymbolization of cultural capital. Resymbolization implies contextually defined forms of democratic cultural environments that allow all groups to participate as coequals without having to defend culturally diverse experiences.

Using cultural capital as a metaphor for analyzing my experiences in American higher education, it seems evident to me that the Chicano community must reclaim its culture on the basis of equal currency with the dominant culture. This will allow the community to advocate for major paradigmatic shifts in the educational system that will address broader social, cultural, and linguistics concerns.

At the personal level, the absence of cultural capital tends to put one on the defensive. Although my early work in academia reflected my own acceptance of the dominant culture, I have deliberately struggled to decolonize my own thinking, particularly by advancing the view of Chicano cultural capital. In addition, I have always been involved in the development and support of ethnic and culturally diverse students. But these activities have placed me in the role of the Other, someone in direct opposition to the status quo of the universities. What I represent as the Other is threatening precisely because I advocate for the inclusion of the Other. Ironically, when it comes time for my worthiness as an academic to be judged, it is done so by conservative and liberal white males who represent the heart of the status quo.

The Bias of Instrumentalism

I have found myself having to defend, explain, or justify my academic work within the university in strictly instrumental terms. Instrumentalism is widely used in American social thought (Giroux 1983), frequently to explain quantitatively the "truth" about anything, everything, and everybody. Instrumental ideology was born of positivism and is reductionist in that it attempts to technocratically rationalize schooling experiences in terms specific to teacher practices, skills, and drills. It incorporates the scientism of eighteenth-century natural science in which all assumptions are derived from a single scientific approach that is indistinguishably applied to the physical and the human sciences. The emphasis of instrumental ideology lies primarily in the efficacy of technical mastery, which fails to enhance the inquiry process by locating it within broader qualitative terms. Deluvina Hernández (1970) provocatively challenged these positivistic, instrumentalist assumptions a generation ago in her monograph *Mexican American Challenge to a Sacred Cow*. She critiqued some of the commonly held notions in the research literature pertaining to Chicanos, as follows:

> In short, through the literature runs a common stereotypic thread which has been taken for truth, built upon and perpetuated by social scientists through the decades. The Mexican American has been portrayed as belonging to a group of people with traits ranging from laziness, lack of achievement, ahistoricism, non intellectualism, fatalism, emotionalism, irrationalism, indiscriminativeness in personal relations, sexually irresponsible, noneducation-oriented, to filling social roles and positions passively and statically, and isolationism from the rest of civilization. (p. 7)

This dominant social science perspective of the Chicano experience has been elevated to a psychological edifice that is framed by dominant notions of morality and socio-ideological apparatuses constructed around monological conceptions of lived experiences. Difference is bereft of its rich plurality and contained within strict dominant social control and scientific management models of linear purpose and function. Thus, to understand the Chicano academic experience within the master social and psychological narratives that dominate common public knowledge (and often social science knowledge) is to misunderstand and undermine it.

At the personal level, these cultural misconceptions manifest themselves when my Euro-American colleagues apply them to me. It has not been uncommon for them to have stereotypical images of me as a Chicano in personal and professional terms. They have asked me questions or made comments based on a stereotypical representation that they hold about my Mexican heritage, such as "It's siesta time" or "Does your machismo get in the way of your teaching?" In some cases, it may simply be a lack of sensitivity or awareness in some individuals, but in other cases it has been overtly intentional. These remarks are a reflection of the individual's culturally overdetermined psyche, and of not understanding or valuing diversity. In some cases, I have taken the time to debate or discuss the nature of their remarks, but in other cases I have chosen not to engage them.

Academic Success

Chicano academic success has increased in recent years in spite of continued high drop out rates, and in spite of the difficulty in gauging academic success given the standard assessment tools used to measure it. Most research on academic performance has used physical science models of measurement rather than humanistic models, thus consigning human agency to totalizing statistical interpretations. Popkewitz (1993) explains that the term *statistics* was derived from the French language and meant "state arithmetics," which were used to control public knowledge. Apple and Christian-Smith (1991) explain that "what counts as legitimate knowledge is the result of complex power relations and struggles among identifiable class, race, gender/sex, and religious groups" (p. 2). What is offered in schools is a decontextualized notion of academic achievement because success is measured through the hidden curriculum that is located within the dominant ideological structures of the educational system.

Dominant culture is reproduced via a discourse of cultural and linguistic codes that are inculcated in majority individuals since birth but to which minority children are not even exposed until reaching school. For these students, accessibility to the dominant cultural and linguistics codes comes with struggle and at a high cost to the native identity and culture of the students. It is usually at the expense of diminished self-respect, especially in the areas of language, culture, and personal location. My personal struggle in the schooling process has been to keep alive the cultural and linguistic codes that I grew up with during my childhood to adolescent years. Yet my involvement in the dominant culture has been continuous and coterminous with my educational attainment. But I believe that it would be highly illusory of me to think that "I've made it because I have a degree." That is not to say that I have not been successful. I have been successful when measured by any reasonable yardstick. But I see myself mostly as a cultural worker (Giroux 1992) struggling to redefine success and to recontextualize it from my own view of ethnolinguistic and sociocultural experience. That struggle in itself may constitute an attempt to move away from the narrowness of hegemonic cultural practices regarding how culture is named and legitimated through dominant cultural capital.

Chicanos in Colleges and Universities

Chicanos have long struggled to improve their employment, retention, and promotion in colleges and universities. Higher education institutions have used a host of ethnic studies and related projects to promote the appearance of caring and extending a hand. But, on the whole, institutions have moved slowly to change their policies and behaviors with regard to minority participation. Fearing the impact of offices such as Equal Employment Opportunity and Affirmative Action, institutions often have moved simply to add accommodative programs.

The participation of the Chicano community in higher education exhibits in the extreme the hostility that we have endured in our struggle to transform our history and socioeconomic status. Yet I feel that we have not "sold out" our values for those of the dominant culture, although some might argue differently. I interpret our behavior more as wanting to recharacterize our role in higher education and in doing so we are pointing to a new role for higher education in general. Therefore, I cannot allow myself to sit comfortably behind my tenure and let the chips fall where they may. Before me lies a dominant hegemonic educational system that is culturally intolerant and still inflexible toward plurality and diversity.

Unequal beginnings do not result in equal outcomes. Although one can vividly see more Chicano and Chicana faculty in colleges and universities, there are proportionately fewer Chicano faculty than twenty years ago, due to the overall growth of the Latino population. The population growth has occurred at a faster rate than their entry into postsecondary educational institutions (Meier & Stewart 1991). Moreover, the academy has treated Chicano faculty poorly and unfairly. In my case, for example, I have always had to fill the "minority slot" in an array of college committees while my Euro-American colleagues have been left to their scholarship. My committee service met affirmative action guidelines, but kept me from my own scholarly pursuits. In the final analysis, I was not given the credit warranted for my service to the university, but in fact I was penalized during my tenure and promotion efforts.

More hiring opportunities have to be made available to Chicanos on the basis of potential—a risk that colleges and universities are not willing to take. At institutions where no or few Chicanos and Chicanas exist, inexperienced but *potentially* productive Chicanos or Chicanas would add a great deal of strength to the institution's commitment to diversity. My sense is that it is acceptable to hire Euro-Americans that have potential but that it is not acceptable to hire Chicanos and Chicanas with the same or more potential. As my friend and colleague Rudolfo Chávez Chávez has noted with some irony: "If it is mediocrity that the gatekeepers are worried about, then Chicanos and Chicanas should have as much right to it as anyone else."

An old adage still prevails in university hiring practices that implies that there are not enough Chicano and Chicana candidates from which to choose. This view begs the question: Why then are there several potentially excellent Chicano and Chicana faculty looking for positions in institutions of higher education? Clearly, institutions must act affirmatively in their hiring practices instead of waiting for something to happen that will reduce the ethnochauvinism that creates so much disparity in the hiring of minorities in higher education. Otherwise, higher education institutions lose out on many opportunities to hire excellent minority persons and fail to diversify not only their faculties but the administration and the curriculum as well.

The issues of race, class, ethnicity, and gender have found their way into American higher education via forms of multicultural education. But as Giroux (1991) points out, the multicultural education discourse "in its varied forms and approaches generally fails to conceptualize issues of race and ethnicity as part of the wider discourse of power and powerlessness" (pp. 224–225). All discussions about multicultural education center around ethnic minorities' abilities or inabilities to become versed in dominant cultural values and norms. Rarely does one find a discourse focused on the issue of Euro-ethnics acquiring minority languages, values, and norms. Most discourses of ethnicity in higher education are presented in depoliticized contexts that focus on the Other as a problem rather than as an opportunity to enhance diversity and enrich the campus. The monolithic and Eurocentric conception of ethnicity garners power from its ability to mask the issues of "whiteness" and Otherness, thus masking the relationships of privilege and power. To counter this situation, Peter McLaren (in press) calls for a critical multicultural education that embraces a transformative political plan and that moves beyond the multicultural models of accommodation commonly used in educational circles.

The need to remap and advance higher education to a poststructuralist perspective that emanates from postmodern theories is imperative. Postmodernism offers the opportunity for ethnicity to become a viable oppositional medium that can see beyond the binary essentialism of modernism (Giroux 1991). The Chicano community can ill afford to continue the legacy of educational neglect in which ethnicity is viewed and understood within a deficit framework that does not identify Difference as a valuable essence for transforming history, culture, and meaning. Chicanos are the fastest growing segregated group in American schools, mostly through ethnic and linguistic identification. Without major changes, such as the ones offered through cultural diversity in governing and organizing schools, little can be expected to change or improve in the schooling conditions of Chicanos. Bringing about changes entails working against the grain of dominant cultural patterns of doing, knowing, becoming, and analyzing in order to rewrite the narratives for shifting the current paradigms.

I was reared in a traditional Chicano family consisting of eight boys and two girls; the oldest sibling was a sister, in a sense my surrogate mother, and then there was a younger sister. Although I did grow up doing the range of chores any sibling grows up doing, and maybe more, I grew up with an indoctrinated image of females as typical and stereotypical as that of the vast majority of males of that era. An array of feminist readings and conversations with feminists are helping me to reconstruct new images of feminism with discernible and holistic views. I do not pretend to understand fully the internal and external workings of Chicana oppression as I am sure that I also am seen as the oppressor, and to various degrees am the oppressor, amid my own struggle to unpack my representations of male-female relations as they are constructed in my sociocultural world. My struggle continues with this issue.

But Chicanas have indeed recast their assertiveness in terms unknown to the academy. Chicanas have created their own identity within metarelationships of gender, race, class, and ethnicity in an effort to reposition themselves in a space and place that does not relinquish their strength or identity. Thus, issues of gender also offer a multidimensional opportunity to rewrite the "canons" of feminism as a more inclusive category in which Chicanas can provide broader knowledge and comprehensiveness to their personal and public positions in institutions of higher education.

Class is a category that keeps close company with gender, racial, and ethnic concerns. Confined to marginal participation in American higher education, the Chicano community's position in the category of social class has played a major role in barrioizing Chicano and Chicana academicians and scholars within universities. There is an overrepresentation of poor and working-class Chicanos in the United States. Nevertheless, being poor does not constitute incompetence. Under dominant canons, perhaps incompetence is highly associated with poverty so that in dominant social thought one cannot exist without the other. Indeed, one role of the dominant class has been to reproduce working-class structures as a homogeneous entity (Apple & Christian-Smith 1991). But working-class oppositional and counterhegemonic struggles have attempted to reconstruct class as a form of resistance to monolithic formations and creations of ruling-class ideology.

I have fought long and arduous battles in university settings to educate my administrative colleagues regarding the educational needs and aspirations of the Chicano community. In the 1980s I was involved in Hispanic dropout committees that frequently operated from a totally ignorant perspective about why minority students were leaving schools. Most committees I worked with viewed the Chicano students as incapable of learning and did not try to broaden their understanding of the cultural paradigms at work within the curriculum that push minorities out of the schools.

My struggle within and against universities has always been located around issues of quality publications, lower salaries for equal work, promotion and tenure, overt ethnochauvinism, and questions about my teaching, research, and service. I am now employed at the third institution in a tenure-track position in the college of education. At each institution, I have encountered what is known as "institutionalized discrimination" or forms of exclusion that systematically work to undermine my personal and professional work. My work as an academician has been questioned frequently by dominant-culture faculty and students whose positivist notions of culture, knowledge, and truth assume I have limited knowledge about what I teach. I do welcome challenges by those students and faculty to the degree that their questions are framed in nondominant forms of inquiry rather than on dominant cultural givens positioned as representations of totalizing truth.

I have sat in faculty lounges where racist and sexist jokes and innuendoes are a common form of expression without regard to the presence of female and ethnic persons. On occasion I remember challenging quite offensive jokes only to be told that I must have a chip on my shoulder. This was designed to trivialize and disarm my rebuttal. Ethnic and sexist jokes are not harmless or trivial, especially when they are being told and one is present, and to boot, the brunt of the jokes. Power and privilege have a way of anesthetizing the oppressor's daily forms of injustice that infantilize, for the oppressor anyway, the real damage caused to the victims of such jokes. Women and ethnic minorities are systematically traumatized and victimized by the cruelty of racist and sexist jokes. On top of this, they are admonished for "not being able to take a joke" when an oppositional voice is raised against such violence.

At the first institution where I was employed, I went up for promotion and tenure a year early with the unanimous support of my department head, dean, associate deans, and the college faculty. But at the level of the graduate college my promotion and tenure were delayed one year because they felt that I had not published in "major journals." Here was a graduate dean, not in the field of education, telling me, and in fact the whole college of education, what he considered to be major journals in education. Yet there had been white faculty members who went up early, and who had fewer publications and service than I, who were tenured and promoted. The following year I resubmitted my application and finally was tenured and promoted. It might have helped that I had spoken to the affirmative action director and indicated to him that I would file a grievance against the institution if I was not awarded tenure and promotion. I made it clear that I should not be receiving such treatment in the first place, if all things were equal and fair. Subsequently I moved to another institution where my tenure and rank were honored, plus I received a substantial raise in salary and additional professional advantages.

Indeed, the opportunities seemed without limit at the second institution. I experienced a wonderful honeymoon period during the first year there. But when I began to question the institution's programs and curriculum, the second year was full of surprises. A "communications problem" appeared in which I was not receiving necessary information within my own program to work productively with students and faculty. As I looked into the matter, it became clear that the source of the problem was located within my very own unit. When I challenged the individual involved (in this case it happened to be a minority female), I was told by the department head and the leadership of the college that there was nothing they could do to improve the situation. They had already agreed, without my knowledge or approval, to assign me to courses in other departments and to place my faculty line in another program. At that point, I began to consider seriously the possibility of relocating to a different university. I was not totally powerless to prevent what was happening to me. I was powerless only to the degree that I had no information to assist my defense. I finally chose not to involve myself in a major defensive battle because I did not feel enough loyalty to the institution to see the battle through. I decided instead to put my energies into relocating to another institution where I could conscientiously make a commitment to work and struggle for the things and ideas needed to achieve a fuller expression of democracy.

I am now at a third institution where common practices of neglect and exclusion exist. However, the difference is that now I have made a commitment to stay in the area and become involved in the broader community. Also, I have several colleagues with whom I can conduct a "reality check" from time to time. As in other institutions, I have to deal with the undermining of my work by dominant-culture students and faculty. I welcome the challenge to my work, but only if it is based on genuine academic concerns and not simply my ethnicity. When students and faculty challenge my work because of who I am and not because of the knowledge that I am offering them, then it is probable that they are using power and privilege, that is, their cultural capital, to challenge my work. If the ad hominem attacks were meted out equally to all faculty without regard to ethnicity, race, and gender, then maybe I could at least learn to live with them. But on several occasions I have found students addressing me in forms and tones that they would never even consider using with Euro-American faculty. Much cultural diversification work is still needed at this institution, and I am committed to making a contribution in this regard.

My struggle has now turn to the reconstruction of how I am viewed within the political context of the academy. I intend to develop and introduce new discourses that deconstruct my location outside of an ahistorical map that is used to define my role as a faculty member. We need to redraw such maps in order to view our presence in American education as a dialectical and democratic challenge rather than simply as a problem in higher education. Clearly, we cannot wait for the hegemonic structures to do that for us. We ourselves need to deconstruct our thinking about our roles in higher education and construct the narratives that will position us as coequal brokers within a democratic sphere. I see myself now in a space and time of great challenges and opportunities both to develop my intellectual capacity and to confront the institutional hegemony that labels me.

Conclusion

The pipeline of opportunities for Chicanos in higher education remains narrow and sometimes plugged. The racial crisis in American higher education remains to be worked out. Issues of race, ethnicity, gender, and class will not go away simply because we want them to. They were constructed as part of the American social and ideological landscape, which failed to include languages of collaboration and incorporation of the Other and Difference. To deny the exigencies of those categories is to risk the danger of losing our identity as a democratic nation. Our struggle as a community has put all aspects of democracy to the test, and in some cases it has failed us. So democracy must be reconstituted as a radical social practice rather than as the practice of a rational good citizenry. A radical democracy asks questions and does not provide ready-made answers. Instead, it allows and encourages a problematic discourse that can be engaged by all.

Academia needs to recognize that the Chicano community, like other communities, speaks with multiple-voiced subjectivities and that there

are no singular notions of cultural identity within it. We are as heteroge-
neous as the next ethnic group in American society. The ethnic identity
"problem" of Chicanos does not lie within ourselves as a community,
but within institutions of higher education that tend to view the Chicano
community stereotypically or as a unitary ethnolinguistic group. Chicano
identity means different things to different Chicanos, but to the dominant society all of us are lumped under one monolithic notion of what
we are, as if scripted in Hollywood.

The Chicano community in higher education often feels the weight
of "one-lump-sum" practices that add to the problem of identity. The
umbrella term *Hispanic* is bestowed on anyone resembling or appearing
to sound or look Spanish-speaking. To ameliorate this problem, institutions of higher education must be willing to reconstruct their Eurocentric
paradigms and further the practice of inclusion. They must create more
radical democratic environments that will become the necessary ingredi-
ent for twenty-first-century educational settings where new questions
will be asked, new social analyses will be conducted, and new metacritical
discourses will be engaged (García 1993).

New languages and new knowledges must be incorporated into the
metalogic of diversity. The language of postcolonialism, postmodernism,
postpositivism, feminism, and other related post-pedagogies needs to be
used to rethink and rewrite the issues of ethnicity, race, gender, and
class in order to reincorporate higher education as a site where all
peoples can attain multifaceted pedagogies. The Chicano community in
higher education, and my own place within it, is in a prime position to
consider seriously this counterhegemonic challenge. ¡Vamos pa'lante!

References

Alvarez, R., Jr. (1986). The lemon grove incident: The nation's first
    successful desegregation court case. *Journal of San Diego History*,
    (Spring): 116–35.
Apple, M., & Christian-Smith, L. K. (1991). *The politics of the text-
    book*. New York: Routledge, Chapman & Hall.
Bourdieu, P., & Passerson, J. C. (1977). Cultural reproduction and
    social reproduction. In J. Karabel & A. H. Halsey, *Power and
    ideology in education*. New York: Oxford University Press.
García, H. S. (1993). Shifting the paradigms of education and language
    policy: Implications for language minority children. *Journal of
    Educational Issues of Language Minority Students*, *12*, 1–7.

Giroux, H. A. (1983). *Theory and resistance in education: A pedagogy for the opposition.* Rawley, MA: Bergin & Garvey.

———. (1991). Postmodernism as border pedagogy: Redefining the boundaries of race and ethnicity. In H. A. Giroux (Ed.), *Postmodernism, feminism, and cultural politics.* New York: State University of New York Press.

———. (1992). *Border crossings: Cultural workers and the politics of education.* New York: Routledge.

Hernández, D. (1970). *Mexican American challenge to a sacred cow.* UCLA Chicano Studies Center, Monograph No. 1. Los Angeles: Aztlan.

McLaren, P. (in press). White terror and oppositional agency: Towards a critical multiculturalism. *Strategies.*

Meier, J., & Stewart, K. J. (1991). *The politics of Hispanic education: Un paso pa'lante y dos pa'tras.* Albany: State University of New York Press.

Popkewitz, T. (1993). Preface. In *Critical theory and educational research.* New York: State University of New York Press.

Rich, A. (1984). Invisibility in academe. In *Blood, bread, and poetry: Selected prose, 1979–1985.* New York: W. W. Norton.

CHAPTER 11

What's in a Name?
Conflict at a University for the
Twenty-First Century

GERARDO M. GONZÁLEZ, FRANCISCO A. RÍOS,
LIONEL A. MALDONADO, STELLA T. CLARK

California State University–San Marcos (CSUSM) is the newest university in the United States. From its inception it has claimed to be an "institution for students who will live most of their lives in the 21st century" ("California Designs a University for Citizens of the 21st Century" 1993). Before opening to students in the fall of 1990, the university's founders crafted a mission statement that stresses multiculturalism, global awareness, and diversity. With recognition of its special role in north San Diego County (locally referred to as "North County"), CSUSM seeks to maintain an international focus and an awareness of its surrounding communities' needs. "The University," says the mission statement, "provides an atmosphere in which students can experience a challenging education in a supportive environment, preparing to live cooperatively and competitively in a world of cultural and ethnic diversity, economic and governmental differences, shared resources, ecological restraints and technological change" (*CSUSM 1992–3 General Catalog*, 7).

This essay represents an effort to analyze the conflict that resulted from naming the university's administration hall in honor of State Senator William Craven. The senator generally is considered the prime force in having the campus located in San Marcos. The controversy arose as a result of statements he made, then steadfastly refused to disavow, comments that showed bias against undocumented workers and, by extension, Latinos generally. The events all took place in the spring term, 1993.

This chapter will point to the clash of perceptions between a Latino organization on campus, the university, and the North County community. It will describe the conflict, provide an analysis of major issues that emerged, and offer suggestions for resolving future conflicts. It will sketch the status of Latinos in the development of the emerging campus and challenge the issue of whether CSUSM is, indeed, a campus of the twenty-first Century.

The Godfather of a University

The need for a university in North County was evident by the late 1960s, when local citizens became aware of the area's potential growth as well as the overcrowded and inaccessible conditions at San Diego State University. After an unsuccessful effort to establish an annex of San Diego State in the city of Vista, area leaders reinitiated the dialogue with California State University System administrators in the late 1970s. Key among these leaders were State Senator William A. Craven (R-Oceanside) and his administrative aide, Carol Cox. The latter represented the "average citizen" affected by the lack of opportunity for North County residents to complete their education. From the passage of Senate Bill 1060, which Craven authored to provide funds for a feasibility study of the North County campus, to negotiations with the central offices of the California State University System, CSUSM became a reality when it opened its doors to students in the fall of 1990.

Called the "father of the university," Craven claimed to have garnered much public support for the project from its inception. The campus, he said before it opened, will be "an educational jewel that will bring everlasting credit to the North County community." Citing a "chauvinistic" interest in developing the area, Craven touted the cultural and economic benefits to the "ordinary citizens" of the region ("North County Poised to Cut Ribbon on University" 1990). In the same edition of the San Diego *Union* (later named the *Union-Tribune*), Lee Thibadeau, the San Marcos mayor, concurred: "it's the greatest thing to ever happen in San Marcos . . . property values have risen, we're seeing higher quality and less-dense [*sic*] residential developments, and several of the top 500 companies in the country have contacted us" (p. B1).

To crown this success story, a community advisory committee and founding administrators proposed that the central building of the new campus be named Craven Hall. After securing CSU trustee approval, the campus moved forward to recognize the contributions of its "father" at the building's dedication in April 1993.

Before setting forth the events surrounding the controversy, however, we will provide a sketch of North County to give the reader some context about the area.

A Stronghold of Conservatism

Los Angeles, the nation's second largest city, and San Diego, which ranks sixth, are about 125 miles apart. Over the past few decades, their urban peripheries have grown closer together. By 1990 the strip approximated one continuous urbanized area, extending from north of Los Angeles, through Orange and North Counties, to the Mexican border. This sustained growth is the result principally of migration and immigration. Immigrants have been both legal and undocumented; they are both Latinos and Asians.

These north/south urban sprawls are checked only by Camp Pendleton, the huge military base in North County. Eastward urban spread is limited to a degree by desert areas. But with San Diego and Los Angeles claiming some of the nation's highest median prices for housing, even these less hospitable desert areas are undergoing a measure of urban settlement.

The economy of North County has experienced rapid change. For a long time an agribusiness and horticultural economy, it boasted extensive amenities appealing to an upper middle class lifestyle and reflective of its conspicuous consumption. Urbanization has brought a range and mix of high-tech and low-tech service industries, the latter requiring a large unskilled labor force. Across the border, *maquiladoras* have multiplied, adding their influence to the area's culture.

The military has had a strong presence in the area. There are myriad naval and marine installations; indeed, the military remains the county's single largest employer. This presence is evident in the number of military retirees who have settled there.

Like Orange County to the north, North County has a long history of political conservatism. Until the 1992 elections, it had been in the Republican column in presidential contests for the past thirty years. Candidate Clinton's margin over President Bush was among the narrowest among California's counties. Ross Perot's support was stronger here than in many other sections of the nation. The area's congressional representatives are well known for their conservative views; they include Republicans Randy "Duke" Cunningham, Ron Packard, and Duncan Hunter. Tom Metzger, a resident of the North County community of Fallbrook, is a former Grand Dragon of the California branch of the Ku Klux Klan and a founder of the White American Resistance, a white supremacist group.

The political conservatism of the area's national representatives is replicated at the local level. For example, a neighboring North County community school board is composed of a Christian Conservative majority whose first order of business upon their 1992 victory was to seek reinstatement of creationism in the science curriculum and the introduction of voluntary school prayer. San Marcos recently captured widespread attention with a council resolution that the city would not fund any federally mandated social programs unless it received federal funds for them, a move interpreted by many as a conservative response to budget woes ostensibly made worse by providing services to the undocumented.

The national recession of the 1990s has been deeper and longer in southern California than in other industrial states. California has had a string of state budgets with major deficits; efforts to balance them have favored cutting social services rather than raising taxes. The unemployment rate for southern California stubbornly has hovered above the nation's average. These factors, combined with the downsizing of the military and its obvious impact on economic dislocations and restructuring, have created vast insecurities among the citizenry.

Rapid social change and economic downturns often result in psychological stress (Bean & Tienda 1987; Jaynes & Williams 1989). These feed, in turn, the common response to affix blame for attendant social ills. A common reaction is to turn that stress and frustration on the most vulnerable segment of the population (Allport 1954; Omi & Winant 1986). In North County, the undocumented have become that scapegoat. Efforts have been made to blame the undocumented for lost jobs, depressed wages, and overburdened educational, health, and welfare institutions. In addition, the number of reported verbal and physical attacks on the undocumented has increased dramatically as the recession intractably lingers on. These reactions, furthermore, often are generalized to other Latinos.

Latinos on Campus

From the first hiring wave, CSUSM appears to have strongly supported diversity within its walls. This has met with a great deal of success. Among the current workforce of more than four hundred employees, over 10 percent are Latinos, and Latinos constitute the largest minority. As a result of the initial thrust, an interest group was formed in the fall of 1990. Baptized the Latino Association of Faculty and Staff (LAFS), it included Latinos at all levels: an assistant vice president, a college dean, faculty at all ranks, and management and clerical staff. Because the university previously had created a community support group of Latinos, the Hispanic Advisory Committee (HAC), the administration welcomed an internal group that would provide guidance and leadership in attracting, hiring, retaining, and mentoring Latinos. At the same time, as a successful reception in May 1991 and scholarship fund-raising efforts proved, LAFS figured prominently in making the university visible to the community at large and bringing in area Latino leaders. As the university workforce has grown, so has LAFS.

LAFS's mission statement stresses the social, educational, economic, and political advancement of Latinos as well as of those who subscribe to the same goals. It encourages diverse points of view and operates with the understanding that Latinos have varied backgrounds, situations, positions, and views. Although they share in common their faculty positions, the authors demonstrate this variety and were members of the executive committee in 1993.

Town-Gown Relations

The events leading to the controversy discussed in this chapter began early in February 1993. California is the destination for large waves of immigrants, both legal and undocumented, and many local officials have voiced concerns over their presence. Many have asserted that the "costs" of providing services—such as education, health, and welfare—to the undocumented place undue strains on already fragile budgets. There has been a push, therefore, to lobby the federal government for some measure of compensation. State Senator Craven, as chair of the Special Committee on Border Issues, was instrumental in funding a study to calculate these costs to San Diego County. His committee held hearings on these issues in San Diego on 5 February 1993. At one point toward the end of the public hearings, the senator discussed with legal counsel from the Department of Education the U.S. Supreme Court decision (*Plyer v. Doe*) that states that every child who resides within the school district is entitled to be educated and must produce only proof of residency, not citizenship. The senator is on record as saying the following:

> There will be a lot of people who will disagree with what I'm going to say and it's just a thought that I had. It's not a philosophy. It seems rather strange that we go out of our way to take care of the rights of these individuals [i.e., the undocumented and their school-age children] *who are perhaps on the lower scale of our humanity for one*

reason or another [emphasis added], and we really spend a lot of time and obviously a lot of money to discommode the people who pick up the tab to take care of the people that the law seems to favor. Is that correct? (Senate Special Committee on Border Issues 1993, 2).

The senator's comments were reported in the San Diego *Union-Tribune* the next morning, 6 February. In addition, the paper reported that he did not understand the offense that many had taken at the House Un-American Activities Committee's (HUAC) inquiries into possible Communist affiliations among American citizens.

The CSUSM faculty is represented by the Academic Senate. At its regularly scheduled meeting on 10 February, the body included a discussion of the newspaper account on its agenda. By a unanimous vote, the senator was invited to clarify the comments attributed to him in the press. A respectful and polite letter was sent on 15 February.

Ten days later, the senator's response arrived. Acknowledging the legitimacy of the Academic Senate's concerns, Senator Craven nonetheless failed to address the HUAC matter. Turning to the central concern of the Academic Senate's letter, Craven readily conceded the statement attributed to him but declared he meant to refer "solely to their [undocumented workers'] economic status." That clarification was not well received by some.

On 9 March, the day before the next regularly scheduled Academic Senate meeting, a Latino faculty member sent a letter to the body that was critical of the senator's response. In it, he noted that the senator seemed to imply that restricting the rights of individuals could be legitimated on the basis of social class. Specifically, the faculty member's letter pointed out that the senator "does not disavow his statement [referring to undocumented workers as the lower form of humanity] but claims that he refers to Mexicans' economic status." In his letter, the faculty member asked whether the senator implied that "Mexicans at the lower reaches of the socioeconomic hierarchy also [are] on a lower scale of humanity? Or do individuals in lower socioeconomic positions, regardless of ethnicity, merit reduced human rights?" The letter pointed out that "it is very troubling to use either ethnicity or socioeconomic status as a basis for differential treatment. That merely substitutes one form of bias (class) for another (ethnicity)."

The faculty member's letter to the Academic Senate also noted that the senator failed to address the HUAC issue. It closed by suggesting that, to foster discussion among academic senators, the body might look into the means by which the name of the administration building might be changed.

The Academic Senate met on 10 March. After discussing Senator Craven's response at length, the body voted unanimously to ask for additional clarification, since his response raised more issues than it resolved. One week later, the second carefully crafted and respectful letter was sent. Signed by the Academic Senate chair, the letter again noted the senator's work on behalf of the university and requested that he meet with the body to explain his position on the two matters: HUAC and the basis on which to withhold rights, social class, and/or ethnicity. At the same time, the Academic Senate sent a memorandum to the CSUSM president informing him that the body would oppose the dedication of the building until and unless the senator clarified his views. Throughout the unfolding drama, the president of the university had remained silent.

The following week, the chair of the Academic Senate received a hand-delivered letter from the mayor of San Marcos. In it, the mayor supported the naming of the campus building to honor the senator and chastised the faculty as interlopers unfamiliar with the folkways of their adopted community. Laced with ad hominem attacks on the Academic Senate chair, the letter stated:

> If this kind of action is representative of what we have to look to in the future, we don't need or want a University; we don't need this kind of thoughtless and cruel behavior in our community. As hard as I've worked and as strongly as I've supported the University, I'll be the first to say, *before this cancer can spread and infect the entire community, cut it out.* (emphasis added)

In his letter, the mayor stated that "[y]ou and your small group of misguided members need to apologize to the Senator immediately."

During all this period, LAFS had been meeting regularly to discuss its own actions regarding the senator's comments and the developing controversy. At the least, several argued, the organization should support the actions of the Academic Senate. Others argued for additional actions. On the day after the mayor's angry letter, though its existence was yet unknown to members, LAFS sent its own letter to the senator. It supported the Academic Senate's call for further clarification and dialogue. In addition, since the senator had not disavowed his comments regarding restrictions on the rights of individuals, whether by ethnicity or social class, the organization's letter requested a public retraction and apology. The group also called on the senator for an appropriation of funds so that rigorous and carefully designed empirical studies on the costs *and* benefits of the undocumented could be carried out. The group also stated that scholarship funds should be made available to the campus to support Latinos' educational aspirations in order to enhance their human capital and thus bolster their economic and social contributions to the local economy. The letter concluded that, failing each of the foregoing, "[a] consummate alternative corrective action is to decline the honor of a university building in your name."

LAFS's letter was sent on a Friday afternoon, with a copy given to the university's president. It immediately captured the attention of the campus administrators. For the rest of that afternoon, members of LAFS's executive committee who were on campus were besieged by representatives of the university's administration to retract their statement or retrieve the letter. The reasoning advanced was that the letter stood to undermine the administration's efforts to resolve the matter between the senator and the Academic Senate. It was suggested to untenured members of the LAFS executive committee that their careers could be jeopardized by their actions. Comments were made in the halls to faculty, and in the presence of staff, that the actions were "stupid" and potentially destructive of careers.

The next day, a Saturday, the San Diego *Union-Tribune* carried an article on the letter by San Marcos's mayor. It quoted the senator as saying that he knew of the letter but had not yet seen a copy. Defending the mayor's right to his views, the senator stated that his personal friend, was "just expressing his opinion and dislike of the attitude of people who have made the comments" ("San Marcos Mayor Rails at CSU Faculty" 1993). The reference was to the faculty's request for clarification.

On Sunday, the Escondido *Times-Advocate*, one of North County's two daily papers, carried a story on the letter to Senator Craven from LAFS. The article quotes the senator as saying that "[g]ood judgment and good taste prevent me from telling them [LAFS] what they should do." He defended his comments of 5 February by saying that they were taken out of context and were in reference to "the poorest of the poor." He continued: "I suppose it [LAFS's letter] reflects the thinking of a small group of people from the Academic Senate. It appears Latino members have banded together and developed a plan of attack and are going to continue until 'I mend my ways' " ("Latino Group Targets Sen. William Craven" 1993). The Oceanside *Blade-Citizen*, published in the Senator's hometown, also carried an article describing the letter from LAFS to him.

By Monday, 29 March, matters had heated up. In an apparent effort to defuse the situation, the president called an emergency meeting of high-level staff and administrators, and included several others: the chair of the Academic Senate, another academic senator, two members of LAFS, and the student body president. The president discussed the escalation of the matter and alluded to his behind-the-scenes effort to resolve it. He asked representatives of the various interest groups what it would take to reduce tensions and deescalate the situation. He indicated his intent to fly to Sacramento, the state capital, to meet personally with the senator to forge a response that would meet the minimum conditions of the diverse interest groups. At the conclusion of the two-hour meeting, the president presumably had a clear notion of each group's position.

For its part, the LAFS executive committee was asked later that day by a member of the administration to draft a letter spelling out its minimum concerns. Members also were asked to refrain from further publicizing their concerns via the press. Having written that letter and having agreed to the "gag rule," LAFS presented the finished product to the administration so that the president could take it to Sacramento.

Sometime after Monday's meeting but unknown to many who had been present, nine members of the original dozen Founding Faculty (the initial group hired in 1988–89 to help plan CSUSM) met in the president's conference room and drafted yet another letter to send to the senator and local newspapers. Its content and import would not be known for several days.

The president did not make his trip to Sacramento, even though the San Diego paper's caption in an article noted that he would be a "peacemaker in the CSU flap" ("Stacy Will Be Peacemaker in CSU Flap" 1993). In that article, the president was reported also to have said that, despite opposition to naming the building after the senator, the 19 April 1993 dedication would proceed as planned. Members of LAFS took this to mean that their concerns and the prior day's agreement for resolution had been put aside.

By this time, an emergency session of the Academic Senate had been scheduled for Wednesday, 31 March. The opportunity to resolve the matter rapidly was closing; positions seemed to be hardening. Actions attributed to the administration suggested that some of the interest groups' concerns were to be dismissed, particularly those articulated by LAFS.

During the emergency meeting of the Academic Senate, the president was granted time to address the body. Members of the senate's executive committee also requested time on the agenda for a motion they sought to bring forward.

Some individuals believed that the president's statement would present the latest response from Senator Craven, a response many hoped would resolve matters. Others believed that the situation would be settled in a way to disempower various segments of the academic community. Many Latinos felt they would be the sacrificial lambs. The latter two opinions were borne out by events that afternoon. The president, kindly but sternly, admonished the faculty for their response to the matter and stated that he was convinced the senator had not meant to disparage any ethnic group. By this time, the HUAC and social class concerns had been brushed aside.

A sharply divided Academic Senate wrangled for nearly three hours. Finally, a series of resolutions were passed. One focused on support for the Academic Senate's chair in carrying out the wishes of the body and defended him against the ad hominem attacks he had received (not just those from the mayor). The second reiterated the continued effort to keep communications open with the senator. Both passed unanimously. More contentious was the motion that the Academic Senate apologize to the senator for the escalation of the matter and find ways to reestablish more cordial relations with the communities offended in the controversy. No mention was made of apologies to the Latino community or of ways to reassure it and the poor that their rights would be protected. This motion passed; one-fifth of the Academic Senate voted nay.

On the same day, 31 March, the Founding Faculty's letter to the senator began to circulate. An e-mail to most of the campus community went out from the president's office that individuals interested in signing the letter could do so in the Human Relations—personnel—Office. Reports began to appear almost immediately that some staff managers had drafted memos urging their employees to sign the letter, though signing was voluntary. Other assertions, later confirmed, were that some who sought signatures were saying that legislative support and funding for the university could be negatively affected and that the letter would mollify legislators.

Whatever the letter's intent, it proved divisive of faculty, staff, and students. Many saw it as a clumsy and crude form of a "loyalty oath." The basis of this judgment was its announcement via campuswide e-mail from the president's office that his representatives went about seeking signatures, and that individuals not personally solicited could sign on in the Human Resources (personnel) office. In addition, there were confirmed reports that an administration representative who sought employees' signatures implied that state funding for the campus was at risk. Other administrators drafted memos urging staff members in their units to sign the Founding Faculty letter. Group meetings were called where employees felt coerced to sign the letter; Latinos felt particularly vulnerable. All this raised questions for many about the tactics for soliciting signatures; it smacked of intimidation, coercion, and bullying.

On 2 April, Senator Craven's response to the Academic Senate's second letter finally arrived. In it, he distanced himself from HUAC tactics as practiced by the late Senator Joseph McCarthy (R-WI, who was censured by the U.S. Senate for his role on HUAC), though not from its initial efforts and strategies by which Communist sympathizers, fellowtravelers, and dupes were to be ferreted out. Craven also noted that he had not intended his comments to be taken as an ethnic slur. And, if his letter is given a charitable reading, it appears that the senator acknowledged the resistance by some to discrimination based on social class factors. Last, he reiterated a defense that had appeared often in the press and among his defenders: that his comments were taken out of context.

Editorials, cartoons, and commentary had been appearing in the North County dailies—*Union-Tribune, Times-Advocate,* and *Blade Citizen*—that were highly critical of the faculty. Charges of "political correctness" and of the faculty as "thought police" were leveled ("Craven's Blooper" 1993). An editorial in the *Times-Advocate* sought to dismiss the faculty's concern as much ado over a "semantic episode . . . that would be laughable if it weren't such an insult to the honor of the man." ("Roses and Raspberries" 1993). An editorial cartoon in the *Blade-Citizen* (fig. 11.1) depicted a cross section of a "multiculturalist's brain" that implied rejection of all apologies by the senator for ethnic slurs. (Indeed, we learned upon requesting permission from the *Blade-Citizen* to reproduce it with this chapter that the original copy of the cartoon had been requested by Senator Craven's office within two days of its appearance, strongly implying the mutual support between the senator's office and the print media.)

Another cartoon, in the *Times-Advocate,* showed the senator on his knees apologizing to an undocumented worker for referring to him as the "quite simply and unfortunately rather poor in general" while being prodded by the lance of a faculty member wearing a badge, presumably a member of the "Thought Police on Political Correctness" (fig. 11.2).

Classes resumed after spring break on 12 April. LAFS met on 13 April and reviewed Craven's second response and the transcripts of the 5 February hearing that had come to the university. Since these documents did not provide any justifying context for his remarks, LAFS decided not to participate as an organization in the 19 April dedication.

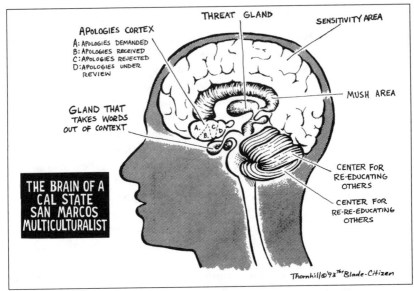

Fig. 11.1 Editorial cartoon, Ocean *Blade-Citizen*, 31 March 1993, p. F6.

Fig. 11.2 Editorial cartoon, Escondido *Times-Advocate*, 28 March 1993, p. A8.

The Academic Senate's executive committee invited LAFS's president to its 14 April meeting and opened it to all interested parties. The senator's latest reply was discussed and its receipt was formally acknowledged and conveyed to him. The executive committee decided that additional efforts for further clarification from the senator would be futile.

A high-level administrator at the meeting reiterated that the senator's comments had been taken out of context. He could not, however, offer any context that would justify saying that "it seems rather strange that we go out of our way to take care of the rights of these individuals who are . . . on a lower scale of our humanity."

The caption on the 15 April San Diego *Union-Tribune* front-page story read: "Latinos to Boycott Ceremony at CSUSM." The article dramatized LAFS's decision not to participate, though it was not a "boycott" as the caption read. In addition, the article reported the controversial tactics used to obtain signatures on the Founding Faculty petition.

The fateful day arrived, 19 April. Few faculty and staff showed up for the dedication. The senator came and was treated to his honor. Local business and community leaders made their appearance. There was a small-scale student demonstration. The day ended like it had begun, quietly and with little or no fanfare.

On the same day, the San Diego *Union-Tribune* carried a feature article on the event. Its headline: "Craven's Goof Still Cries Out for Apology." The columnist recounted some of the events highlighted here. Prominent was the deep hurt and legitimacy of LAFS in articulating its protest over Craven's remark, though it singled out the scholarship issue as having hurt the group's cause (while ignoring the other recommendation for funds to carry out empirical studies on the costs and contributions of the undocumented to the county). The story also noted that faculty were unreasonably "bashed." It concluded that the president's tardy effort to deal with the matter after it had escalated, perhaps beyond his abilities to redress matters, was unwisely divisive, though it might have earned him a small measure of credit with the external community ("Craven's Goof Still Cries Out for Apology" 1993).

Lessons Learned by Latinos

An analysis of the events surrounding the naming of Craven Hall brings into focus eight themes regarding LAFS and Latinos at CSUSM: (1) the administration's tacit acceptance of the discriminatory comments; (2) the sanctimoniously harsh overreaction by the print media to LAFS's concerns and letter; (3) the rallying of forces to support the Senator and to isolate LASF; (4) a lack of understanding and outright disregard for the university's mission statement; (5) the drift in the university's leadership; (6) the neglect of freedom of speech; (7) the social control and intimidation surrounding the event; and (8) the unanticipated positive outcomes for Latinos on campus and the LAFS.

Tacit Acceptance of the Discriminatory Comments

Without doubt, one of the biggest issues that fell by the wayside during the crisis was the fact that Craven's comments were, in fact, prejudicial. The entire matter began with his sponsorship of a study by which undocumented immigrants could be shown to contribute to the state's economic problems while ignoring their contributions. This helped set the stage to make them scapegoats for economic woes. It ended with Craven's comments and his explanation—first, that what he meant to say was that poor people were on the lowest scale of humanity whose rights could be ignored, and second, that these comments were taken out of context. In either case, his comments were prejudicial. It is difficult to imagine any context in which such statements are acceptable. Moreover, if it were critical that his remarks did not reflect bigotry, the senator should have informed the faculty about that context. Instead, he merely repeated the claim without providing any proof. Regrettably, the range of issues that were generated by his initial comments remains to be adequately addressed.

Among LASF's members, however, the comments are impossible to forget. At all the meetings held during the controversy, members poignantly and movingly reiterated how the comments were burnished on their memories, recalling the pain and harsh treatment their family members had experienced for their ethnicity, historically and up to the present. Indeed, a good portion of the LAFS letter detailed the strong negative effect caused by the senator's remarks.

It is interesting to note that, in contrast to the sanctions imposed on other public figures who have voiced racial slurs, the Senator was re-*warded* with a building in his name. For example, Al Campanis said in 1987 that Blacks simply did not have the "necessities" to lead in sports and was removed from sports; Jimmy "The Greek" Snyder in 1988 stated that Blacks were created different from whites, which accounted for their athletic ability, and was released as a commentator; and Cincinnati Reds' owner Marge Schott told people in 1992 about her "million dollar niggers," resulting in her being suspended for one year from direct involvement in baseball and fined $250,000. Comparing these to the senator's veneration with a building in his honor supports the point that there was more than tacit acceptance of his remarks by the university and surrounding community.

Overreaction by the Local Press

Another theme that emerged from this controversy was the degree to which the local press overreacted to the issues that LAFS raised. In a sense, this seemed to draw out conservative forces in support of the senator. The press's vitriolic attacks, perhaps giving voice to community values, lashed out at the faculty generally and the "multiculturalists" specifically. These attacks came by way of written editorials and editorial cartoons detailed earlier. What is most important here are the racial overtones in these editorials (it is important to understand that the chair of the Academic Senate, who carried out its wish and was most visible, is African American). Thus, the "multiculturalists" to whom these editorials alluded are people of color.

Rallying behind the Senator

The press, in addition to making vicious attacks on the "multiculturalists," served to rally support for the senator. In fact, several individuals stepped forward to lend their support by way of championing the senator's work and attacked those who took offense at his remarks. Most prominent among these individuals were the mayor of San Marcos and the president of the university. The mayor sent his support in the form of the letter mentioned above. He indicated "disappointment and disgust" at how "a group of uninformed educators try to make something so hateful out of a newspaper story." And while his letter was so personal in its attack that it elicited disavowal the next day by several members of the city council, it nonetheless reflected the values of someone elected to high public office who ostensibly represents that community's interests.

The university's president also remained a staunch supporter of the senator. In his remarks to the Academic Senate, he sought to clarify the meaning and intent of the senator's remarks on the basis of alleged private conversations between them. Many in LAFS felt that, if indeed he had met with the senator early in this episode and been convinced no slur was intended, he should have met with the group to pass along that information. Yet he issued no public statement on the matter for nearly two months.

Disregard for the University's Mission Statement

Throughout the initial development of the university, the administration consistently had looked to its mission statement to unify the campus community and to develop a set of common goals. Explicit in that statement is the notion of inclusiveness. To be sure, many of the Latinos hired early in the history of the university felt that their perspective was sought out, respected, and in many instances acted upon. But with the campus's first crisis, the high-minded principles in the mission statement quickly gave way to the politics of resentment and exclusion. University officials neither sought advice from LAFS nor tried to learn their views. Rather, a serious rupture developed between the university and Latinos on campus, creating a "we-versus-they" atmosphere, of in- and out-groups.

The chain of events brought into question the function of diversity and the administration's commitment to the mission statement. Its actions did not exemplify the principles embodied in the statement. Indeed, it distanced itself from that idealistic statement by its very actions. This raised questions about the degree to which the document actually guides efforts to build a university for the twenty-first century. It was difficult not to conclude that principles were sacrificed in an apparent move to appease political elements in the community. The president's touted role as "peacemaker" was, in reality, to appease the senator at the expense of the faculty, but particularly LAFS. In essence, these actions suggested that hierarchical, not cooperative, social and power relationships would emerge with the campus's first crisis. The exercise of power would be the means by which compliance would be enforced, rather than the vaunted common values from the mission statement.

Lack of University Leadership

The university administration did not display constructive leadership in the resolution of the Craven controversy. It largely remained silent for fifty-one days—from 6 February (when the senator's comments were reported in the press) to 31 March (when the president addressed the Academic Senate). Its members apparently either failed to recognize how deeply Latinos on campus might have been affected by Craven's remarks or dismissed their legitimacy. Moreover, it appears that the press was used to express the harsh attacks on LAFS, rather than engage the organization directly in the dispute's resolution. Subsequent to LAFS's public stance, actions were taken that effectively isolated and discounted the organization. The president, through the press, expressed regrets over bruised feelings but did not meet with campus Latinos until the eleventh hour.

The administration also apparently allowed the scapegoating of LAFS by use of the Founding Faculty letter, which reiterated deep gratitude for the senator's efforts on behalf of the university and offered to seek ways to reestablish cordial and constructive relations with him and the local community. Members of the LAFS executive committee suspected that the president, or someone in his office, had advanced the idea of a Founding Faculty letter as a device to appease some of the angered interest groups, particularly those off-campus. That view is supported by the fact that the meeting of the Founding Faculty took place in the president's conference room, that their letter's existence was made known via an e-mail message from his office to the entire campus, and that one Founding Faculty member who had been recently appointed as the president's special assistant was most aggressive in seeking faculty and staff signatures.

Freedom of Speech for Latinos on Campus

The administration did not publicly acknowledge the legitimacy of LAFS's position. There was no indication of support for the group's right to voice its concerns. Some administrators attempted to pressure LAFS to retract its letter to the senator. Upon learning that LAFS's letter had been sent, the organization's leadership came under intense pressure. These attacks sometimes led to self-doubt and uncertainty among the LAFS executive committee; members perceived the attacks as a means of isolating and dividing the group. LAFS, in essence, became the out-group and its members the targets of intense negative feelings. As a result, the LAFS executive committee decided to censor itself by not talking with the press. Apparent administrative actions, such as the Founding Faculty petition, merely served to silence and divide other faculty and staff. This contributed to a public perception that most at the university supported the senator and that a few trouble-makers had created the crisis. The administration sought to downplay LAFS's concerns about the senator's statement and focused instead on LASF's so-called demands, referring to them as "extortion" and "blood money." Indeed, the blame was shifted to LAFS as the group that started the controversy and thwarted a possible resolution. An additional example of "blaming the victim" (Ryan 1976) was the assertion that LAFS's actions had created an environment in which town-gown relations had become strained, requiring extraordinary measures to repair them. It was, in the view of Latinos on campus, a time of siege, isolation, and alienation.

Social Control and Intimidation

The social control of Latinos was demonstrated in ways to inhibit the legitimate rights of employees to voice their concerns. The administration's

tactics to divide and control the university community included rumors
that losing Craven's support would result in budget cuts and potential
layoffs. Intimidation was explicitly used, particularly against untenured
faculty and staff vulnerable to dismissal. That probationary employees'
jobs were on the line or that tenured employees were jeopardizing others'
jobs certainly forced many to restrict their actions. The manner in which
the controversy was dealt with created a deep sense of vulnerability, inse-
curity, and estrangement as described by Apple (1979).

Positive Outcomes: United We Stand

The events described led to a strengthening of the bond among the LAFS
membership. Despite the diversity of perspectives in LAFS, there was strong
support for the group's leadership. And while there was no consensus
initially on the contents of LAFS's letter to Craven, the principle of taking
a strong stand was never in question and the executive committee was
endorsed overwhelmingly in the aftermath. Members who generally had
not participated in the organization used the incident to further distance
themselves. At the same time, the remaining members appeared to have
stronger unity than ever, particularly over the attacks on the leadership.
This unity was shown in the increased attendance at subsequent meetings,
especially as the organization took a strong stand on the manner of acquiring signatures for the Founding Faculty petition.

LAFS underwent several changes as a result of the controversy.
Initially perceived by many outsiders as a "fellowship" group that organized *pachangas*, *tardeadas*, and fiestas, the group emerged with the
public recognition of having lived up to its own mission statement in
the face of strong opposition and possibly high personal costs. Also, the
administration grudgingly began to acknowledge the organization's advisory role. This became apparent at a subsequent meeting between
LAFS and the university's president.

A major aspect of the controversy related directly to matters of
Latino empowerment. LAFS strove to express a voice and to gain recognition. There was no reason to be complacent. The path toward empowerment was initiated by the organization's stance on the Craven
matter. This resulted in conflict because the administration would not
perceive that stance as acceptable. In the ensuing siege of LAFS, there
was an attempt to discredit the organization as a legitimate representative voice of Latinos. On the other hand, a few members of the Hispanic Advisory Committee were portrayed as satisfied with Craven's
explanation of his remarks, this in an apparent effort to force compliance by LAFS or otherwise dismiss the group.

Implications

Upon reflection, we realize how much we have learned about ourselves, our Latino community, the university, and the community at large as a result of this event. One lesson learned is that lofty principles can be quickly set aside for political expediency. Another lesson is that, during its developmental stage, a university must clarify the vision upon which it is built. Until these general and idealistic aims are clarified and made specific, perhaps by identifying the practical principles that stem from that vision, individuals will be allowed to use the mission statement to validate their behavior. This can entail tolerating the discriminatory remarks made by a senator who has a building named in his honor, or taking a leadership role to oppose such remarks even if it means isolating oneself and one's community from the larger social context.

Another lesson learned is the need to use the media to disseminate one's views. We felt used by the media for its own agenda; as a consequence, we censored ourselves. The result, of course, was that our views were spelled out in one letter to the senator and the varying interpretations the press gave to those views. The community at large did not hear our concerns as the crisis unfolded. The need is clear for a strategy whereby our views are presented clearly, repeatedly, and systematically. In short, we need to be active in shaping public perception regarding our concerns rather than letting others do so.

Perhaps the most important lesson is how little social relationships have changed in a university touted as "one for the twenty-first century." During the civil rights era, the byline was that increasing our numbers in various institutions was key to empowerment. When that proved less than fully effective, it was hypothesized that, additionally, greater representative democracy was attainable by a more equitable representation across the spectrum of institutional positions. Clearly, both those dicta were not enough in this instance.

Our suggestion is that effectiveness may be more realistically linked to adding coalitions with other groups and organizations, both within and beyond the university. In short, the incorporation of minority views and interests may lie in forging bonds with other social, political, and economic interests, including professional organizations. These links, moreover, should span widely to include regional and national organizations. Attempting to operate solely within an organizational structure such as a university might not lead to the results one envisions in a society or institution governed by power relationships rather than by consensus reached through enlightened vision and the open debate of issues.

Another suggestion we would make is that the means by which
names of university buildings and monuments are made should be reviewed. This also might include sources from which funds for various
university activities and structures are received. Much of the controversy
over Craven's remarks could have been averted if a building had not been
designated in advance to reward the man's efforts in locating the campus
in North County. Indeed, this issue is not unlike efforts over the past few
years to divest from companies and nations whose practices and patterns
are counter to the ideals of the university (Freire 1983).

Summary and Conclusions

This chapter has presented the natural history of a controversy that arose
at a new public university over open remarks made by a state politician.
They were regarded as racist and restrictive of rights. Latino faculty and
staff reactions to these comments met with efforts by the administration to
circumscribe their right of dissent. The means of handling the controversy
proved highly divisive of faculty, staff, and students; it served to alienate
Latinos from administrators and colleagues. This created in-groups and
out-groups; it served to disenfranchise members of the out-group and,
further, blame them for the situation. It was a climate exacerbated by
actions of the area's print media and politicos who rallied to the defense of
the offending state senator, even distorting the issues in that support.

Latino faculty and staff viewed the administration's reaction as break-
ing covenant with the campus's lofty mission statement. That declaration purports to provide a supportive environment for a challenging
education that will prepare students to live cooperatively and competitively in a world of cultural and ethnic diversity, as well as economic
and governmental differences and rapid social change. Thus, rather
than the pluralistic society articulated in the mission statement, the view
more realistically is one that looks backward to hierarchical and asym-
metrical power relations, where the rights of the minority are restricted
and circumscribed. Moreover, it raises questions about honesty in recruiting prospective faculty, staff, and students when there is such a
glaring disjunction between lofty values and the freedom to dissent,
particularly when dissent is voiced by an ethnic minority.

The experiences of this episode also suggest a continuing necessity
for minority groups to practice coalition politics, seeking allies and
support across institutional and ethnic boundaries. Specifically, our experience has convinced us that our vulnerability might well have been

lessened had we actively sought the support of off-campus organizations and groups. These could include area politicians sympathetic to minority concerns as well as business and trade groups that cater to minority constituencies. Most certainly, these links to the world beyond the academy should include the media, both print and electronic. Belatedly, we learned that we should have been more astute in getting our views before the public, both in English and in Spanish. There undoubtedly are other institutional structures with which we should forge alliances, including professional associations. It is important to note that the siege under which we operated clearly called for external help. Our efforts to keep the matter within the limits of the university did not serve us well.

Latinos in academia continue the struggle to establish their voice and to become empowered. The events described in this chapter might be unique to this university, but the conflicts over issues surrounding the institutional response to questions of affirming diversity parallel those at many universities. Without a doubt, Latinos in higher education need to be aware of ways in which institutions say they value diversity while responding to critical incidents such as these in hostile and divisive ways. These conflicts are inevitable; thus, there is the need for strong organizations that represent Latino interests and that, in conjunction with other university groups, offer support and unified effort. Only then will we be able to respond to these conflicts with words we long to hear: "¡venceremos!"

Bibliography

Allport, G. (1954). *The nature of prejudice*. Cambridge, MA: Addison-Wesley.

Alvarez, R. (1985). The psycho-historical and socioeconomic development of the Chicano community in the United States. In C. Bonjean, R. Romo, R. Alvarez, & R. de la Garza (Eds.), *The Mexican-American Experience* (pp. 920–42). Austin: University of Texas Press.

Apology sought. (1993, 30 March). Oceanside *Blade Citizen*, pp. A1, A7.

Apple, M. (1979). *Ideology and curriculum*. London: Routledge & Kegan Paul.

Bean, F. D., & Tienda, M. (1987). *The Hispanic population of the United States*. New York: Russell Sage Foundation.

California designs a university for citizens of the 21st century. (1990, 21 February). *Chronicle of Higher Education*, p. A3.

Craven defends remarks. (1993, 12 March). Oceanside *Blade-Citizen*, pp. A1, A11.

Craven deserves to have building named after him [commentary]. (1993, 25 March). Oceanside *Blade-Citizen*, p. B9.

"Craven Hall" in trouble? (1993, 19 March). Oceanside *Blade-Citizen*, pp. A1, A7.

Craven says he meant no racial insult. (1993, 7 April). San Diego *Union-Tribune*, pp. B1, B6.

Craven's blooper: Thought police exact a toll at CSU San Marcos [editorial]. (1993, 3 April). San Diego *Union Tribune*, p. B14.

Craven's goof still cries out for apology. (1993, 19 April). San Diego *Union-Tribune*, pp. B1, B2.

CSU founding faculty's letter praises Craven. (1993, 3 April). San Diego *Union-Tribune*, p. B2.

CSU San Marcos panel addresses Craven dispute. (1993, 1 April). San Diego *Union-Tribune*, pp. B1, B7.

Freire, P. (1983). *Pedagogy of the oppressed*. New York: Continuum.

Jaynes, G. D., & Williams, R. M. (Eds.) (1989). *A common destiny: Blacks and American society*. Washington, DC: National Academy Press.

Latino group targets Sen. William Craven. (1993, 28 March). Escondido *Times-Advocate*, pp. B1–B2.

Latinos to boycott ceremony at CSUSM. (1993, 15 April). San Diego *Union-Tribune*, pp. A1, A12.

Lee, A. M., & Lee, E. B. (1972). *The fine art of propaganda*. New York: Farrar, Straus & Giroux.

Massey, D. S., & Denton, N. A. (1993). *American apartheid: segregation and the making of the underclass*. Cambridge: Harvard University Press.

McCarthy, K., & Burciaga Valdez, B. (1985).*Current and future effects of Mexican immigration in California*. Santa Monica: Rand Corporation.

Migrants a burden on local budgets? Hearing is heated. (1993, 6 February). San Diego *Union-Tribune*, pp. B1, B4.

Omi, M., & Winant, H. (1986). *Racial formation in the United States*. New York: Routledge & Kegan Paul.

Opinion [cartoon]. (1993, 4 April). Escondido *Times-Advocate*, p. A12.

Question not academic [editorial]. (1993, 4 April). Escondido *Times-Advocate*, p. A8.

Roses and raspberries. (1993, 23 March). Escondido *Times-Advocate*, p. A12.

Ryan, W. (1976). *Blaming the victim* (rev. ed.). New York: Random House.

San Marcos mayor rails at CSU faculty. (1993, 27 March). San Diego *Union-Tribune*, pp. A1, A19.

Senate Special Committee on Border Issues. (1993, February 5). California State Senate Archives Office. Transcripts available from authors.

Senator Craven defends remarks about migrants. (1993, 26 March). San Diego *Union-Tribune*, pp. B1, B2.

Senator will receive regret but no apology. (1993, 1 April). Escondido *Times-Advocate*, pp. B1, B2.

Stacy will be peacemaker in CSU flap. (1993, 30 March). San Diego *Union-Tribune*, pp. B1, B2.

Held to a Higher Standard: Latino Executive Selection in Higher Education

ROBERTO HARO

Are there perceptions among people at American colleges and universities that impede minorities,[1] especially Latinos,[2] from attaining academic executive-level positions? And if such perceptions exist, are they intentional, unintentional, or a product of other factors? The issues surrounding these questions are emotionally charged and may be a source of considerable debate and speculation. What is important to consider, however, is whether negative perspectives toward Latinos might help to explain why so few Latinos are selected for key leadership roles in higher education. Most of the available, reliable data indicate that Latinos are seriously underrepresented in top leadership jobs in colleges and universities.[3]

It is essential for Latinos to begin questioning their limited numbers in leadership roles in higher education. Why are so few in senior-level academic executive jobs? The path to academic leadership roles—deans, academic vice presidents and presidents—at colleges and universities requires successful candidates to be tenured, full professors. And information provided elsewhere in this book reveals numerous obstacles that Latinos have to overcome to secure a tenured faculty role and recognition for their scholarship. Imagine, therefore, the challenges Latinos face as they apply for academic leadership jobs in higher education, especially in predominantly white institutions.

Before continuing, some key terms must be identified. I choose to limit my discussion of executive positions to presidencies and academic vice presidencies. The president of a college or university is the chief executive officer (CEO) for the institution and usually serves at the pleasure of a board of regents or trustees. The academic vice presidency is a key executive position on any campus, and an important pathway to a presidency. In the absence of the president, the academic vice

189

president (AVP) is usually in charge of the campus. More CEOs in higher education seem to have come to the presidency from the role of academic vice president than from other types of vice presidencies (Ross, 1993). I will also use the popular term *glass ceiling* to identify a process that limits the upward mobility of an administrator to a certain organizational level and can result in professional stagnation. With these definitions in mind, it is appropriate to delve into the topics associated with the two questions raised earlier.

Numerous studies have been done to gather data for analysis on (1) the number of women and minorities serving as presidents (Leatherman, 1991), and (2) the selection and appointment of women, and even less frequently minorities, as presidents (Sturnick, Milley, & Tisinger 1991; Esquibel 1977). And there are many articles, reports, and guidebooks on selecting academic leaders (Birnbaum 1988; Bolman 1965; Kaplowitz 1973; Marchese 1987; McLaughlin 1985, 1990). However, fewer studies have been done to determine the number of women and minorities in academic vice presidencies. And even less attention has been devoted to studies about the selection and appointment of minorities as academic vice presidents. A few organizations regularly (some annually) gather data on the number of new women presidents,[4] with very modest tracking of minority progress. Most of the current activities result in quantitatively oriented studies and reports. There are several reasons for this. By capturing quantitative data, usually as a product of strictly controlled questionnaire surveys, the outcomes lend themselves to a form of sanitized statistical analysis. The "hard" data gathered in many of these studies provides ways to address the questions raised earlier. And while an analysis of the data might not provide us with complete answers, it may be inferred from such investigations that the representation of women, and particularly minorities, in leadership roles at American colleges and universities is significantly less than for white males. Many of the studies conclude by stating that there is a severe underrepresentation of women, and especially minorities, in top executive jobs in higher education.

A follow-up question to the above is, Why? Not satisfied with the research on the limited numbers of Latinos in top executive positions in higher education, I decided to conduct a study on the selection and appointment of presidents and AVPs at twenty target campuses. The study took almost four years to complete. Five more institutions were added to the original group. This was done to include multicampus systems at the two- and four-year levels. Several control factors were involved. First, all of the institutions had to be coeducational and have at least a 60 percent white student enrollment. Second, the target institutions had to include two- and four-year colleges, and research universities. Third, the four-year institutions had to include privately and publicly supported ones. Fourth, the institutions had to be located in different parts of the United States where Latinos were at least 9 percent of the region's population. The target sites were eventually located in ten mainland states. Institutions in Puerto Rico were not included in this study. Finally, a case-study method was adopted that included a structured interviewing technique for data collection (Yin, 1984). Target sites were selected as soon as a public job announcement was available. No *formal* contact was made with the campus during the screening and interview phases of the search for a president or academic vice president. However, unofficial visits were made to the target sites during the final phases of the search process. A discreet gathering of different types of information available to the public during this part of the search was possible. Formal contact occurred after an offer of employment was made and accepted, or the search had been canceled. Structured interviews were conducted with different people at the target campuses. Where an off-campus consultant or executive search firm had been retained to assist with the search or screening process, only the resource persons from that firm involved in the screening were asked to participate. Strict confidentiality was the key criterion to guarantee cooperation, along with the opportunity to review the outcomes draft.[5] Finally, no indication was given to the interviewees about the researcher's ethnic background.[6]

Target Institutions

Twenty colleges and universities were contacted in 1986. The breakdown of institutions is as follows:

- Five community colleges (two year institutions)
- Five four-year private liberal arts colleges—two with small graduate professional programs in business, a health services profession, or law
- Five publicly supported regional universities with graduate programs at the master's level only
- Five research universities (public and private) that offer the doctorate

The enrollment categories for the institutions ranged from a low of 1,500 full-time-equivalent students (FTES) to over 25,000 FTES. In 1989, five additional institutions were added to the target group. Among them were presidencies and academic vice presidencies at systems that included two or more campuses (e.g., the superintendent of a community college district that included two colleges.) Data collection was completed late in 1990.

Data Collection Methodology

A structured questionnaire was developed to solicit information from different people involved in the search process at the target campuses (Yin 1984). And an interviewing strategy was developed to control the investigator's intervention into the observational setting (Webb et al. 1966). Human subject guidelines were strictly adhered to at this writer's home institution and at the target sites. The questions were designed to capture specific data about the subject's role and status on the campus, or as a consultant/search firm representative. Conversations with the interviewees occurred after the searches were completed and a candidate had been selected or a new search was required. People interviewed included faculty, staff, students, administrative personnel, trustees, and off-campus consultants. Six out of 129 candidates for the positions in question were also contacted;[7] and then only to follow up on allegations of discrimination. But the information from those conversations was not factored into the results of this study.

A total of 130 people were asked to participate in the study. Ninety-six (73 percent) agreed to be interviewed.[8] The interviews were done, for the most part, in person. However, several subjects preferred to talk on the telephone. Follow-up conversations were done mainly by telephone. Of the 96 interviewees, 37 were involved in AVP searches and 59 were involved in presidential searches.

Every campus or system office was visited. A process of walking around and randomly talking with student leaders, faculty, and staff— and in a few instances off-campus people—was used to gain a sense of the institution's culture and some of the prevailing attitudes about the search. This was particularly helpful in cases involving presidential selection. David Riesman mentions this technique in his report on choosing a college president (McLaughlin & Riesman 1990). Public information about the search and the finalists also was gathered—for instance, from newspaper articles, letters to the editor of campus and off-campus news-papers, and flyers.

In four out of the twenty-five case studies (16 percent), there was a failure to make an appointment. Where a finalist rejected the offer of employment, that person was contacted and asked to be interviewed. Almost all of them agreed to be interviewed. Again, this information was not factored into the results of the study.

Data secured from the interviews with members of the search or screening committees, and other sources, were compiled and structured into five major categories to allow for computer manipulation:

- Academic preparation
- Experiential background
- Scholarly/teaching accomplishments
- Matters of style
- Interview impressions

The following discussion will focus on these categories and provide infor-mation about outcomes.

General Outcomes

Looking at the appointments of presidents and academic vice presidents at the target institutions by ethnic background and gender, the numbers—and their statistical values—offer some interesting outcomes (Table E.1). Even though the sample size is small, the results do allow for a limited amount of supposition and intriguing conjecture.

Among the 21 candidates appointed as new presidents or academic vice presidents, 13 (62 percent) were white males, 5 (24 percent) were females, 2 (10 percent) were Latinos, and 1 (4 percent) was a non-Latino minority male. Most of the white males appointed as presidents or super-

Table E.1 Appointments by Ethnicity and Gender

Category	Number	(W) Males	(W) Females	Latinos	Non-Latino Minority
President	13	8	3	1	1
Academic VP	8	5	2	1	0
Totals	21	13	5	2	1

Table E.2. Finalist Pool (n = 129)

White Females	White Males	Latinos	Non-Latino Minorities
42	56	19	12

intendents of community colleges or districts were sitting presidents.[9] At the four-year colleges and universities, approximately 34 percent of the presidential appointees were already CEOs at other institutions. Among the academic vice presidential appointments, 63 percent were white males.

There were 129 finalists within the 25 case studies (Table E.2). All of the target institutions had a finalist pool that included one or more women. However, among the 25, only 23 had a finalist pool that included one or more minority males. And out of the 25, only 19 had a finalist pool that included a Latino, male or female. Overall, white women outnumbered minority males by about two to one in the applicant pool of finalists for presidents and vice presidents. Latinas were not represented in the finalist pools for presidencies. They were in the AVP pools only. White male finalists were almost three times as likely as females to be selected as presidents, and two and a half times as likely to be selected for AVP jobs.

Specific Outcomes

Academic Preparation

After the data on the academic preparation of the candidates were tabulated, notable differences surfaced. People were encouraged to respond to a question that asked, "How important is the academic reputation of the institution that awarded the finalists' doctorate?" Three responses were possible: not important, important, and very important. The 96 respondents answered in the following manner. For white males, the caliber of the institution that granted the doctorate was very important for 55 (57 percent) of the respondents. For white females it was very important for 75 (78 percent) of the respondents. For Latinos it increased to 80 (83 percent). However, if the finalist was a sitting president, it was very important for only 35 (36 percent) of the respondents. All of the sitting presidents were white.

The type of academic subject background or area of concentration of the candidates was part of another question asked of the interviewees. There were several broad categories.[10] The general academic area cited most often by the respondents as the ideal background for the AVP candidates was the sciences (biological and physical), particularly at the four-year and research institutions. This criterion would have eliminated all but two of the minority finalists and over 70 percent of the white females. In some of the searches, it did result in the elimination of several women and minority finalists.

Experiential Background

For the AVP jobs, people (*n*=37) were asked to rank how important it was for a candidate to have been a dean and a department chair. The results are intriguing. For white males, only 20 (54 percent) of the respondents believed it was very important for these finalists to have been *both* a department chair and a dean. For white females, it was very important for 29 (78 percent) of the respondents. And for Latinos, it was very important for 30 (81 percent) of the respondents.

A similar question was asked about the experiential background of candidates for presidencies. People (*n*=59) were asked to rank the importance of having served as an academic vice president or a dean.[11] Thirty-six (61 percent) of the respondents felt it was very important for presidential candidates to have been a vice president and a dean. However, if the candidate was a sitting president, only 18 (31 percent) of the respondents felt it was very important. Forty-six (78 percent) of the respondents felt it was very important for a white female to have served as a dean and a vice president. And 51 (86 percent) of the respondents felt it was very important for a Latino to have served in *both* capacities.

Scholarly/Teaching Accomplishments

This category was divided into two parts, one dealing with scholarly publication, and the other with recognition as a teacher. At the research institutions and regional universities, scholarly activity was an important criterion for presidential candidates, whereas teaching was given a less significant value. At the community colleges and most of the liberal arts colleges, the concerns were almost reversed.

Twenty-eight (47 percent) of the respondents believed it was very important for a presidential candidate to have demonstrated scholarly activity. However, if the candidate was a sitting president, only 17 (29 percent) considered it very important. Thirty-nine (66 percent) of the respondents believed it was very important for a white female to engage in scholarly activity. And 43 (73 percent) of the respondents felt it was very important for a Latino candidate.

In the searches for the AVP jobs, the results were striking. twenty-three (62 percent) of the respondents believed it was very important for a white male finalist to have a record of scholarly accomplishment. Twenty-eight (76 percent) of the respondents indicated that it was very important for a white female to have a record of scholarly accomplishment. And 31 (84 percent) of the respondents believed it was very important for a Latino finalist.

With respect to performance as a teacher, in the presidential searches only 23 (39 percent) of the respondents felt it was very important for white males to be recognized as successful teachers. If the candidate was a sitting president, less than 5 (9 percent) considered it very important. However, 34 (58 percent) considered successful teaching a very important criterion for white females. Forty (68 percent) indicated it was very important for Latino candidates.

In the AVP searches, 18 (49 percent) of the respondents said it was very important for a white male to be a recognized teacher. For white females the response was 23 (62 percent), and for minorities it was 26 (70 percent).

Matters of Style

Style proved to be a very difficult topic for discussion. Style was interpreted to mean different things by different people, ranging from management behavior (or style) to choice of apparel. It was next to impossible to avoid some overlap between this criterion and the interview impressions. With this in mind, the category of matters of style is defined to represent the following: communication with people; how well the person works with staff and clerical employees, senior officers, and faculty; some personal mannerisms—like a sense of humor—and, for want of a better descriptor, emotional stability.

Matters of style were considered very important in the searches for a president. Many of the respondents volunteered information about what presidents should look like or how they should behave. Consider some of the responses:

- Presidents should be tall and attractive.
- They should dress conservatively and in good taste.
- They should be polished speakers.
- They should be very gregarious and friendly.
- They should have a firm hand shake.
- They should be good listeners and thoughtful.

- They should fit in at any social setting.
- They should be leaders with vision and direction

The subjective nature of these responses may indicate how difficult it was to quantify style as a key part of the selection process. However, for the respondents, matters of style became a very important criterion by which to rank the presidential finalists.

After the data were tabulated, several intriguing things surfaced. A major concern vocalized by faculty, administrators, and trustees at different campuses was the "style" of Latinos. Ambitious Latinos, regardless of how effective they might have been, were often regarded as "presumptuous," "contentious," and "lacking seasoning." A senior faculty member at a research university said that a Latino finalist who had not been selected for the presidency at his campus was "young" and "too ambitious." Yet after other members of the selection committee were canvassed, it was learned that they admired the "drive" and "determination" of the younger white male who got the job.

The way Latino candidates for presidencies were perceived by some of the respondents was fascinating. The chair of the trustees at a college said he "could not read the man" (the Latino finalist). He elaborated by saying the Latino did not appear to be dynamic and did not seem to be an outgoing person. Moreover, he indicated that it was difficult to know what he (the Latino) was thinking. Yet when the background of the successful candidate was examined (a white male), he was identified as a "reserved" person, described as a "poker player," and considered taciturn. Why was it acceptable for the laconic white male to be reserved, and not so for the Latino?

At a regional university, a Latino finalist was not considered for the presidency because members of the search committee were uncertain how this candidate might "interact" with well-to-do white alumni and donors, and benefactors for intercollegiate athletic teams. Several Latino candidates for presidencies were considered at a disadvantage by white respondents who "felt" they would be unable to communicate and "get along well" with people in intercollegiate athletics and agribusiness. One respondent even categorized a Latino finalist as "not fully in touch with American athletics."

In the AVP searches, respondents at several four-year institutions were concerned that a Latino might not be able to work well with white male presidents and mostly white male academic deans. The perceptions were that a Latino in an academic vice presidency would "continually need to prove himself" to the deans. One of the interviewees indicated that Latinos were not strong leaders and tended to pursue a path of less resistance in their decision making, particularly at predominantly white institutions. This respondent referred to a Latino finalist as a "wimp." Some interesting attitudes toward Latinos surfaced during the study. Criticisms of Latina candidates for AVP jobs stressed that their "interpersonal skills" are different, and their "communication skills" needed improvement. When the respondents were asked to define what they meant by "different," they hesitated, and many became evasive in their responses. A few indicated that they thought Latino, male and female, finalists spoke with an accent. They considered this a disadvantage. As for "communication skills," this stylistic characteristic ranged from speaking too loudly to being barely audible, and not making frequent eye contact, a criticism most often applied to Latinas.

Interview Impressions

This is a very gray area because it involves relatively brief encounters between the candidates and members of the search committees. However, some strong and definite attitudes surfaced when the data were analyzed.

In the AVP searches, faculty, and especially department chairs and academic deans, played an important role in evaluating the candidate, as did the heads of faculty senates and unions. Most of the people interviewing the candidates were white males.

The number of interviews that finalists had to attend ranged from six at one campus to twelve at another. Breakfasts and luncheons were particularly important sessions. One campus took pride in its full interview schedule for the finalists, beginning at 7:15 A.M. and ending with an evening meal at 7:30 P.M. The search committee chair indicated that the full schedule was designed to test the finalists and determine how well they did under stress!

Three of the most significant types of impressions mentioned by the respondents in the AVP searches were these: how well the finalists dealt with faculty concerns; how well they responded to budget questions; and how well they responded to questions regarding academic planning. Twenty-nine (78 percent) of the respondents considered white male finalists best prepared in the interview process. Twenty-five (68 percent) considered females to be well prepared in the interviews, and 23 (62 percent) considered Latinos well prepared in the interviews.

In the presidential interviews, the schedules were usually long and with a broad grouping of campus and off-campus people. Some of the key concerns raised during the interviews with the presidential finalists included fund-raising activities, community liaison, dealing with alumni groups, working with boards and policy bodies, and relationships with parents and students.

Three critical areas where significant differences between types of candidates surfaced involve fund-raising, alumni relations, and working with boards and policy bodies. White male finalists were considered very knowledgeable about fund-raising by 49 (83 percent) of the respondents. White females were considered very knowledgeable in this area by 36 (61 percent) of the respondents. Latinos were considered very knowledgeable by 30 (51 percent) of the respondents. In alumni relations, the respondents indicated that 52 (88 percent) of the white male finalists had satisfactory experience. Thirty-seven (63 percent) of the respondents believed white women finalists had a satisfactory level, and 28 (48 percent) considered Latinos satisfactory in this area. As for working with boards of trustees and policy-making bodies, 46 (78 percent) of the respondents considered white male finalists satisfactory, 40 (68 percent) believed white women were satisfactory, and 32 (54 percent) thought Latinos satisfactory.

Analysis

In nearly every category mentioned above, the level of accomplishment required of finalists by screening-committee members was almost uniformly more stringent for women and especially Latinos than for white males. In sixteen of the twenty-five case studies, people on the selection committees indicated that they expected Latino finalists to achieve at the highest level. And they said this was to "help Latinos" be competitive. Several of the people who held this opinion were white women and non-Latino minorities. While the credentials of white males had been reviewed carefully by the different screening groups, they were not, as a whole, held to the higher standards demanded in some case for women and Latinos.

The level of experience required for Latinos was almost stringently prescribed. The same was nearly the case for white women. White males, however, were finalists for AVP jobs even though they might not have served as a department chair or an academic dean. In a few cases, white males were presidential finalists even though they had not been an academic vice president.

After analyzing the data on experiential background, an interesting pattern emerged. For an applicant to be a finalist for an AVP position, she or he needed to have served as the chair of a teaching department and an academic dean. Among the exceptions to this pattern were four white males. For presidencies, the pattern included serving as a teaching department chair, as an academic dean, and as an AVP. Unless the Latino candidates had served in all three capacities, they were not considered "viable" finalists for a presidency. The females selected as presidents had served in all three capacities. And the Latino appointed to a presidency had served in all three capacities. However, among the white males appointed to presidencies, two had not served as department chairs, and one had been a vice president, but not in academic affairs.

The level of expectation by which Latinos were evaluated for AVP and president jobs was always higher than for white males and females. Even when the experiential background of Latinos was as good as or better than that of other finalists in the pool, their chances for appointment were much less than for their white male counterparts.[12]

The scholarly/teaching accomplishments of the finalists were what may loosely be referred to as a "limited swing factor." The respondents did not consider these matters to be of the highest importance at some of the target institutions. However, they could play a determinative role; and more often than not, a negative one. In a few cases, particularly at the research universities, lack of distinction as a scholar would seriously compromise a candidate's chances to become a finalist for either an academic vice presidency or a presidency. However, a review of the data shows that women and minorities were eliminated from consideration as finalists if their scholarly accomplishments or teaching was not of the highest caliber. This was not the case for some white males. Even when a Latino had the most extensive list of scholarly publications among the finalists, he was passed over in favor of a white male. In this particular case, two respondents considered his scholarly productivity a disadvantage.

When the data regarding matters of style were analyzed, some fascinating things surfaced. Style issues were very important in the selection of a president. The appearance of the finalists, their track records in working with different groups, especially alumni and institutional benefactors, and participation in key networks were considered very significant by the respondents.[13] The abilities of the finalists to communicate easily and work closely with different campus constituencies was critical. Any rifts between finalists and their home campus groups, especially faculty, would work negatively against them. And it did in several cases. A finalist's candidacy was compromised because a few disgruntled faculty at his home institution volunteered negative information about his style. While the information volunteered was impressionistic, it was taken seriously by key members of the screening committee. Matters of style, nebulous factors at best, often worked negatively against Latinos in presidential searches.

For the AVP positions, matters of style encompassed a different set of variables. Here respondents were very interested in how well the finalists worked with faculty and other senior administrators. The finalists were rated on their success in lobbying for resources to benefit the academic program and curriculum. At the research institutions, the ability to work closely with the human apparatus of funding bodies was a priority. At some of the four year-institutions, faculty were very insistent that the AVP be like them and have progressed through the ranks. Several of the faculty respondents expected the AVP candidates to serve as their spokesperson. Some of the respondents, particularly at the two- and four-year colleges, believed that the AVP finalist selected *might* become a president. Consequently, they expected additional stylistic qualities from the finalists, many not unlike what might be required of a president. When the data were tabulated, it became clear that matters of style and the interview process were highly subjective criteria that could be manipulated by the appointing group to condition the selection of a particular finalist.

Interview impressions were the most difficult things to identify and quantify. However, the results are very important. For the finalists, how well they interviewed and dealt with prepared or spontaneous questions and requests for information on different issues could make or break them. Here the impressions of the respondents— and, in some cases, their biases—became very apparent. A white male finalist was "grilled" extensively by a minority group on the campus. Toward the end of the interview his response to a question on staff diversity indicated that too many questionable appointments may have occurred because of affirmative action.[14] He carefully evaded the follow-up questions posed by the minorities. He was praised by two of the male respondents for his "tough stand" on this "questionable issue." The trustees selected him for the presidency.

Overall, women and Latinos did not seem to fare as well as their white male counterparts in the interview process. A female candidate for an AVP position was asked about using faculty funds to pay the salaries of some coaches in the basketball, baseball, and football programs. She indicated the need to review the matter and determine how it had been decided and if the arrangement included female coaches. Several of the members of the search committee later received calls and notes that the female AVP finalist was "fuzzy-headed" and "anti-athletics." She did not get the job.

A Latino finalist was asked whether, given his positive work on diversity, he would appoint minorities as senior people to his management team. He responded that highly qualified women and minorities would be encouraged to apply for openings within the president's management team. His answer was interpreted by some of the respondents to mean that minorities only would be hired in these roles. He was not offered the presidency.

The vagaries associated with the interview process, very much like those for matters of style, tended to work against women and Latinos. Any reservations that campus people might have toward these finalists surfaced during their visits to the institution. Some were subtle and even benign, while others reflected a guarded distrust of women, and Latinos in leadership roles.

Conclusion

The information available from the twenty-five case studies yields a disturbing pattern of hesitation and even resistance to the selection of Latinos and some women for presidencies and academic vice presidencies. Numerous "added" requirements or "higher achievements" than were the norm for the finalists at the target campuses were "expected" of Latino finalists. The level of confidence by respondents for the accomplishments of Latinos was not as good as for their white male or female counterparts. An underlying suspicion about the credentials and accomplishments of Latino finalists was apparent from the remarks of numerous respondents who were interviewed. A few comments were made that categorized Latinos as emotional, unpredictable, and unstable. In four cases, white females on the search or screening committees agreed with this categorization and were diffident toward Latino finalists. This is an intriguing development and should be the subject of another investigation.

When the results of this study are compared with national data about the appointment of new presidents, the figures correlate well. Women represent about 18 percent of the CEOs at regionally accredited colleges and universities. Their numbers are gradually increasing in these executive capacities. However, progress for Latinos, especially females, is slow and their paths to presidencies often contain serious obstacles. In a few cases, the hostility of white males and females toward the appointment of Latinos in leadership roles defies explanation. In one case, a white female faculty member initiated a vicious, gratuitous letter-writing campaign to humiliate a Latino executive from her campus who was a finalist for an AVP position at another college. The tragedy was that a few key members of the search committee did consider this negative information in their decision making and passed over the Latino candidate, even though his credentials and accomplishments were as good as or better than those of the white male who eventually was offered the position. The Latino finalist was never allowed to comment on the gratuitous allegations made against him. This is but one of several scenarios where there was a troublesome reluctance to appoint a Latino to an executive role in higher education.

The data paint a disturbing picture for Latino candidates. They are held to a much higher level of preparation and achievement than are either white males or white females. The attitudes of several respondents reflected a perfunctory suspicion of Latino finalists for presidencies and AVP jobs. Some referred negatively to Latinos as "affirmative action products." A few people implied that Latino finalists may have been "coddled" or "helped" through their doctoral studies and then given "preferential treatment" in the tenure and promotion process. Unfortunately such attitudes were held by several influential search and screening-committee members who conveniently ignored the genuine accomplishments of these finalists.

While the appointment of Latinos to executive and leadership positions in higher education is improving gradually, it is painfully slow and filled with examples of subtle, and in some cases overt, biases that work against them. The same is true for some white females. Latino women, however, bear a double burden—being considered less desirable because they are women and people of color. In areas of the country where Latinos have, for demographic or sociopolitical reasons, begun to achieve recognition, opportunities might improve for them to serve as college or university executives. In a few cases, the influence of minority trustees, particularly at two-year colleges, might enhance the chances for a Latino or a person of color to become a president.[15] Most recently, the influence of Latino elected officials at the state and local levels has improved opportunities for the appointment of Latinos in publicly supported colleges and universities. However, such off-campus political influence is soundly criticized by many Anglo administrators and faculty.

The results of this study add to the body of evidence that suggests that a glass ceiling for Latinos does exist in higher education—and particularly that the advancement of Latino women is seriously hindered by negative perceptions and stereotypes. The data reflect attitudes on the part of responsible people involved in the selection of AVPs and presidents that may have impeded the appointment of Latinos, some females, and people of color for leadership roles at colleges and universities.

It is important to share some personal information from situations in which I was a candidate for an academic vice presidency and a presidency. As a participant observer, I perceived definite reactions to my ethnic background, along with a subtle dissatisfaction with my academic preparation and Chicano-oriented scholarship. While none of the information from the searches in which I was a finalist was factored into this study, the outcomes represent a consistent collateral pattern of ambivalence toward Latinos.

The academic credentials and scholarship of Latinos, especially if they have been strong advocates for ethnic studies teaching and research, might be viewed skeptically by many white scholars. During a final interview for an academic vice presidency at a regional university, one of the screening committee members, a full professor, arrogantly tossed a copy of my list of publications on the table and said cynically, "Do share with us why so many of your articles are in ephemeral publications." When I asked him to be specific, he said, "Well, after all, ethnocentric publications can hardly be compared to scholarly and refereed journals." He and others on the screening committee were surprised to learn that I made it a practice to send some of my writings to developing minority serials, even though many had been solicited by scholarly journals. And I pointed out that about 80 percent of my writings were in scholarly and refereed journals.

In a presidential search where I was a finalist, the faculty, students, and staff identified me as their top choice. However, the trustees—eight whites and one non-Latino minority—were being influenced by two external groups. Several white presidents associated with a national organization were encouraging some of the trustees to select a white male finalist. The other was a network of white women in national associations lobbying for the appointment of a white female. The trustees offered the presidency to the white female. Later when I asked the student member of the board of trustees in confidence why they decided to do so, the response was dispiriting. The student trustee indicated that the white female network on and off the campus lobbied and persuaded the trustees, key alumni, and local political leaders that it was "time for a woman to be president." In the final analysis, it was not the suitability or the accomplishments of the top three finalists that mattered. It was the personal and professional pressure the white female network was able to apply. Ironically, Latinos have been chided by many Anglo academic leaders and researchers for resorting to "the political process" to gain tenure, promotions, anc leadership jobs. Yet why is it acceptable for them, including white females, to play the political game and not so for us? This appears to be a fascinating double standard.

While more extensive and exhaustive studies are recommended, sufficient reliable information exists to underscore perceptions about the existence of a glass ceiling for Latinos. Organizations like the American Council on Education (ACE) should initiate efforts similar to ones they have for women (the Commission on Women in Higher Education and the National Identification Program) that will identify and help prepare Latino academic administrators, and monitor the selection and appointment of Latino executives in higher education. Executive search firms should meet with major Latino organizations such as the Hispanic Association of Colleges and Universities (HACU) to help identify qualified Latinos, especially females, for leadership roles. Latinos should take steps to secure appointment or be elected as trustees for colleges and universities. Latino elected political leaders should play a more active role in supporting qualified and talented Latino candidates for executive roles in higher education. The major foundations should consider funding studies and research activities that will identify barriers to the promotion and appointment of Latinos in executive roles in higher education, and then offer realistic alternatives to overcome them. A firm commitment and a national resolve is needed to identify and help qualified Latinos achieve leadership roles in higher education. This valuable human resource should not be ignored. Latinos need to be better utilized in American higher education. They will bring new and valuable ideas, insights, and solutions to many of the pressing challenges that exist on our campuses. In these times of declining resources and mounting pressure to enhance diversity on our campuses, their contributions may be invaluable.

Notes

1. The denotation of the term *minorities* will include U.S. domestic-born people of African American, Asian American, Latino, and Native American heritage.

2. The term *Latino* will be used to denote men and women of Cuban, Mexican, Puerto Rican, and Central or South American descent, and those from other Spanish-speaking regions of the world.

3. The American Council on Education's Office of Minorities in Higher Education has information on the number of minorities in executive roles. Dr.

Antonio Esquibel completed an extensive study on Chicano Administrators in the Southwest (Esquibel 1993).

4. The American Council on Education has efforts that regularly capture information on women in executive roles and encourage their appointment as CEOs: the Presidents Study, the Commission on Women in Higher Education, and the National Identification Program.

5. All interviewees were given the opportunity to review the pertinent section of the first draft of the report dealing with the search on their campus.

6. For the purposes of the study, all communication between the interviewees and this writer was under the name *Robert* Haro. No intimations were given that the writer is Latino.

7. From the data received at the target sites, overt discrimination was mentioned in a few cases. Six finalists—one white male, three women, and two minorities—were contacted and asked to comment on allegations of bias against them.

8. The 130 persons contacted do not include the six finalists for CEO or AVP jobs who were separately interviewed.

9. The term *sitting president* is used to mean a candidate who is a president at another institution.

10. The broad categories were these: arts, humanities, social sciences, engineering, education, science (biological and physical), the professions (law, medicine, etc.), and other.

11. At some of the community college settings, the dean of instruction was equivalent to an academic vice president. This officer was in charge of the campus whenever the president/superintendent was away.

12. It is interesting to note that the Latino appointed as an AVP was moved laterally after two years, and left the campus to assume a dean's position at another institution.

13. Yolanda T. Moses (1993) discusses exclusion from key networks, and other barriers that work against minority administrators.

14. This candidate's remarks indicated that minorities and some women had received preferential treatment in the academy, even though their qualifications and experiences were not of the highest caliber.

15. Most of the Latina presidents are at community colleges; one is at a two-year college that has been absorbed by the state and changed to a four year institution.

References

Birnbaum, R. (1988). "Presidential searches and the discovery of organizational goals." *Journal of Higher Education*, 59(5), 489–509.

Bolman, F. (1965). *How college presidents are chosen*. Washington, DC: American Council on Education.

Cohen, M. D. and March, J. G. (1974). *Leadership and ambiguity: the American college president*. New York: McGraw-Hill.

Esquibel, A. (1993). *The career mobility of Chicano administrators in higher education*. Boulder, CO: Western Interstate Commission for Higher Education.

Kaplowitz, R. A. (1973). *Selecting academic administrators: the search committee*. Washington, DC: American Council on Education.

Leatherman, C. (1991, November 6). "Colleges hire more female presidents, but questions linger about their clout." *The Chronicle of Higher Education*, pp. A19–A21.

Marchese, T. J. (1987). *The Search committee handbook: a guide for recruiting administrators*. Washington, DC: American Association for Higher Education.

McLaughlin, J. B. (1985). "From secrecy to sunshine: an overview of presidential search practice." *Research in Higher Education*. 22(2), 195–208.

McLaughlin, J. B. and Riesman, D. (1990). *Choosing a college president: opportunities and constraints*. Princeton: Carnegie Foundation for the Advancement of Teaching.

Moses, Y. T. (1993, January 13). "The Roadblocks confronting minority administrators." *The Chronicle of Higher Education*, pp. B1–2.

Ross, M. (1993). *The American college president*. Washington, DC: American Council on Education.

Sturnick, J. A., Milley, J. E. & Tisinger, C. A. eds. (1991). *Women at the helm: path finding presidents at state colleges and universities*. Washington, DC: American Association of State Colleges and Universities.

Webb, E. J., et. al. (1966). *Unobtrusive measures: nonreactive research in the social sciences*. Chicago: Rand McNally.

Yin, R. (1984). *Case study research: design methods*. Beverly Hills, CA: Sage.

Contributors

Adalberto Aguirre, Jr., is an Associate Professor of Sociology at the University of California, Riverside. He earned a doctorate in sociology and linguistics from Stanford University. His research publications cover such topics as Chicanos and intelligence testing, Chicano faculty in higher education, sociolinguistic features of Chicano bilinguals, cross-national mass communication systems, and sociolinguistic perspectives on bilingual instruction. He has coauthored with Rubén Martínez the book *Chicanos in Higher Education: Issues and Dilemmas for the 21st Century*.

Rudolfo Chávez Chávez is an Associate Professor in the Department of Curriculum and Instruction in the College of Education at New Mexico State University. Currently, he is serving as Associate Department Head. He teaches courses in multicultural education as well as in curriculum and instruction at the graduate and undergraduate levels. His research interests focus on the application of critical theory in multicultural education and curriculum. His most recent works deal with teachers and multicultural education and racism.

Stella T. Clark is Mexican born and raised, becoming a naturalized American citizen in 1960. She received a Ph.D. in Spanish and Latin American Literature from the University of Kansas. She joined the faculty at California State University, San Marcos, as a founding member of the Foreign Languages Program. Previously, she was Professor of Spanish at California State University, San Bernardino, where she served in several administrative capacities, including Chair of the Department of Foreign Languages and Literature and Interim Dean of the School of Humanities. Her research areas are Latin American literature, Mexican literature, culture, and art, and Spanish language and pedagogy.

A. Reynaldo Contreras is a Professor of Administrative and Interdisciplinary Studies at San Francisco State University. Formerly he was Professor of Educational Leadership and Policy Studies at Indiana University, Bloomington. Professor Contreras received his Ph.D. from Stanford University, where he studied administration and policy analysis. His research interests include policy studies in education, minority educational leadership, and education in emerging metropolitan contexts. He has contributed to journals and books on urban education and educational leadership.

Dulce M. Cruz is a Dominican American and an Assistant Professor of English and Cultural Studies at George Mason University in Fairfax, Virginia. She attended City University of New York and Indiana University, Bloomington, where she completed a doctoral program on Language, Literature, and Literacy. Her dissertation is titled *High Literacy, Ethnicity, Gender and Class: The Case of Dominican Americans*. Dr. Cruz's teaching interests include literacy, feminist and composition theory, contemporary United States Latino literature, and literature written by Third World women. Her current research examines the role of writing and reading as seen in the literature produced by highly literate yet socially and culturally marginalized women.

Hermán S. García is an Associate Professor of Education in the College of Education at New Mexico State University, Las Cruces. He is also coordinator of bilingual education and ESL studies in the Department of Curriculum and Instruction. He has been incorporating various critical pedagogy discourses into bilingual education, ESL, and cultural diversity.

Gerardo M. González is an Assistant Professor of Psychology at California State University, San Marcos. He earned his doctorate in clinical psychology at the California School of Professional Psychology, Fresno. He completed a predoctoral and postdoctoral clinical internship at the University of California, Berkeley, and a postdoctoral clinical-research fellowship at the University of California, San Francisco. Among his research interests are multicultural mental health issues (particularly among the Spanish-speaking), computerized clinical assessment, and the cognitive prevention and treatment of clinical depression. He is former President of the California State University, San Marcos, Latino Association of Faculty and Staff.

María Cristina González received an M.A. degree in Communication from SUNY at Buffalo and a Ph.D. in Speech Communication from the University of Texas at Austin. As a Fulbright scholar, she held a professorship at La Universidad Autónoma de Chihuahua, where she conducted multimethods research on modernity, the extended family, and women's roles in Chihuahuan society. She says, "I am committed to developing avenues for alternative voices and forms of representation for ethnographic research." She has completed a book of ethnographic poetry, *Painting the White Face Red: Non-Indians in Search of Their Spiritual Selves*.

Roberto Haro, a Chicano scholar, has served in different capacities in American higher education. He earned a B.A. and two graduate degrees from the University of California at Berkeley. His doctorate is in higher education and policy studies. Haro has worked and taught at the State University of New York, the University of Maryland, the University of Southern California, and several campuses of the University of California. He is a Professor of Mexican American Studies at San Jose State University, and Director of its Monterey County Campus.

Lionel A. Maldonado earned his Ph.D. in Sociology at the University of Oregon. Before joining the faculty at California State University, San Marcos, as Professor of Ethnic Studies, he was Deputy Executive Officer and Director of Minority Fellowship Programs at the American Sociological Association. Previously he was Associate Professor of Sociology at the University of Wisconsin, Parkside. He has conducted research and published on the Mexican American population, focusing on labor force participation, stratification, and social mobility.

Ana M. Martínez Alemán, a native born Cubana, is an Assistant Professor of Education and the Concentration in Gender and Women's Studies at Grinnell College, a small liberal arts college in rural Iowa. She teaches courses in the areas of feminist pedagogy and educational philosophy. Her current research focuses on the cognitive value of women's friendships. She begins each midwestern morning with a cup of *café Pilón*.

Tatcho Mindiola, Jr., is the Director of Mexican American Studies and an Associate Professor of Sociology at the University of Houston. His publications and research deal with race relations, political behavior, and the demography of racial and ethnic groups. His current research focuses on the relationship between Mexican and African Americans.

Raymond V. Padilla is a Professor in the College of Education at Arizona State University. He earned a Ph.D. in Higher Education from the University of California, Berkeley. His research interests include Chicanos in higher education, bilingual education policy, and the use of computers in qualitative research. Recent publications include a book, *Critical Perspectives on Bilingual Education Research*, and an article, "Using Qualitative Research to Assess Advising", which appeared in *The Review of Higher Education*.

Francisco A. Ríos is an Assistant Professor in the College of Education at California State University, San Marcos. He taught communications, psychology, and international/intercultural relations at Waukesha County Technical College in Wisconsin from 1978 to 1991. He received his doctoral degree from the University of Wisconsin in Educational Psychology. His teaching specialities include learning and instruction and multicultural education. His research interests focus on teacher cognition in multicultural contexts.

María E. Torres-Guzmán is Associate Professor and Director of the Program in Bilingual/Bicultural Education at Teachers College, Columbia University. She has published numerous articles and chapters, co-authored *Learning in Two Worlds*, and developed computer-based and curricular materials in Spanish.

Richard R. Verdugo is a Senior Policy Analyst with the National Education Association in Washington, D.C. He earned a doctorate in sociology from the University of Southern California. His substantive areas of expertise are the sociology of education, labor markets, and racial stratification. Dr. Verdugo's most recent publications appear in *Social Science Quarterly*, the *Journal of Human Resources*, the *Encyclopedia of Education Research* (6th edition), the *Journal of the Association of Mexican American Educators*, *Contemporary Education*, and the *Economics of Education Review*. Dr. Verdugo is currently completing a book that is an historical case study of a Chicano community in Texas.

Index

213